W9-AEZ-518

LIFE

OF

FRANCIS PARKMAN.

CHAMPLAIN EDITION.

The Champlain Edition of Francis Parkman's Works is limited to Twelve Hundred Copies.

No. 896

Francis Parkman.

From a Photograph taken in 1889.

A LIFE

OF

FRANCIS PARKMAN.

BY

CHARLES HAIGHT FARNHAM.

BOSTON:
LITTLE, BROWN, AND COMPANY.
1901.

University Press:
JOHN WILSON AND SON, CAMBRIDGE, U. S A.

This Memoir is Dedicated

TO

ELIZA W. S. PARKMAN

AS A TOKEN OF ESTEEM

AND

A MEMORIAL OF HER DEVOTION TO HER BROTHER.

C. H. F.

PREFACE

THE chief interest of Francis Parkman's life was not his connection with the great events, important questions, or celebrated people of his time, his life being singularly devoid of external and tangible elements available for a biography. The main attraction of the subject lies in his picturesque, manly character, his inspiring example of fortitude and perseverance, and his training and achievements as historian. As a man he was even greater and more interesting than his work. It is therefore the man himself that I have tried to keep everywhere in view, as the chief object among the experiences of his somewhat uneventful life.

This purpose early brought on a conflict between a sentiment and a conviction, — respect for Parkman's extreme reserve and a belief that this must be ignored by his biographer. He never admitted any one to his inner life, nor did anything to make himself known to the public;

on the contrary he greatly preferred retirement, and believed that the public had no legitimate concern with the private life and character of an artist. It is clearly out of accord with his nature and feelings to write a biography of him worth the reading, and many may suppose that to lift the veil ever so little would be entirely against his wishes. Yet good reasons have led me in this memoir to be as explicit and intimate as possible.

First, I do not agree with him that the public has no concern with the private life and character of the artist. No man, in any form of activity, can elude his personal equation, or produce work that is disconnected from its helping and hindering forces. As the artist thus depends on the man, a knowledge of the man is the indispensable key to his productions. While living the artist has an undoubted right to his retirement; it may even be indispensable to his free activity. But after he has left us, there is nothing but benefit in making known the qualities and defects, the capacities and limitations from which his works took their birth. What perfection of senses had he for perceiving men and things? To what degree did his health affect his sensuous and mental activities? What were the nature and trend of his intellectual faculties? What powers of sympathy or imagination secured his intimate relations with his work? What were the force and range of his moral sensibilities? These are among the most vital questions in estimating an artist's labors, and they can be answered by studying his character in the numerous relations of life, far better than by considering only his productions. A perfect biography would be the strongest testimony a sound reputation could ask, or a false one could fear.

Second, Parkman gave an example in his own person of the utmost thoroughness and sincerity. I am convinced that he would desire his biography to be written, if at all, in the frankest way. Also, he has put himself on record in two autobiographic letters, as if wishing to make his experience useful to any student who should meet with unusual difficulties. To this end he wrote of his conditions and trials with a fulness that he never even approached in daily intercourse with friends. Finally, there is nothing to hide in writing Parkman's life, and it would thus appear that his biography should be as free as was his character from all shams and concealment.

The materials for a life of him are extraordinarily scanty. When I began the work he seemed to me almost a mythological person, so little matter was there sufficiently interesting for publication. Being obliged to save his strength and sight for historical labors, he wrote very few letters, diaries, or papers of general interest. Moreover, while his external life was too uneventful to serve as the main dependence, his real inner life was never revealed to any one. Nor is it easy to show his personality in his works, for they are singularly impersonal; he kept to the facts of the story, avoiding all expression of his philosophy, tastes, opinions, or feelings. Furthermore, he felt little sympathy with the political, social, religious, or other reforms of his time; and though his views were very decided, he seldom had eyesight or strength to expend in opposing these movements. Again, he held but little intercourse with noted people. The singular lack of personal elements in his life thus made it impracticable to paint him in a picture of his times surrounded by important characters. He could be presented only as he was — a solitary, often a pathetic, figure in the silence and shadow of his study. And in turning thus to the most interior source of interest — the growth of his mental and moral nature — there was yet found comparatively little to say; for his opinions, tastes, and character were formed when quite young, his inelastic, conservative nature changed but little with the passage of years, and he left no autobiographic record of the forces and methods concerned in this development. Then, partly because he was not one of those men who say and do quotable things, reminiscences of his friends were somewhat disappointing. They could give few anecdotes, few witticisms, few important thoughts, few noteworthy actions. And lastly, my own personal intercourse with him seemed too brief to justify his family in selecting me as his biographer. Our acquaintance began in 1885, and my departure from Boston in 1890 put a stop to our social relations. In common with all his friends I often regretted that his illness made frequent visits impossible. I enjoyed, however, one exceptional privilege and opportunity, in camping with him for a month on the Batiscan river, near Quebec — a good occasion for getting data and impressions of value.

But all these unfortunate hindrances to a complete knowledge of him were to some extent offset by the strong picturesqueness of the man, and by the distinct self-revelations made by his unconscious, perhaps unwilling, pen.

My thanks are due, first of all, to Mr. Parkman's family, from whom I have received all possible aid. I should like also to express my gratitude to his many friends, both classmates and those of later years, who have in different ways given me much valuable help. And I am indebted to Dr. Titus M. Coan for assistance in revising the manuscript.

The chief publications concerning his life are: "Francis Parkman," by the Rev. O. B. Frothingham, written for the Massachusetts Historical Society, 2d series, vol. viii.; "Memoir of Francis Parkman," by Edward Wheelwright, in the Publications of the Colonial Society of Massachusetts, vol. i.; and by the same author a life of Mr. Parkman in the history of Harvard College, class of 1844; "Francis Parkman," by Barrett Wendell, in the Proceedings of the American Academy of Arts and Sciences, vol. xxix.; the remarks made at a special meeting of the Massachusetts Historical Society in November, 1893, by Dr. George E. Ellis, Dr. Oliver Wendell Holmes, Hon. Robert C. Winthrop, Hon. George S. Hale, Hon. John Lowell, Hon. Martin Brimmer, and Hon. Leverett Saltonstall; an article by Prof. John Fiske, and one by Mr. Justin Winsor in the "Atlantic" for May, 1894; articles by Rev. Julius H. Ward, in "McClure's Magazine," January, 1894, and in the "Forum," December, 1893; "Francis Parkman," by Abbé H. R. Casgrain; "Francis Parkman," by C. H. Farnham, in the "Critic," February 27, 1886; "Francis Parkman," the beginning of a biography by Lowell in the "Century" for November, 1892; an obituary notice in the "Nation" for November 16, 1893; an article by George Willis Cooke, in the "New England Magazine," November, 1889.

There is very little unpublished matter from Parkman's hand. Though he kept a diary of each of his vacation journeys from 1841 to 1846, he used the best portions of them in writing the "Scalp Hunter," "Exploring the Magalloway," "A Convent at Rome," and "The Oregon Trail." His letters are disappointing to the biographer; few in number, they are still more inadequate by their shortness, and by their limitation to the seeking and copying of historical material, or to the most external matters connected with his condition and movements when travelling. But something has been gleaned from Parkman's letters to Abbé H. R. Casgrain and others in Quebec and elsewhere.

Fortunately there exist materials more helpful. First should be mentioned the two extremely interesting autobiographic letters to his friends, Dr. George E. Ellis and the Hon. Martin Brimmer. These papers are poignant revelations of his experiences and of some of his traits. Then the reader who has already some knowledge of Parkman's character, will find many autobiographical touches in the novel

"Vassall Morton." "The Oregon Trail" gives some striking scenes in his life, — the last of the manly adventures he loved so much, and that he gave up only on account of his subsequent infirmities. The prefaces to certain of his books contain personal references of value, especially as to the difficulties and methods connected with the writings of the histories; while his few miscellaneous articles, on Universal Suffrage, on Woman Suffrage, on Our Common Schools, give direct glimpses on important lines of his thought and feeling.

A word may be said about the plan of this memoir. As in the case of many other scholars, Parkman's external life was unimportant compared with the more interior interests of his education, his method of work, his historical productions, and the growth of his character. It seemed advisable, therefore, to depart from the tradition that accepts chronological narrative as the backbone of biography. I have tried to simplify the reader's labor and gain vividness of portraiture, by confining chronology chiefly to one chapter, thenceforth viewing facts and experiences as bearing mainly on achievement and development. This method naturally leads to some repetitions and returns; but it enables one to bring many of the details of mere biography into closer and more significant relations with the deeper interests of life. The book thus divides itself into three parts: (1) Parkman's preparation, (2) the reflection of his personality in his works, and (3) the story of his moral growth.

SILVER BAY, LAKE GEORGE,
June, 1900.

CONTENTS.

LIST OF ILLUSTRATIONS

A LIFE OF

FRANCIS PARKMAN

CHAPTER I

INTRODUCTORY

If we seek to trace Francis Parkman's individuality to its source in any of his ancestors, we shall be disappointed. Whether regarded as the outcome of his antecedents or as a member of his community, he was an original man, marked indeed by some of the strongest antipathies for the nature, training, and pursuits of his progenitors. Like many other distinguished New Englanders, he sprang from a clerical family, all members of the early Puritan colonies. Many of them were people of energy, capacity, and position; a goodly number were scholars and divines graduated from Harvard College.[1]

[1] Mr. Parkman's descent in the paternal line, through eight generations, is as follows:

1. Thomas Parkman, of Sidmouth, Devon, England.
2. Elias Parkman, born in England, settled in Dorchester, Massachusetts, 1633, married Bridget ——.
3. Elias, b. in Dorchester, Mass., 1635, m. Sarah Trask, of Salem.
4. William, b. in Salem, Mass., 1658, m. Eliza Adams, of Boston.
5. Ebenezer, b. in Boston, 1703, minister at Westborough, Mass., m. (2d) Hannah Breck.

Parkman's great-grandfather, the Rev. Ebenezer Parkman, a graduate of Harvard, 1721, was a man of note. "He is spoken of as a good example of the New England minister of the olden time. He magnified his calling, and was careful not to lower its dignity, wielding almost despotic power with firmness guided by discretion and tempered with kindness. He was largely concerned in making the history of the town, and also in writing it. The records of the church were kept by him on diminutive pages and in a microscopic hand during the whole of his pastorate. He also kept during the same period a private diary written in the same almost undecipherable characters. A portion of this diary is preserved in the library of the American Antiquarian Society

6. Samuel, b. in Westborough, m. (2d) Sarah Rogers.
7. Francis, b. in Boston, 1788, m. (2d) Caroline Hall.
8. Francis, b. in Boston, 1823.

The following is his descent on the mother's side, through the same number of generations, from John Cotton:

1. John Cotton, b. in England, 1585, m. (2d) Sarah Hankredge, of Boston, England, widow of William Story. Came to Boston, 1633.
2. John Cotton, b. in Boston, Mass., 1639, m. Joanna Rossiter.
3. Rowland Cotton, b. in Plymouth, 1667, m. Elizabeth Saltonstall, widow of Rev. John Denison.
4. Joanna Cotton, b. in Sandwich, 1719, m. Rev. John Brown, of Haverhill, Mass. (H. C. 1714).
5. Abigail Brown, b. in , m. Rev. Edward Brooks, of Medford.
6. Joanna Cotton Brooks, b. in , 1772, m. Nathaniel Hall, of Medford.
7. Caroline Hall, b. in Medford, 1794, m. Rev. Francis Parkman, of Boston.
8. Francis Parkman, b. in Boston, 1823.

(From *Memoir of Francis Parkman*, by Edward Wheelwright, in *Publications of the Colonial Society of Massachusetts*, vol. i. pp. 304–305.)

at Worcester; other portions have been distributed among his descendants. Its quaint humor was a never-ceasing delight to his great-grandson, the historian."[1]

This excellent divine was worthy of the colonial times, not only for his masterful spirit, but also in being the father of sixteen children. His third son, William, was the boy of seventeen who is mentioned by Lowell, and who at Ticonderoga, in 1758, as Parkman tells us, "kept in his knapsack a dingy little notebook in which he jotted down what passed each day." Another son, Breck, was one of the minute men who marched from Westborough on the 19th of April, 1775.

Samuel Parkman, the twelfth child of this minister, was the grandfather of the historian. He came to Boston as a poor boy, and by his assiduity and talent rose to eminence and opulence among the merchants of Boston. He was a liberal benefactor of Harvard University.

The Rev. Francis Parkman, father of the historian, was born in Boston in 1788, graduated from Harvard in 1807, received the degree of *Sanctæ Theologiæ Doctor* in 1843, and was installed in 1813 as pastor of the New North Church in Boston, corner of Hanover and Clark streets. This charge he retained to the end of his pastorate in 1849. From 1819 to 1849 he was one of the Overseers of Harvard University. He added a donation to his father's gift to the College,

[1] Mr. Wheelwright's *Memoir*.

and thus helped to found the Parkman Professorship of Theology. As a student he showed "a strong desire for knowledge and an aptitude to avail himself of all means which presented for general improvement."[1]

"Every aspect of suffering touched him tenderly. There was no hard spot in his breast. His house was the centre of countless mercies to various forms of want; and there were few solicitors of alms, local or itinerant, and whether for private necessity or public benefactions, that his doors did not welcome and send away satisfied. The processes of his mind were practical, however, rather than speculative. His style was not wanting in force, but distinguished rather for clearness and ease. For many years he has been widely known and esteemed for his efficient interest in some of our most conspicuous and useful institutions of philanthropy. Harvard University . . . was very near to his heart, and its concerns touched his personal pride."[2]

Another writer says of him:

"Whether he conversed on theology or politics or manners or individual character, or recorded some sad or pleasant experience of his own, the wise and genial humorist was always observable, softening, enlivening, enriching everything he touched; his practical discernments were so sure and keen, his knowledge of the world was so extensive and his perception of character and motives was so quick and deep that it was impossible to impose on him by any pretense or deception."[3]

[1] Dr. Isaac Hurd. [2] Bishop Huntington.
[3] Edwin P. Whipple.

Lowell says of him:[1]

"He still survives in traditions of an abundant and exquisite humor, provoked to wilder hazards, and set in stronger relief (as in Sterne) by the decorum of his cloth."

His genial temper, however, was often shadowed by attacks of melancholy. In spite of a nature that was generous, free even to eccentricity in certain directions, he was very conservative in feeling and opinions, — an excellent Bostonian of those days.

When he died, in 1852, the Boston Association celebrated him as "one who loved his calling and discharged all its duties with untiring devotedness. As a preacher he was practical and evangelical; as a pastor tender and affectionate. He was a man of active and useful charities, a friend to learning, a punctual member or an energetic officer of many literary, philanthropic, and religious associations, as well as a true friend of the worthy poor." One of the best tributes paid to him was Dr. Ephraim Peabody's saying that he was particularly kind to the unattractive. And finally, it is pleasant to add that "He was a kind and indulgent father, and though he did not sympathize with all his son's aspirations and pursuits, he never thwarted or opposed them."[2]

Francis Parkman's maternal branch sprang from the good old Puritans, John Cotton of Boston and of Plymouth. His great-grandfather was the Rev.

[1] *The Century*, November, 1892.
[2] Mr. Wheelwright's *Memoir*.

Edward Brooks, of Medford, Massachusetts, who graduated at Harvard in 1757, and was "called to the church at North Yarmouth, Maine, where, however, he remained only five years, having been dismissed on account of his too liberal views."[1] This is the only person among Parkman's ancestors who is mentioned as having liberal tendencies. "On the 19th of April, 1775, he went over to Lexington, on horseback, with his gun on his shoulder, and in his full-bottomed wig."[2] His chief exploit on that eventful day appears to have been saving the life of a wounded British officer. Parkman records that through the sister of Peter Chardon Brooks he himself shared in the Huguenot blood that often played so prominent a part in the history of New England.

Parkman derived more traits from his mother than from any other of his ancestors. She was Caroline, daughter of Nathaniel Hall, of Medford, Massachusetts. Mr. Frothingham wrote of her:[3] "She was a fine example of the best type of New England woman . . . She was a Unitarian by inheritance, but quite uninterested in speculative or dogmatic matters. With questions of doctrine she did not concern herself, and took no part in the controversies that were raging around her, though she had a profound respect for spiritual things and an undoubting faith in the cardinal principles of religion. Her devotion

[1] Mr. Wheelwright's *Memoir.*

[2] Peter Chardon Brooks.

[3] *Francis Parkman,* by the Rev. O. B. Frothingham, Boston, 1894. *Proceedings of the Hist. Soc. of Mass.,* vol. viii. p. 521.

to her husband and children was with her a sacred duty. Humility, charity, truthfulness were her prime characteristics. Her conscience was firm and lofty, though never austere. She had a strong sense of right, coupled with perfect charity toward other people; inflexible in principle, she was gentle in practice. Intellectually she could hardly be called brilliant or accomplished, but she had a strong vein of common sense and practical wisdom, great penetration into character, and a good deal of quiet humor." And Miss Parkman says of her: "She had a strong unselfish and gentle nature, a calm and steady temperament, with deep feeling, yet great, though never cold reserve. She had abundant common sense and excellent judgment, great penetration in discerning character, shrewd and humorous, but never sharp in her criticism of it. She was too retiring and self-distrustful to share her husband's marked social tastes, but in her large circle of friends and relations she was a great favorite. She was very simple in her tastes, loved her home, and never wanted to leave it, and was its centre, the sure and loving dependence of all in it. The strength and sweetness of her nature were all expressed in her face. Whatever characteristics Frank inherited from his parents came from her. He was like her in many ways, and the expression of his face grew more and more like hers. She had, I think, always a peculiar tenderness toward him, her oldest child." Mrs. Parkman brought into the family most fortunate elements, — a mental steadiness and moral earnestness that elevated and purified as much as it sweetened.

This superficial account of Parkman's ancestry, is, however, almost useless, nor would a much fuller one help us where we most desire help, — in comprehending the personality we are about to study; our data and insight are still utterly inadequate to a solution of the mysteries of heredity, and we cannot trace many of Parkman's peculiarities to their sources. Yet there is a certain interest, if no certain knowledge, in these glimpses; they enable us to mark some traits that might be overlooked without such hints to arouse and direct curiosity. They will enable us to see how vigorously and independently he disagreed with many of the tendencies and traditions of his family; how, on the other hand, he faithfully adhered to many of them; and again, how he often wished to free himself from some of the most fundamental inherited forces of his character.

A biography to be worth anything should have its basis in a thorough knowledge of the subject's character, since all the practical accomplishments of his life spring from that source. The fundamentals of his physical and mental being are the only keys to his aims, tastes, abilities, limitations, and achievements. We need these keys at the start, justly to appreciate, as we go along, the life to be described. Parkman's physical organism was strangely compounded of strength and weakness. It lacked that equilibrium of forces which secures health and makes consecutive labor possible. His eyes failed him in college, and ever afterwards refused their usual service; his brain was affected by some disorder that limited, and often entirely prevented intellectual activity; in short, he had to endure a great deal of pain and suffering nearly all his life. In the intimate question of the body's relation to mental action, it must be noted that his senses were not highly developed; he was more or less insensible to delicate impressions from sound, color, odors, taste, and touch. His physical organism thus imposed on him many limitations, although it gave him the advantages of exceptional energy, a great love of activity, and a very tenacious vitality and power of endurance.[1]

The mental make-up of the man corresponded with his physical development, his character being marked by a few simple and elementary powers rather than by delicacy, subtlety, and variety of sensibilities and emotions. His entire personality was moulded by the master quality of manliness. Impetuosity, courage, honesty, energy, reserve, a practical turn of mind, and an iron will were his chief forces. A lack

[1] "In personal appearance Mr. Parkman was distinctly noticeable. He was about five feet eleven in height, square-shouldered, and firm-set. He had a strong, clear-cut face, always closely shaved, with a chin and jaw of marked vigor of outline. His forehead was rugged and broad; his whole carriage and expression was that of a modest but resolute man, capable, spite of whatever drawbacks and infirmities, of hard work and the persistent prosecution of difficult undertakings." (E. L. Godkin, in the *New York Evening Post*, Nov. 9, 1893.)

of certain elements of spirituality constituted his chief defect; a matter to be more fully dwelt on in a later chapter.

These, then, were the raw materials of the human entity, Francis Parkman — the marble that his gifts, ambition, and experience were to carve into the historian, the citizen, the friend, the father.

Mr. Parkman's Residence, from 1838 until his marriage, Bowdoin Square, Boston.

CHAPTER II

CHRONOLOGICAL

FRANCIS PARKMAN, eldest son of the Rev. Francis Parkman and Caroline (Hall) Parkman, was born in Boston, Mass., on the 16th of September, 1823. He was born in a house that still exists, though much altered, — the "Lyndhurst," No. 4A Allston Street. About 1829 the family moved to No. 1 Green Street, where they resided until about 1838, when they took possession of the house that Samuel Parkman, the historian's grandfather, had built for himself. This stately colonial mansion, No. 5 Bowdoin Square, was one of the landmarks of Boston.

"It was an excellent specimen of the Colonial residences once so common in and around Boston, a large square house, three stories in height, and built of brick. . . . Within was a fine entrance hall, and a noble staircase with spiral balusters. When the house was demolished the historian caused these balusters to be removed, and placed on the stairs of the house which he built for himself at Jamaica Plain. . . . There was a 'front yard' enclosed by a light and simple iron fence with tall square pillars at the corners. In the rear was a large paved courtyard, and beyond that, where the land sloped rapidly to the north, a garden, divided into terraces, one below the other, and devoted to the cultivation of fruits rather than of flowers. The flavor of a certain choice variety of bergamot pear which grew there still lingers in the memory of those who were ever so fortunate as to taste it."[1]

Later we see Parkman as a child from eight to thirteen years of age, living on his grandfather's farm at Medford, where he developed his love of nature by roaming the woods of the Middlesex Fells; and again as a schoolboy, serious over his books in the Chauncy Hall School, or with equal earnestness studying nature more intimately in chemistry and the natural sciences.

In 1840 he entered Harvard College in the class of '44. During his college course he devoted himself with ardor and concentration to his special interests, — the study of rhetoric and history, the pursuit of physical development, and a knowledge of the American wilderness. His diaries of these years enable us to follow his vacation trips to the wilds of New England and localities of historical interest; but no record offers much information as to the formative forces of his life. In his freshman year he "chummed" with his classmate Benjamin Apthorp Gould in No. 9 Holworthy Hall. After that he had a room to himself, — a condition better suited to his reserved and studious nature. When sophomore he lived at Mrs. Ayers's on the corner of Garden Street and the Appian Way; in the junior year he lived in

[1] Wheelwright.

24 Massachusetts Hall, during the senior year in 21 of the same building.

For the first year of his law course, 1844–5, he occupied No. 7 Divinity Hall; after that date he generally lived with his parents, until his marriage in 1850.

It was in 1841 that he began the researches and experiences that were to fit him for his work, making his first trip to the wilderness with Daniel D. Slade, passing through Portsmouth to Alton, thence along Lake Winnipesaukee to Centre Harbor; on to the Notch and up Mount Washington; thence to Franconia Notch, Lancaster, Colebrook, Dixville Notch, thence to the Androscoggin river near the mouth of the Magalloway, and up this river to its junction with the Little Magalloway.

The next year, in company with Henry Orne White, he made a second trip to the Magalloway. They passed through Albany, Saratoga, and Glens Falls to Lake George. After studying the battle-fields about Caldwell they hired a rowboat and spent a week camping along the shores of the lake, — fishing, shooting, climbing mountains, and hunting rattle-snakes. At Sabbath Day Point he tarried a day to gather from an old Revolutionary pensioner, Captain Patchen, traditions connected with the region. After a careful examination of Ticonderoga the two crossed Lake Champlain to Burlington, and there began their walk to Canada and the head-waters of the Magalloway. They passed through Essex, Jericho,

Underhill, Cambridge, Johnson, Troy, Stanstead, Barnston and Canaan, and finally reached Connecticut Lake. From this point onward their journey is described in "Harper's Magazine" for November, 1864. Parkman often expressed a particular fondness for Lake George; it was perhaps, after his home, the corner of the earth most dear to him. As the object of his first literary pilgrimage, it stirred his imagination strongly both by its beautiful scenery and its exceptional wealth of historical traditions.

In the winter vacation of 1843 he visited his classmates Hale and Perry, at Keene, N. H.

"'It was doubtless with recollections of this visit and of others in his mind, that in the last published volume of his histories, Parkman speaks of Keene as 'a town noted in rural New England for kindly hospitality, culture without pretence, and good breeding without conventionality.'[1] His two classmates were not the only acquaintances he had in this delightful New Hampshire town. Two years before, while with Slade in the White Mountains, he had fallen in with a lively party of travellers from this place, and one young lady in particular had charmed him by the 'laughing philosophy' with which she had taken 'a ducking' in his company while passing through the Notch on the stage and in a pouring rain. Still more was he pleased by the 'strength and spirit and good-humor' she had shown in the ascent of Mount Washington. With this lady, who afterwards married a distinguished citizen of her native State,[2] Parkman kept up a lifelong friendship."

[1] *A Half Century*, vol. ii. p. 230. [2] Wheelwright.

There is no reference in diaries or letters of 1843 to any journey to the wilderness. But he made a trip to Canada for historical materials, examining again on the way the battlefields of Lake George and Lake Champlain, going on to St. Johns and Chambly, and visiting Montreal. He gathered notes of the Hope Gate and other important localities at Quebec, and on his way back to Boston through the White Mountains, noted many stories of frontier life and border warfare. Perhaps it was at this time that he made the trip to which he refers in "Montcalm and Wolfe":

"I once, when a college student, followed on foot the route of Rogers from Lake Memphremagog to the Connecticut."

He then went to Maine to study the Indians near Bangor and to collect the traditions of their wars with the Mohawks. This vacation was evidently something else than the collegian's usual season of idleness. This nineteenth summer of his life, the beginning of his exclusive devotion to historical labors, witnessed the birth of the deep enthusiasm that later overcame such remarkable obstacles, and infused his persistent industry with heroism.

In September he visited Europe, making the tour we shall follow in his diaries.

In 1844, after a creditable though not brilliant college career, he graduated from Harvard and entered the Harvard Law School.

"He was a member, while in college, of the Institute of 1770, of the I. O. H., of the Hasty Pudding Club, — of which he was successively Vice-President and President, — of the Harvard Natural History Society, — of which he was Corresponding and Recording Secretary and Curator of Mineralogy, — of the C. C. or Chit-Chat, of the short-lived R. T. D., and of the Phi Beta Kappa." [1]

The vacations of this year he devoted to historical research. Taking his rifle he tramped alone over the hills of western Massachusetts, to study the routes followed by the French and Indians in their attacks on that region. He passed through Springfield, Cabotville (old name of Chicopee), Chester Factory, Lee, Stockbridge, Great Barrington, Mount Washington, Lebanon Springs, Stephentown, the Hopper and North Adams.

The diary of 1845 shows that he had now focussed his ambitions on a definite work — the Conspiracy of Pontiac. In April of that year he made a trip to St. Louis, and spent the summer in collecting materials for this volume. He visited Lancaster, Paradise, Harrisburg, Williamsport, Trout Run, Blossburg, Corning, Seneca Lake, Rochester, Buffalo, Detroit, Windsor, Sandwich, Mackinaw, Sault Ste. Marie, Palmer, Newport, Niagara, the Devil's Hole, Fort Niagara, Oswego, Syracuse and Onondaga Castle. In all these journeys he showed indefatigable energy and alertness, and while his main interest was historical research, in which pursuit he noted the scenery of historic places, examined family papers and other

[1] Wheelwright's *Class of 1844*, p. 162.

documents, and wherever it was possible interviewed descendants of the actors in his historic drama, his diary reveals almost as much of interest in nature, human nature, and civilization. The sketches he contributed to the "Knickerbocker Magazine"[1] show something of these tendencies crystallized in literary forms.

In the winter of 1846 he made a trip through Pennsylvania, visiting Trenton, Philadelphia, Washington, Baltimore, Harrisburg, Carlisle, Chambersburg and Pittsburg. This year is marked also by his most adventurous and important expedition, the trip of the Oregon Trail.

His classmate, Mr. Wheelwright, has given us the following glimpse of Parkman's social life in college:

"His boarding-place during the greater part of his College course was at Mrs. Schutte's, a lady who kept an excellent table at what was thought a very moderate price even in those days. The company was numerous, comprising representatives of all the classes. Much lively and interesting talk went on there, at and after meals, and not a little good-natured chaffing. Almost all the guests had some soubriquet conferred upon them, more or less indicative of their characters, or of some peculiarity of appearance or manner. Some of these, from their happy appropriateness, soon spread beyond the coterie where they originated, and have even clung to their recipients through life. Such was not the case with that

[1] See the list of his works in Appendix.

bestowed upon Mr. Parkman. From being oftener an amused listener to conversation than an active participant in it, he was called *lucus a non lucendo*, 'The Loquacious,' a title so absurdly inappropriate that his college friends to-day recall it with difficulty. Far from being the unsocial character this ironical nickname would imply, Mr. Parkman keenly enjoyed the society of his fellow-students. Never boisterous in his mirth, he was by no means averse to taking part in merrymakings and festivities. He was catholic in his likings, and had already begun to develop that keen insight into character which is one of the striking features of his historical writings. He could penetrate within the outer covering of mannerisms and affectations, and see the man himself. He enjoyed with equal zest the wild exuberance of William Morris Hunt and the placid philosophy of George Blankern Cary. He took a lively interest in all that went on in College, and was always ready to do his share in protesting against abuses and redressing wrongs. An instance of this is recorded in the contemporary journal of a classmate. At one time, in the Sophomore year, the Latin professor, Dr. Beck, adopted the arbitrary and novel practice of calling the roll in his recitation-room at precisely the hour, instead of five minutes after, as had been the immemorial custom, and also of marking as absent all who simply came late. Parkman thereupon drew up a memorial, remonstrating against the innovation, obtained the signatures of the principal members of the class, and sent it to the Faculty. And the remonstrance had the desired effect." . . . "Though rather fond of calling upon his classmates, with whom he was always popular, he rarely asked them to visit him in return. One reason probably was that he was very little in his own room, except at night for the purpose of sleeping. His constant craving for bodily exercise kept him out-of-doors or at the gymnasium the greater part of the day. Moreover, as is now known, he had already begun to read such books as he thought suited to help him toward the attainment of his great object, already well outlined in his mind. He did not care to have these secret studies interrupted by chance callers, who might also discover in his room some traces of the 'lucubrations' which he says he pursued at this time 'with a pernicious intensity,' keeping his plans and purposes to himself, while passing among his companions as an outspoken fellow." [1]

Parkman's reserve as to his literary ambition was somewhat exceptional. He not only published his first productions anonymously, but he persistently denied any such ambition as late as 1845. In the following letter to his classmate, George B. Cary, he said:

CAMBRIDGE, Dec. 15, '44.

DEAR GEORGE, — Here am I, down in Divinity Hall (!) enjoying to my heart's content that *otium cum dignitate* which you so affectionately admire; while you, poor devil, are being jolted in English coaches, or suffering the cramp in both legs on the banquette of a French diligence. Do you not envy me in my literary ease? — a sea-coal fire — a dressing-gown — slippers — a favorite author; all set off by an occasional bottle of champagne, or a bowl of stewed oysters at Washburn's? This is the

[1] Wheelwright.

cream of existence. To lay abed in the morning, till the sun has half melted away the trees and castles on the window-panes, and Nigger Lewis's fire is almost burnt out, listening meanwhile to the steps of the starved Divinities as they rush shivering and panting to their prayers and recitations — then to get up to a fashionable breakfast at eleven — then go to lecture — find it a little too late, and adjourn to Joe Peabody's room, for a novel, conversation, and a morning glass of madeira — while you are puckering your lips over bad *vin ordinaire* in a splendid café, and screaming *garçon* in vain hope of relief. If I am not mistaken, George, this is leading a happier life, by your own showing, than to be encountering the hard knocks and vexations of a traveller's existence. After all, man *was* made to be happy; ambition is a humbug — a dream of youth; and exertion another; leave those to Freshmen and divinities. I think the morbid tendency to unnecessary action passes away as manhood comes on; at any rate, I have never been half so quiescent as since I was qualified to vote against Polk and Dallas.

Perhaps you may imagine me under some vinous influence in writing thus. Not at all; yet if I had written this a few nights ago, perhaps it might have smacked more of inspiration. We had a class spree! where, if there was not much wit, there was, as the Vicar of Wakefield says, a great deal of laughing, not to mention singing, roaring, and unseemly noises of a miscellaneous character. There was Gould, and Farnsworth, Wild, Batchelder, and numbers more of the same renown. Joe also gave an entertainment not long ago, where, if there was not so much noise made, there were better jokes cracked and better champagne opened. And now, what are you doing; a cup of coffee at Véry's, perhaps; then a lounge, quizzing glass at eye, in the Louvre, followed by a ditto on the Italian Boulevard, and a fifty-franc dinner at the Trois Frères. What supplement shall I add to this? You will not be sorry, I dare say, to hear a word of some brethren of your *noctes ambrosianæ,* though I imagine that those *noctes* do not now appear very ambrosial on the retrospect. Hale vibrates between Law and Gospel. I fear the chances are a little in favor of the Devil. Snow is established in Graduates' Hall, with two pianos, Shelley, and a half-cask of ale. He now and then appears at the one o'clock lecture, rubbing his eyes and gaping. Clarke is here, taking boxing lessons. Ned is in town, a counter-jumper by day, and a literary character by night; on the way to make a very sensible and accomplished man. Perry has been *hunting* deer and *killing* partridges, and would fain persuade a quiet fellow like me to leave Cambridge and join him; but I preferred a pleasant fireside. Old Treadwell is splashing about in the muddy waters of politics and law. Our brothers, whilom of X X, accused me in the beginning of the term of an intention of authorship! probably taking the hint from the circumstance of my never appearing till eleven o'clock, à la Scott; but I believe they no longer suspect me of so ill advised an intention. It would run a little counter to my present principles, though I *do* remember the time when G. B. C. meditated the Baron of B——; and Snow felt sure (in his cups) of being Captain General of Transatlantic literature, while your humble servant's less soaring ambition aspired to the manufacture of blood and thunder chronicles of Indian squabbles and massacres. But I have discovered a new vein of talent, which I think you did not suspect. In fact, *I* did not dream I could play the hypocrite so well as to deceive your discerning eye, on my return from Europe. I think I did, however: and I believe you embarked in the impression that foreign travel had wasted all its charms on my incorrigible idiosyncrasy. You will answer this, will you not? I am very eager to hear from you.[1]

Yours truly,

F. Parkman.

Parkman still concealed the master passion of his soul when writing to another of his most intimate friends, the next year:

"By the way, what do you mean by charging me (for the fourth time, is it ?) with a design to write a novel, or a poem, or an essay, or whatever it is ? Allow me to tell you that though the joke may be good, it is certainly old. . . . If you catch me writing anything of the sort, you might call me a 'darned fool' with great propriety as well as elegance."[2]

In answer to his friend's charge of deception, he wrote:

"He [a mutual friend] tells me besides that you threaten me with vengeance for deceiving you as to my intention of 'publication,' to which charge I most emphatically plead not guilty, and deprecate your wrath. I think an occasional 'posterior,' as Perry calls them, in the 'Knickerbocker' will hardly put me in the predica-

[1] Letter to G. B. Cary.

[2] To G. S. Hale, Feb. 13, 1845.

ment of a publisher, and I did not suspect that 'literary intentions' had with you so comprehensive a signification."[1]

Although the following letter is not important for its contents, it has a certain interest as the only autobiographic offset to the Spartan spirit that ruled his life.

He wrote to G. S. Hale, Nov. 24, 1844:

"We wanted you the other night. Joe got up one of his old-fashioned suppers, on a scale of double magnificence, inviting thereunto every specimen of the class of '44 that lingered within an accessible distance. There was old S. and Snaggy, N. D., Ned W. (who, by the way, is off for Chili!), P., etc., etc. The spree was worthy of the entertainment. None got drunk, but all got jolly; and Joe's champagne disappeared first; then his madeira; and his whiskey punch would have followed suit, if its copious supplies had not prevented. At first, all was quiet and dignified, not unworthy of graduates; but at length the steam found vent in three cheers for '44, and after that we did not cease singing and roaring till one o'clock. Even my hideous voice grew musical; I succeeded in actually singing in the chorus to 'Yankee Doodle,' without perceptibly annoying the rest. At length, all deserted, except a chosen few. Old S. sat on the rocking-chair, with one foot on the table, and the other on his neighbor's shoulder, laughing and making execrable puns. He had the key of the door in his pocket so that nobody could get out. The whole ended with smashing a dozen bottles against the Washington [word

[1] To G. S. Hale, April 24, 1845.

illegible], and a war-dance with scalp-yells in the middle of the Common, in the course of which several night-capped heads appeared at the opened windows of the astonished neighbors."

As Parkman was already guided by the literary ambition that governed his entire career, we can appropriately take that purpose as the thread on which to string the facts of his subsequent external life. Such a course is all the clearer since he rarely made a journey or undertook any labor disconnected from his work. But unfortunately there is little material out of which to spin this thread, and the thread itself is rarely met with in our scanty biographical details.

At the close of the year 1846 he had seen most of the remnants of Indian tribes to be found from Maine to the Rocky Mountains, visited nearly all the localities connected with his theme, and gathered what could be procured of family papers and traditions, besides official and published documents. Thus he had made a good beginning in the collection of materials for his great work when hardly more than out of college. Early in his researches he had in view not only the general theme of the Old French War, but the special topic of the Conspiracy of Pontiac. Although this subject was the last one in his epoch of history, he wrote it the first, — perhaps regarding it as easier to deal with than the others, and more certain of success because of its picturesqueness.

Finding his health in a deplorable state at the

close of his Oregon Trail journey, he devoted himself largely to medical treatment during 1847 and 1848. He spent the greater part of these years in New York and at West New Brighton on Staten Island, under the care of an oculist, also at a water cure in Brattleboro, Vt., to improve his general health. But literary ambition was not to be put aside on account of illness and poor sight. With the help of friendly eyes and hands he first dictated "The Oregon Trail" in the autumn of 1846, then took up "Pontiac." A gentleman[1] who as a boy knew Parkman when the latter lived on Staten Island, gives me these recollections of him:

"With regard to Frank Parkman, I do remember him very distinctly when he was down here for treatment of his eyes about 1847.

"At the same time were gathered there for the same purpose — my father's ministrations — a goodly number of disenchanted dreamers of Brook Farm, then in process of disintegration — Mr. Dana, Mr. Ripley, and many others less experimentally philanthropic or more purely literary, among whom were Longfellow, Willis, Morris, while for a time the Rev. Charles Lowell, his son James, and his daughters were, with Professor Youmans, members of the household.

"Frank Parkman, or 'Cousin Frank,' as he was called by the Shaw family, was a great favorite with the boys; with whom he played and to whom he told wondrous tales of adventure by field and flood — he having recently returned from one of his frontier expeditions. Later his

[1] Dr. S. R. Elliott.

stories began to vary from the strictly historical, and to take on the guise of fictions. And at last one evening when we were out rowing on the river in front of our house 'Cousin Frank' told of a frightful struggle which he and his companions had with sharks, in the Bay of California, which lasted over two hours and during which he and his two companions — Mexican pearl divers — were in 90 feet of water, so that when the party reached the surface, they were all nearly out of breath. We boys looked at each other silently for a while, until Bob Shaw, who being a relation was less shy of speech — did ejaculate 'g'long'! so forcibly that the passage from the credible to the incredible was recognized. On another occasion — also in the boat — he told us about a row among the animals at an Eastern menagerie, during which he had tied the trunk to the tail of the biggest and most savage elephant, under his belly, till he surrendered by holding up his paw and purring. We were never quite sure after that whether the tales of adventure so freely narrated were meant to be taken literally or not, as 'Cousin Frank's' face gave no outward or visible sign for grave or gay. . . . He was an excellent talker among his peers, the adults, and we boys liked him even better than James Russell Lowell, who had taken more notice of our adolescence, but who somehow appeared condescending and Bostony to our untutored fancy."

He returned to his father's house in 1849, having reaped but little benefit from the efforts of the doctors — the "medical faculty," as he used to call them. With the help of his friend, Charles Eliot Norton, in reading proof, he was able to prepare "The Oregon

Trail" for publication in book form. In 1850 he married Catherine Scollay, a daughter of Dr. Jacob Bigelow. His marriage was a very happy one, yet this epoch of his life was not free from severe strain. With a small income — up to the death of his father in 1852 — he found some difficulty in meeting the expenses of a domestic establishment and those of historical research. His first home was a cottage, still standing on Dorchester Avenue, at Milton Lower Falls; afterward he occupied for a year or two a house in Brookline, on Cottage Street, generally spending the winter season in Boston with his parents or his father-in-law. When at the death of his father he came into the possession of money, he bought about three acres of land on the shore of Jamaica Pond. Here was the cottage which he occupied for half the year until he rebuilt it in 1874; and he continued to live there through the summer and autumn for the rest of his life. In 1853 "the enemy" again became too aggressive to be ignored, and again he resorted to water-cure, at Northampton. He was always willing to give the doctors every facility and to undergo any method of treatment, following faithfully the advice he sought — excepting in regard to giving up writing.

Meanwhile, with the help of his wife and her sister, Miss Mary Bigelow, as amanuensis, he pushed along his literary labors. As soon as "Pontiac" was off his hands — 1851 — he began collecting materials for his historical series, and also wrote a few reviews of historical works for the "Christian Examiner." He now tried his hand at fiction, publishing "Vassal Morton" in 1856. In this year he made a trip to Montreal, Quebec, and Nova Scotia.

But even this limited and precarious activity was greatly hindered and finally arrested; for arthritis attacked one of his knees in 1851, and by depriving him of his usual walks greatly impaired his general powers. Horseback riding relieved him to some degree, but even this was not always possible. His family now numbered three children: Grace, born in 1851, Francis, born in 1854, and Katharine, in 1858. The first great bereavement of his life fell with the death of his promising son in 1857. The next year profound grief again came upon him in the loss of his wife. His sister-in-law, Miss Bigelow, now took his daughters to her home, and relieved him of personal responsibility as to the care and education of them. This arrangement was the more fortunate since the state of his brain made it out of the question for him to work in anything but the utmost quietness, or to occupy himself with the details of domestic economy. But he enjoyed having his children with him a portion of each year, and made himself very companionable to them. As one was of a jovial, and the other of a more philosophical turn, he used to say that he had one daughter for his amusement, the other for his instruction.

Shortly after the death of his wife he went abroad, and spent the winter of 1858–59 in Paris, at the

Mr. Parkman's House and Grounds,
Jamaica Plain, Mass.

Mr. Parkman's House and Grounds,
Jamaica Plain, Mass.

Hôtel de France et de Bath. His brain was then in such a condition that the most eminent specialists of Paris warned him against insanity and forbade him all literary labor; but while spending his time chiefly in observing the life of the streets from the tops of omnibuses, he yet managed to make some investigations in the archives, and to arrange for the copying of documents. Returning to Boston without any improvement in his alarming condition, he joined the family of his mother and sisters, living with them in winter, at No. 8 Walnut Street until 1864, and thenceforth at No. 50 Chestnut Street. They in turn passed the summer with him on the shores of Jamaica Pond.

Parkman was now approaching the worst epoch of his life. The condition of his brain made the least literary labor suicidal; he was called upon to face the certainty of permanent invalidism and the probability of never reaching the goal of his ambition. The way in which he met "the enemy" was characteristic of his courage, cheerfulness, and common sense. Out of the most depressing circumstances he not only wrung a notable success in the conduct of his life, but contributed greatly to the happiness of others. Seeing the temple of fame closed against him, he turned to Nature for consolation. Horticulture became his exclusive occupation for several years — until his health permitted him to resume his pen. His success in this field is the more noteworthy, because he had neither scientific training nor much money to devote to the undertaking. After mastering the principles of the science by reading, he threw into gardening the same ardor and painstaking perseverance that subsequently carried him to success in writing history. He was not long in surpassing his neighbors who had the advantage of him both in material means and experience. It is noteworthy that two other American historians, Bancroft and Prescott, turned their attention to gardening and became celebrated as growers of roses.

Parkman prepared his grounds for horticulture by building a greenhouse, making beds, and planting trees and shrubbery. He employed a good gardener and one or two subordinates to till the soil, but directed everything himself, giving the closest attention to practical details.

When able to walk, he would go at a rapid gait from place to place, and sit down on a stool carried for the purpose; he would then do some of the lighter work, such as sowing seeds, planting borders, weeding, and cultivating. He often cut the grass of the borders when sitting in his wheel chair, and used a rake or hoe in this inconvenient attitude. Sometimes the sensitiveness of his eyes prevented him from being out-of-doors in the sunlight; yet in spite of all such opposing conditions, he soon became so well known among his friends and neighbors as a successful grower of flowers that the Massachusetts Horticultural Society elected him a life member. His reputation brought him an important opportunity. In

1860 or 1861 Mr. Francis L. Lee, of Chestnut Hill, when enlisting for the war, turned over to Mr. Parkman, as the most competent person, a lot of plants and bulbs he had received from Japan and partially brought to flowering — among them the *lilium auratum* and the Parkman Crab. This stroke of fortune thus placed in his hands new and interesting materials, stimulated his ambition to further study, and laid a good part of the foundation of his fame as a horticulturist. In 1862 the possibilities of the case induced him to form a partnership with a horticulturist, with a view of purchasing more land and developing his gardening as a business venture. This scheme, however, was abandoned at the end of a year, though he thriftily turned his labors to some profit by selling plants. Persons who bought of him, still speak of the fairness and generosity of his dealing and the excellence of his wares.

Although Parkman cultivated a variety of flowers, he devoted himself chiefly to the growing of roses and the hybridization of lilies. It is said that he had at one time a thousand varieties of roses in his garden. His most important contribution to horticulture was the magnificent *lilium Parkmanni*, which he sold in 1876 to an English florist for a large sum. He brought out also new varieties of delphinium, phlox, poppy, and other flowers. His garden, especially in the season of flowering shrubs, delighted the eye by its wealth of blossom and glow of color. The flowers themselves rather than the study of arrangement and effect — which did not so much interest him — made its great attraction. The Bussey Institute thought it worth while to publish a list of these when his property was taken by the city of Boston, as part of Jamaica Park. His eminence in horticulture is well attested. The reports of the Massachusetts Horticultural Society show that he received, between the years 1859 and 1884, no fewer than 326 awards — a large proportion being first prizes — besides one bronze and sixteen silver medals. In that society he served as Chairman of the Library Committee from 1863 to 1874; he was Vice-President from 1871 to 1874, and President from 1875 to 1878, when he had to decline re-election. He published a few articles in Tilton's "Journal of Horticulture" in 1867 to 1871. In 1866, at the request of a publisher, he wrote "The Book of Roses," which still holds its position as one of the best guides in the cultivation of that flower; and he wrote a valuable paper on the hybridization of lilies.[1] In 1871 Harvard appointed him Professor of Horticulture to the Bussey Institute — a position he resigned at the end of a year. His duties there were agreeable and not onerous: no preparation being needed to go twice a week to the greenhouses and talk to a class of young women about the cultivation of flowers. He gave up special efforts in horticulture about 1884, when his lameness increased, and thereafter simply maintained his garden for the pleasure of it. He was generous with his flowers, glad to fill the hands

[1] *Bulletin of the Bussey Institute*, No. 15.

of any passer who showed an interest in them. He was very considerate of the feelings of his employees, and patient with them; the humor of a blunder generally outweighed the annoyance of a mistake, but when really vexed he walked away in silence.

Horticulture thus gave him his most intimate contact with nature; it was indeed the only means by which his love came in from the wilderness to a homely and affectionate regard for individual objects. Parkman's general feeling towards gardening and the benefits he himself derived from it are well expressed in the following extract from his presidential address of 1875:

"You have placed me at the head of a society whose sole aim is the promotion of that gracious art which, through all time, has been the companion and the symbol of peace: an art joined in closest ties with Nature, and her helper in the daily miracle by which she works beauty out of foulness and life out of corruption; an art so tranquillizing and so benign; so rich in consolations and pleasures; and one, too, which appeals to all mankind and finds votaries among rich and poor, learned and simple alike. Let us be grateful to the three deities who preside over these halls, and let us not fail to yield them a fitting homage. Horticulture, which in their serene and graceful trinity they combine to represent, is not one of the mechanic arts. It is an art based on a science, or on several sciences. When pursued in its highest sense and to its best results, it demands the exercise of a great variety of faculties, and gives scope to a high degree of mental activity. On the other side of the Atlantic, horticulture, as a profession, stands to-day in a position of eminence. It has proved an avenue to social consideration and public honor. Ability, energy, and self-knowledge can lead men to distinction by the pathways of the garden as well as by the dusty road of what are rather invidiously called the learned professions . . . Horticulture, broadly pursued, is an education in itself, and no pursuit can surpass it in training the powers of observation and induction. The mind of the true cultivator is always on the alert to detect the working of principles and carry them to their practical application. To read the secrets of nature and aid her in her beneficent functions is his grateful and ennobling task."

But we must return to the historian. His restrictions now prevented him from doing much serious historical labor for fourteen years — from the publication of "Pontiac" in 1851 to the appearance of Part I. of his series, "The Pioneers," in 1865. During this trying epoch he was now and then able to gather and arrange some of his material; and he produced several works of minor importance — a few book reviews, the novel "Vassall Morton" in 1856, and "The Book of Roses" in 1866. At the close of the war he visited Washington and Richmond, that he might at least see the battlefields where he would have fought with so much zeal. The Boston Athenæum voted him $500 to buy rebel documents and publications; and he brought back some valuable papers to that institution. In 1866 he made a journey to Montreal, Two Mountains, the Long Sault, the

Chaudière; and then to Quebec to study in detail the scenes connected with Wolfe's attack. Feeling the need of once more seeing the Indians in their native state, he made a journey to Fort Snelling in 1867, visiting on the way Keokuk, Peoria and the Illinois River, Prairie du Chien, and St. Louis, and at the latter place hunting up his old guide and friend, Henry Chatillon, with whom he had continued to correspond since the Oregon Trail trip. The Ottawa and Lake Nipissing were the only important historical locality that he did not see. 1868 was a year of exceptional suffering, rendering all work impossible, although he accepted election as Overseer of Harvard College. Finding that complete idleness now seemed necessary, and preferring Paris to any other place for such a life, he went abroad for the winter, establishing himself in lodgings at No. 21 Boulevard Saint Michel. Here he was vainly sought after by some of the writers of Paris and the élite of the Faubourg St. Germain. In the course of the winter his health improved sufficiently to enable him to enjoy sight-seeing and even make some researches, so that at his return in the spring of 1869 he resumed his labors and saw "La Salle" through the press.

This year Parkman resigned his position as Overseer of Harvard, and accepted an appointment as Professor of Horticulture. In 1872 he went again to Europe for historical materials. Desiring some personal knowledge of the French Canadian people, he spent some weeks of 1873 in visiting several families living on their seigniories along the shores of the St. Lawrence below Quebec. It is unfortunate that we have nothing characteristic to tell of his frequent visits to Canada. He made many pleasant acquaintances at Montreal and Quebec, among both the English and the French writers, lay and clerical. 1874 is marked by the appearance of the "Old Régime." In 1875 he was chosen one of the Fellows of the Corporation of Harvard. "Frontenac" was published in 1877. Again he explored the region between Lake George and Quebec, studying minutely the battlefields along the route. The state of his health prevented him from accepting the Presidency of the Archæological Institute in 1878, but the following year finds him once more in Quebec and Louisburg. In 1880 he helped to organize the St. Botolph Club — an association of the literary men and artists of Boston. The club chose him for the first President, and re-elected him for six successive years, as long as his strength allowed him to serve. His occasional utterances on public questions, showing how deep an interest he took in our national growth, led a Civil Service Reform Association to invite him in 1881 to be one of its Vice-Presidents. "Montcalm and Wolfe" appeared in 1884. In 1885 he made a journey to Florida to examine the places of historical interest in that region; stopping on the way at Beaufort, South Carolina; then going on to Fernandina, Jacksonville, Fort George, Palatka, Ocklawaha river, Ocala

The Camp on the Batiscan River, Province of Quebec.

From a photograph taken in 1886.

and St. Augustine. In 1886 he camped with me a month on the Batiscan River — the first time this lover of wild life had been to the woods in forty years. A delightful companion he was, interested in all the labors and pleasures of camp life, cheerful and patient under all circumstances. Despite his lame knee, he insisted on helping me complete the roof, the fireplace, and the tables we needed, and in doing what he could of camp work. In washing the dishes he always used water far too hot for his hands, saying "It's so much more effective" — a characteristic word of his. When I had chopped down some trees and cleared a little piece of land for a garden on the river bank, he gave the finishing touches to the soil and sowed the seeds. He had bought for the trip a Winchester rifle and a bamboo fly-rod. The mere possession of the rifle was the chief pleasure he anticipated from it, since he could not walk enough to do more than fire a few rounds in a camp at a target. He was a fair shot, even at that age and after so long disuse of firearms. Although a good bait fisherman, he now took his first lessons in casting the fly, and always thereafter showed much appreciation and respect for the fine art of angling. One day we went up the river in canoes to a large pool at the foot of a rapid where the currents were strong and the waters rather tumultuous. When I had worked up the pool and dropped anchor close to the cascade I beckoned him to follow. Being unused to canoeing and to rough waters, he evidently thought the attempt somewhat dangerous; but after casting a penetrating glance at my face, he came up into line with a certain martial obedience. He often talked of the French-Canadians, viewing them as the result of forces manifest in their history and their religion. He now and then spoke of the noted literary people of Boston, setting forth with great certainty of touch and sharpness of outline their salient traits; his criticism, while kindly and impartial, was always keen and firm. The most interesting manifestation of his personality was his mute approaches to nature after so many years of separation. He would look up at a bold bluff that arose several hundred feet above the river, as if fain to scale once more such lofty cliffs. Often he would get into the canoe and float down the river for a glimpse of our neighbors, a family of beaver. I recall most vividly his expectant look off into the depths of the forest as I once took my rod and paddled away to give him a day of solitude. His sojourn at camp was so agreeable and beneficial that he wished to remain longer, but his fidelity to Harvard did not allow him to be absent from Commencement. On leaving for Boston he took with him a box full of ferns for his garden. As circumstances prevented him from carrying out his intention of returning to camp, he went in July to the Rangeley Lakes, and built a log cabin at the Bemis Camp, hoping that he and his sister might sometimes go thither; but his infirmities never allowed him to make the journey a second time. He went with his sister to Europe in the summer of 1880 and again in 1881 — his purpose being both to see his daughter who was then living in Paris and to get historical material. His last journey to Europe was made in 1887, in the hope of getting benefit from some of the German spas. He went with his friend, Dr. Algernon Coolidge, by steamer to Santander, and thence to Madrid. He had barely reached the latter place and attended a bull fight, when a fresh attack of insomnia and lameness induced him to return home by way of Paris, after an absence of only a few weeks. His maladies compelled him in 1888 to resign his office of Fellow of the Corporation of Harvard, after a service of thirteen years. He was now spending a good part of every summer with his daughter and son-in-law, Mr. J. T. Coolidge, Jr., at their summer residence, the old Wentworth mansion at Little Harbor, Portsmouth, N. H. It was there that he wrote a part of "Montcalm and Wolfe," and finished "A Half Century of Conflict," published in 1892.

The close of Parkman's life was both happy and characteristic; — his work done, his reputation still in the ascendant, his friends increasing in number and appreciation. He had always hoped to die before reaching the lingering weakness and decrepitude of old age, for such a soul could not but dread anything that even pointed towards a diminution of power. When a friend once spoke with pride of the work he had done, his energy flamed out with the promise to do still more if he should live. His last summer was a very happy one; comparative freedom from pain and the absence of anxiety as to the completion of his work brought both comfort and peace. He spent the season where he most enjoyed it, at the Wentworth mansion and in the midst of his children and grandchildren. In the autumn he returned to his home at the Pond, to amuse himself with the late flowers or with his boat on the lake. On coming in from his last row, on a Sunday, he felt ill and took to his bed. Peritonitis set in, but he rallied so much by Tuesday evening that a successful surgical operation was thought possible. This hope had to be dismissed when he began to sink on Wednesday morning. He died peacefully about noon of that day, on the 8th of November, 1893, and was buried in the Mount Auburn Cemetery. The last book he read was "Childe Harold," and his last words were to tell that he had just dreamed of killing a bear. Though suffering extremely, he yet maintained to his last hour an impressive degree of dignity, firmness, gentleness, and serenity.

The honors that Parkman reaped were numerous. Laval University discussed conferring on him the degree of Doctor of Letters in 1878, though sectarian opposition defeated the project. McGill made him an LL.D. the following year, Williams in 1885, and Harvard in 1889. His official connections with Harvard will be explained later. He was a member of the following societies: Corresponding Member of the Royal Society of Canada, 1884; Honorary Member of the London Society of Antiquarians, 1878; Member of the Royal Historical Society of London, 1876, — resigned; Member of a score or more of American and provincial historical societies; Member of the Massachusetts Historical Society; Fellow of the American Academy of Arts and Sciences; Honorary Member of the Literary and Historical Society of Quebec; Member of the American Antiquarian Society, of the Archæological Institute of America, of the New England Historic Genealogical Society, of the Bostonian Society, of the American Folk-Lore Society, of the Massachusetts Horticultural Society, of the St. Botolph Club, and of the Colonial Society of Massachusetts.

The more intimate honor of personal esteem was abundantly shown him on the occasion of his seventieth birthday; and still more widely and publicly at the time of his death. By the initiative of his friend, Professor Sargent, a generous fund was subscribed at once for erecting a memorial that is to mark the site of his house and garden at Jamaica Pond.

Part I

PREPARATION

CHAPTER III

PARKMAN unconsciously began his preparation for historical writing in boyhood. From an early day he so directed his efforts as to secure in the happiest proportions the study of nature, books, man, life, and history; and we shall see that he also met with a very exceptional spiritual discipline, the result of an iron will and immense energy encountering great difficulties and sufferings.

He commenced his study of nature on Boston Common, by sounding the mysteries of Frog Pond with a pin hook, where he and his cousin caught horned pouts which they seasoned with ground cinnamon and broiled over a fire in his father's garden. But soon he passed on to larger fields. When eight years of age, having a delicate and sensitive physique, he was turned loose on the farm of his maternal grandfather, Nathaniel Hall, at Medford, Mass. There the boy enjoyed four years of wholesome freedom in fields and woods. He says of this time: "I walked twice a day to a school of high but undeserved reputation, about a mile distant in the town of Medford. Here I learned very little, and spent the intervals of schooling more profitably in collecting eggs, insects, and reptiles, trapping squirrels and woodchucks, and making persistent though rarely fortunate attempts to kill birds with arrows."[1] The woods, indeed, were so seductive as to be responsible for considerable truancy on his part, and some consequent fibbing. Those years at Medford were counted among his happiest, for the manifold interests and activities of country life were very congenial to his tastes; but the woods of the Middlesex Fells, at that time quite wild, were especially fitted to develop one of the boy's strongest passions, — the love of nature. There were hills that seemed mountains to his youthful mind and legs; cliffs of rock and uncertain marshes to arouse his spirit of adventure; wild animals to trail, shoot, or trap; ravines where the Indian warrior may have lain in wait for his victims; streams that caught up the fancy and whirled it along on bubbles to the rapids; ponds where the birch canoe could glide away through sunset clouds; and above all a forest having something of the silence, solitude, and mystery of primeval nature. The region thus reduced to a boy's grasp the boundless American wilderness and made him familiar with many elements of his future histories.

[1] He refers to the boarding-school for boys and girls, kept by Mr. John Angier; the Rev. O. B. Frothingham, a fellow student, speaks well of it, and Mr. Wheelwright says that many people of note received their early training in it.

But Parkman's mental energy led him, even at this early age, to probe still deeper into the natural sciences. He began, at Medford, a collection of minerals for which his father gave him a cabinet that he kept all his life, and in which he placed the rarer specimens met with in subsequent journeys. This study remained an active pursuit with him through his college days, resulting in a collection sufficiently important to be presented in 1847 to the Harvard Natural History Society. In fact, he seems never to have lost this interest, for a young friend who in his later days frequently rowed with him about Portsmouth says that his talk of the rocks there was entertaining even to a young man fresh from the geological course of Harvard.

Zoölogy was naturally attractive to the young sportsman; and, though in after years his observations were limited to civilized regions and domestic animals, it always remained a pleasant pastime. The only anecdotes remembered of his early youth relate to this subject. His omnivorous pockets scorned nothing they could hold, dead or alive. Once a snake that had revived in the warmth of the schoolroom stuck his head out of Frank's coat pocket, to the consternation of a little girl sitting near. Before throwing it out of the door, as commanded by the master, he made sure of the specimen by giving its neck a fatal wring. On another occasion his love of natural history seems to have been mingled with a good degree of humor. His father used to drive out to Medford and bring him home every Saturday to spend Sunday. These weekly returns to town were not at all to the boy's taste, and were said to be the only occasions on which he ever descended to any pretence; he used to stare blankly at familiar town sights, wishing to pass for a green country lad. It is easy to believe that he preferred roaming the woods rather than going to church. One Sabbath morning he chanced on a compensation. While the Rev. Dr. Parkman in his black silk gown with his wife on his arm was walking down Hanover street in all the dignity that became his cloth, the boy following behind them, Mrs. Parkman observed a queer smile on the faces of those they passed. Turning to find the cause, she beheld Frank carrying by the tail, at arm's length, a dead rat. His explanation that he wished to take it home to stuff did not avail; he was obliged to relinquish the rat and resume his walk with more decorum.

Parkman's fondness for animals by no means ceased when the graver duties of life replaced the plays of boyhood. In later years, "when visiting a friend residing in the country, the thing he found most to admire in the house, that which interested him most, was a rug made of the skins of three raccoons that had been trapped on the premises. He seemed never to tire of contemplating the tails of the wild creatures as they lay side by side on the floor, reconstructing in his mind, no doubt, their agile former owners, and following them in imagination to their secret haunts among the rocks and trees, or accompanying them on predatory excursions to neighboring hen-yards."[1] Cats in particular were a favorite source of amusement. His friends so often sent him Christmas cards representing feline subjects, that he once counted in his study forty-two pictures of pussy. He particularly delighted in a life-sized cloth cat which he used to place by the side of the fireplace; and on returning from the Rocky Mountains in 1846 he brought in a box made of buffalo hide a horned frog, which after its death he gave to the Agassiz Museum. Still, oddly enough, Parkman's relations to animals were not exactly affectionate. Though he liked to have them about him, and found endless entertainment in watching them, he did not wish to be bothered with the care of them, and never had any real pets. Rifle shooting was one of the passions of his youth, as is seen by his eager and reckless buffalo hunting on the Oregon Trail. In spite of a rule of the college forbidding students to have firearms in their rooms, Parkman's quarters were those of a sportsman rather than a student. But he was not sportsman enough in his maturity to make journeys for the mere purpose of shooting; or, perhaps, the infirmities that often made such an undertaking impossible, finally obliterated this taste. On the other hand, fishing remained, to the last, one of his favorite recreations. Circumstances favored this quieter kind of sport; and it gave him great

[1] Wheelwright.

satisfaction to catch a good string of fish for the table — as though his sympathy with savage life were gratified by winning his food directly from the surrounding waters. He also brought himself early into close contact with nature through the study of botany, and while yet a boy found one more outlet for his energy in the growth of silkworms.

Parkman's study of science separated him for a time from his natural haunts of fields and woods. In his autobiographic paper, in which he speaks of himself always in the third person, he says that "at the age of eleven or twelve he conceived a vehement liking for pursuits, a devotion to which at that time of life far oftener indicates a bodily defect than a mental superiority. Chemical experiment was his favorite hobby, and he pursued it with a tenacious eagerness which, well directed, would have led to some acquaintance with the rudiments of the science, but which, in fact, served little other purpose than injuring him by confinement, poisoning him with noxious gases, and occasionally scorching him with some ill-starred explosion." This turning from the outdoor world to the mystery of science took place when he left Medford and came to live again in Boston under the paternal roof. His father had a laboratory fitted up for him in a shed at the rear of the house. His comrades say that he became a fair manipulator, and showed considerable mechanical skill in constructing his apparatus. Among other things he made a well-finished electrical machine of wood, brass, and glass, with which he liked to administer shocks to rows of girls holding each other by the hand. He even gave lectures on chemistry and electricity. The following announcement may furnish a taste of his quality at this epoch:

"Grand Exhibition! Mr. F. Parkman, grateful for receiving, and always desirous of returning the favors of his friends and of the public in general, begs leave to announce, most respectfully, that at the request of a large proportion of the citizens of this 'great metropolis' he has consented (at a great expense and labor) to exhibit his truly astonishing, not to say wonderful and amazing exhibition of *Phisyoramic Pyrotecnicon!* or *Pyrric Fires!* Mr. Parkman having studied many years under Maelzel, the original inventor, can assure the public that they are fully equal to his. The performances will comprise, The pyramids and globes, the full sun (this piece cost $200), magic wheel, Transparency of Lord Nelson, etc. The whole to conclude with his powerful *magic lantern*, containing eighteen glasses comprising elegant and beautiful forms."

Naturally the youthful instructor drew an audience composed chiefly of his youthful friends and relations, but he attracted also some who were no longer young, and people of good memory testify to the entertaining quality of the boy's demonstrations.

The strength of Parkman's early interest in science is shown by his own words in the following school composition, written in August, 1839. The paper, moreover, has an interest as evidence that the boy was studying the English language to good purpose;

and it is the earliest bit of his composition that has been preserved:

"'Studies of Nature. Of all pursuits the cultivation of natural science tends most to enlarge the mind and improve the understanding. Nature affords for our contemplation subjects from the minutest to the most grand. We may study the animalcule contained in a drop of water, or observe the motions of the planetary bodies as they revolve in their unchanged orbits. No class of pursuits affords so vast a variety of subjects and none is capable of awakening a deeper interest. Nature cannot be exhausted. The farther we investigate her secrets the wider appears the range she opens to us. The nearer the view we take of her, the more captivating does she appear.

"We all are born with an instinctive fondness for the beauties of nature. We all take pleasure in viewing a lofty mountain, a fertile valley, or a clear stream. But most of us look upon such objects as we would upon a beautiful picture, we imagine no pleasure to be derived from them farther than that which arises from the clearness of the stream or the picturesque contrast of mountain and valley.

"But suppose a man who has made nature his study, who, while searching into the great laws that govern her, has not neglected the tribes of living and inanimate beings to which she is indebted for life and beauty, — suppose him to be placed where we were, and to be looking upon the same objects. The black and precipitous rocks which lie piled in confusion above him, remind him of the period when that mountain emerged from the plain impelled by some irresistible subterranean power. He notices the deposits which through successive ages have accumulated about its base, and compares the present appearance of that valley, enlivened by grazing herds and sparkling rivulets, with its aspect in former ages, when it perhaps formed the bed of a stagnant lake, the abode of monsters, now happily extinct. The plants and animals about him next engage his attention, and in observing their appearances and watching their motions, he finds an inexhaustible source of innocent gratification.

"'But,' say some, 'of what use are such pursuits, or what man of sense can take pleasure in studying the habits of a paltry insect, or in classing and arranging an insignificant shell?' I answer that whatever tends to increase our knowledge of the globe we inhabit is of use, and that objects which appear too trifling to be noticed may, at some future day, be found of great benefit to mankind.

"When the great chemical discoveries of Davy were published, it was said by some, 'Such discoveries are curious and wonderful, but to what possible use can they be applied?' Of what use is the spring of a watch? It is the agent by which the motion of the other parts is produced, and unless it had first been invented, a watch could never have been made. The principle of the spring was known long before any one thought of applying it to the construction of time-pieces. It is the same with such discoveries. They point out the principles which sooner or later will be made the agent in some great improvement in art. The application of the principle may not immediately be discovered, but we should not on this account condemn it as useless.

"Why then should the naturalist be accused of spending his time in useless pursuits? Use, of which we have no idea may yet be made of his researches, and in the meantime there is no pursuit more innocent, more interesting, or more agreeable than the study of Natural History."

But Parkman needed a broader knowledge of nature than was to be had in the details of natural science, and before long he directed his steps to wider and more genial fields. He said in his autobiographical letter:

"The age of fifteen or sixteen produced a revolution. At that momentous period of life retorts and crucibles were forever discarded, and an activity somewhat excessive took the place of voluntary confinement. A new passion seized him, which, but half gratified, still holds its force. He became enamoured of the woods, a fancy which soon gained full control over the course of the literary pursuits to which he was also addicted."

His return to nature was at first directed chiefly by a boy's love of activity in the open air. He enjoyed long walks with a companion about the suburbs of Boston. But soon, at the age of seventeen or eighteen, the purpose of writing the history of the French and Indian War became the controlling power of his life, and he at once began a remarkable concentration of all his powers and activities on this one aim. With a breadth of view unusual in so young a mind, he saw that for this theme would be needed a much wider range of experience and knowledge than the study could give; and he wisely estimated a knowledge of the wilderness and its life as among the most important elements of his preparation. His chivalric nature, too, was easily fired with an ambition to emulate Cooper's dusky heroes, who were then popular personages with many other readers besides himself; and on his tramps in the woods, he was continually living and acting their characters. Finally, one of his strongest characteristics, a love of stir and movement, also pushed him to the excessive activity of which he speaks in the above-quoted passage from his autobiography.

He now began, on entering Harvard, a course of physical training by which he hoped to acquire the utmost strength, agility, and endurance; furthermore, he made his contact with nature serve his literary projects. He took long walks at a pace his companions found it hard to keep up; he practised rifle shooting at birds, chipmunks, and other animals; he also worked in the gymnasium and riding school with great energy and success. Thus he systematically prepared himself for trips in the wilderness. From his freshman year onward he devoted every summer vacation to journeys about the United States and Canada, partly in inhabited regions to collect historic material, and partly in the wilderness to study its features and the experiences of life on the border and in the woods, recording his observations in a few small diaries kept from 1841 to 1846.

Parkman's journals, significant though they are

of his mind and character, make their revelations quite as much by their omissions as by their notes; and if we would see their whole significance and bearing we must keep in mind the writer's peculiar nature.

They sprang from no impulse to record the movements of his inner life; they are only the exercises of a young man bent on cultivating his powers of observation and description. Singularly reticent in regard to feelings and intentions, these notes are almost exclusively a record of external phenomena. Yet, while as autobiographic material they are disappointing, they do now and then cast light on Parkman's individuality. Their force comes from his sticking simply to facts, and from his good judgment in selecting the effective and characteristic in whatever he sketches; having been written, moreover, without any thought of publication, their style has the charm of simplicity and naturalness sometimes absent from his first books. They are everywhere entirely free from the grandiloquence so frequent in the collegiate's pages. In offering some extracts it is, of course, impracticable to maintain a rigid division of subjects; we shall have to keep as a clue our chief aim of revealing Parkman's personality and growth, and let the headings blend more or less under this general purpose.

The following entry in his diary at the White Mountain Notch shows with what nerve and ambition the youth was setting out in life·

"This afternoon I achieved the most serious adventure it was ever my lot to encounter. I walked down the Notch to the Willey House, and out of curiosity began to ascend the pathway of the avalanche on the mountain directly behind. This pathway is a deep ravine channelled in the side of the mountain, which in this place is extremely steep. In the bottom of this gulf a little stream comes down from a spring above, and renders the precipitous rocks as slippery as clay. The sides of the ravine, which runs directly up and down the mountain, are a decaying granite, while the bottom is formed by a trap-dike. I ascended at first easily, but the way began to be steeper and the walls on each side more precipitous. Still I kept on until I came to a precipice about forty feet high and not far from perpendicular. I could see that this was followed by a similar one above. Professor Silliman, a year or two ago, ascended in this place until, as he says, 'further progress was prevented by inaccessible precipices of the trap-rock.' The exploit of the Professor occurred to me as I stood below, and I determined that the 'inaccessible precipices' which had cooled his scientific ardor should prove no barriers to me. I began to climb, and with considerable difficulty and danger, and with the loss of my stick, which went rattling and bounding down the ravine many rods before it found a resting-place, I surmounted both precipices. I climbed on, but finding that I was becoming drenched by the scanty stream, and seeing, moreover, a huge cloud not far up, settling slowly towards me, I bethought me of retracing my steps. I knew that it would be impossible to descend by the way I had come, and accordingly, I tried to get out of the ravine to the side of the mountain which was covered with wood which I could grasp hold of to assist me. But I was inclosed between two walls of fifty feet high and so steep, and composed of such materials that an attempt to climb would only bring down the rotting granite upon my head. So I began to descend the ravine, nothing doubting that I could find some means of getting out before reaching the critical point. But it was impossible, and I found myself at the top of the precipice with no alternative but to slide down, or clamber the perpendicular and decaying walls to the surface of the mountain. The former was certain destruction, as I proved by suffering a rotten log to slide down. It glanced by the first descent like an arrow, struck at the bottom, bounded six feet into the air, and leaped down the mountain, splintering into twenty pieces as it went. The other method was scarcely less dangerous, but it was my only chance, and I braced my nerves and began to climb. Down went stones and pebbles, clattering hundreds of feet below and giving me a grateful indication of my inevitable fate in case my head should swim or my courage fail. I had got half way up and was climbing to the face of the precipice, when the two stones which supported my feet loosened and leaped down the ravine. My finger ends, among the rotten gravel were all which sustained me, and they, of course, would have failed had I not thought on the instant of lowering my body gradually, and so diminishing its weight, until my feet found new supporters. I sunk the length of my arms and then hung for the time, in tolerable safety, with one foot resting on a projecting stone. Loosening the hold of one hand, I took my large jack-knife from my pocket, opened it, with the assistance of my teeth, and dug with it a hollow among the decayed stones, large enough to receive and support one foot. Then thrusting the knife as far as possible into the wall to assist my hold, I grasped it, and the stones with the unoccupied hand, and raised my foot to the hollow prepared for it; thus, foot by foot, I made my way, and in ten minutes, as time seemed to me, I seized a projecting root at the top and drew myself up. During the whole time of climbing I felt perfectly cool, but when fairly up I confess I shuddered as I looked down at the gulf I had escaped. A large stone, weighing, perhaps, a hundred pounds, lay on the edge. I thrust it off with my foot, and down it went, struck the bottom of the ravine with a tremendous crash, and thundered down, leaping from side to side, until it lodged at last, far below against a projecting rock. I descended the mountain by means of the trees and bushes, cut a fishing-pole at the bottom, and having amused myself with an hour's fishing, went to the tavern and astonished the company with a recital of my adventure. Crawford expressed considerable astonishment at my escape, and the young lady in whose company I got my ducking on the stage transferred an account to her journal, but refused to let me see it, promising to send me a copy the moment her book was out of press."

A letter to his father, written July 22, two days before this event, shows that his adventurous spirit caused some anxiety at home. The happy traveller said:

"I write, as in duty bound, to relieve your spirit of the overwhelming load of anxiety which doubtless oppresses you, seeing that your son is a wanderer in a strange land, — a land of precipices and lakes, bears, wolves, and wildcats. Not only has my good genius borne me in safety through such manifold perils, but he has also infused into my heart such a spirit of contentment with my lot that I should be in no wise reconciled to any manner of change."

It was his way to make light of hardship, fatigue, peril, and suffering; he rarely mentioned them in either his diaries, conversations, or the few letters he wrote.

He wrote again later:

"The worst thing I have yet encountered in the way of danger was an attack from an old he-goose backed by a little bitch puppy, who assaulted us on the highway, but was soon put to flight without loss of life on either side."

Here is one of his earliest pictures of the wilderness he was later to portray so vividly:

"We passed the meadows at length, and again our way was through the forest, and a most wild and beautiful appearance did the river shores present (the Magalloway). From the high banks huge old pines stooped forward over the water, the moss hanging from their aged branches, and behind rose a wall of foliage, green and thick, with no space or opening which the eye could penetrate. . . . Soon the moon came up and glistened on the still river and half lighted the black forest. An owl, disturbed by the glare of our fire, sent forth a long, wild cry from the depths of the woods, and was answered by the shrill bark of some other habitant of the forest."

This practical study of the wilderness and the life men led in it was the most congenial of all his labors of preparation; but it was cut short when he had finished his journey on the Oregon Trail.

Such trips furnished amusing incidents as well as trying ones, and the youth showed his patience and good humor by making equally light of both kinds of experiences. This diary of 1841 tells of his friend Slade and himself crossing a "guzzle" on their tramp up the Magalloway:

"I said before that our road was of a structure somewhat unelaborate, but as yet we had encountered no difficulties like that which now presented itself. A muddy creek two rods wide and of uncertain depth extended back from the river directly across our path. There had once been, as we were assured, a trunk felled so as to form a sort of bridge across this slough of despond, but now the only means of passing were three or four slender poles projecting from each side and meeting in the middle where a floating log contributed to their support. We stood in horror and amazement, in vain endeavoring to solve the problem how a man of ordinary weight could place his foot on such a structure without 'slumping in' at once. We determined to put the matter to the test of experiment. I excused myself from making the first essay on the plea that I carried a heavier weight than my friend, upon whom, then, the first responsibility devolved. Seated on the bank I watched his operations. With a countenance of direful import, he strapped his knapsack firmly on his back, grasped a long pole, one end of which he planted firmly in the mud at the bottom to support his tottering footsteps, and cautiously advanced his foot upon the frail bridge. He had gotten about two yards from the bank, when the poles began gradually to sink beneath his weight, yet by a certain fatality he continued to advance until he gained the log in the middle. The water was above his knees, and fast rising to his waist. The poles began to glide like eels from beneath him; if he stood still the bridge was too weak to sustain him, if he moved he lost his foothold. He felt his fate inevitable, and with a dismal imprecation sprang desperately toward some loose logs and brush-wood that floated near the opposite bank. The logs tilted up, there was a heavy splash, and my friend appeared struggling and floundering amid the ruins of the demolished bridge. He grasped a root that projected from the bank, and drew himself up wet and beslimed from head to foot, but with a temper in no wise affected by his misfortune, for he responded most heartily to the laughter with which I saluted him. My companion being over six feet high, and yet feeling as he declared, no bottom to the gulf, I felt my own situation rather awkward. I set about making a new bridge while he arranged his toilet as best he might on the other side. Strapping my gun and other equipments to my back I managed to get over, though wet to the knees."

In all his wanderings Parkman never made an aimless journey; even now, when a freshman out on his summer vacation, he had a very practical purpose in view:

"My chief object in coming so far was merely to have a taste of the half savage kind of life necessary to be led, and to see the wilderness where it was as yet uninvaded by the hand of man."

And at the close of the trip:

"I regard this journey but 'as the beginning of greater things,' and as merely prefatory to longer wanderings."

In 1842 he went again to the Magalloway. Naturally such an ardent lover of forest life was pained by all elements of civilization that destroyed the wilderness and altered primitive, or at least simple, methods of living. Thus he said at the beginning of this trip of 1842, while in the train *en route* for Albany: "Of all methods of progressing, that by steam is incomparably the most disgusting." The sights of Saratoga put him into an "unmitigated temper," while at Glens Falls, so degraded from their natural beauty, his "wrath mounted higher yet." He was equipped this year for the wilderness better than before, having among other things, his much-loved rifle "Satan." There is little to quote concerning his study of nature on this trip; the best of his diary is to be seen in the article in Harper's, "Exploring the Magalloway." Here, however, is a good touch concerning Lake George:

"We kept down the lake with a fierce wind sweeping down after us and driving the mists before it. The water was a dark, glistening blue, with lines of foam on the crests of the waves; huge shadows of clouds coursed along the mountains. The little islands would be lighted at one instant by a stream of sunshine falling on them, and almost making their black pines transparent, and the next moment they would be suddenly darkened, and all around be glittering with a sudden burst of light from the opening clouds."

The following passage is exceptional for him, dealing, as it does, explicitly with sentiment, and reading into nature his own mood:

"The air was full of mists, rolling along the hills, and entangled among the trees. Every mountain was hidden among clouds. We passed through tracts of half burned forests, steaming and smoking, some blasted trunks standing upright, others prostrate among charred trunks and tangled underwood, all looking supernaturally dismal through mist and rain. . . . At last we saw Lake Memphremagog, — a direful composition of great sheets of leaden water, scarce distinguishable from the fogs that enveloped it, and a border of melancholy trees which stood apparently lamenting, and pouring forth copious tears above it. All nature was in a fit of the blue-devils."

Forest trees were evidently very dear to him; they were the chief beings composing his favorite world of the wilderness, and they, more than any other single element of a landscape, seem to have kindled his imagination to the heat of poetic figures. He thus recorded his sympathy with these mute witnesses of his future dramas:[1]

[1] *Harper's Magazine*, Nov. 1864, p. 736.

"Around us was an innumerable host of trunks straight and crooked, smooth with youth, or bepatched with the mosses and lichens of rugged old age; erect in pristine vigor, or staggering for support against their neighbors; knotted and gnarled, infected with goitres and tumors, warts, and hideous fungi; or dribbling pitch or turpentine from frost-rent crevices and the stumps of wind-amputated limbs. Their dead comrades in every stage of dissolution and every variety of posture, cumbered the earth below, overgrown with a vile mesh-work of vines and creepers, scrub oaks, scrub savins, matted junipers and trailing wintergreen. Looking upward we could enjoy at intervals a hand's breadth of sky between the leaves, and the surrounding circle of vision varied from three yards to fifteen. Now and then there was a 'windfall' — a disgusting feature of forest scenery, owing its origin to the passage of a whirlwind, sweeping down the trees and piling them in masses. One of them, in a hollow place, where a gorge opened from the mountain, presented an aspect singularly unpleasing. It was of old date, for the forest had grown up around and over it. Some of the trees had their heels in the air, some their heads, some were prostrate, and sprawling, and the rest pitched together at every angle which the tyrannical caprice of the tornado had ordained. All were more or less rotten, according to their nature and position. Some were a mass of pulp, delicately coated over with a sleek green moss, which, pressed with the finger, oozed like a sponge. Others not as perishable or lifted higher from the earth still showed fight against the elements, and scores of red cedars in particular bristled out of every part of the pile in an execrable chevaux-de-frise."

In his diary of the summer of 1843 is this passage relating to scenery:

> "I write at the bottom of a den more savage than the last. Turn to the left as you approach Crawford's, enter a gateway of rock, and you will reach two dens that look like the very bottom of hell. Nothing but great piles of damp mossy rocks, rotten timber, huge black cliffs, fencing you in with trees stretching across from their edges. A stream is plunging somewhere underground and breaking out into a black pool among the moss. Behind is a great heap of rocks where you descend. In front a steep descent, choked with fallen timber, and such a tangled mass of vegetation that a bear could scarce get through."

Under a pressed flower, still preserved between the pages, he wrote: "This delicate little flower, whatever it be, I place here in memory of the grimmest, dismallest den on earth, where it grew among moist precipices and rotting logs."

In the autumn of 1843 Parkman sailed for Europe from motives connected with his health. This diary of 1843–44 is more interesting than the earlier ones, his mind now being more mature and the field of his observations more varied and extensive. Not even seasickness could repress his energy and interest in the phenomena about him. "A turtle," he wrote, "came up at the ship's side to sleep on the quiet surface, but prudently sunk back to the depths just as Mr. Hansen was lowering me by a rope to take him prisoner." But he was attracted chiefly by the grander aspect of the sea:

"As soon as it was daybreak I went on deck. Two or three sails were set — the vessel scouring along, leaning over so that her gunwale scooped up the water; the water in a foam, and clouds of spray flying over us, frequently as high as the mainyard. The spray was driven with such force that it pricked the cheek like needles. I stayed on deck two or three hours; when, being thoroughly salted, I went down, changed my clothes, and read 'Don Quixote,' till Mr. Snow appeared at the door with — 'You 're the man that wants to see a gale of wind, are ye? Now's your chance: only just come up on deck.' I went. The wind was yelling and howling in the rigging in a fashion that reminded me of a storm in a Canadian forest. . . . I got hold of a rope by the mizzen mast, and looked about on a scene that it would be perfect folly to attempt to describe. . . . The sailors clung, half drowned, to whatever they could lay hold of, for the vessel was, at times, half inverted, and tons of water washed from side to side of her deck. . . . As for the usual horizon it had disappeared — we seemed imbedded among moving mountains. . . . It was a noble sight when at intervals the sun broke out over the savage waste, changing its blackness to a rich blue, almost as dark; while the foam that flew over it seemed like whirling snow-wreaths on the mountains."

The voyage was tedious with bad weather; from storms they passed to exasperating calms when almost in sight of Gibraltar, and he reported in this way the captain's complaints:

"'A head wind and none of it,' groans the Captain: 'if ever I see the beat of this!' This is but the nucleus of his remarks, so to speak, which he surrounds and adorns with a host of forcible and ornamental forms of expression which I refrain from recording."

But at last they landed at Gibraltar, and Parkman rested his observant eyes on European scenes. As he visited no places that are new to readers of to-day, we pass by most of his descriptive pages; but here and there a passage is noteworthy as a reflection of his tastes and characteristics. He gave in these few words an admirable picture of Palermo:

"After taking a last look at the ancient and moss-grown church and the black cliffs around it, I left Monte Pellegrino. As we waded through the snow down the mountain the view of Palermo was noble. The valley was as smooth and level as the ocean, and set between the immense arch of snow-covered mountains, as green and bright as an emerald. The city was but a very small part — there were forests of olive trees, and immeasurable gardens, all dotted with white houses, and the palaces of the nobles. It was the King's birthday, and the city was half covered with the smoke of cannon."

Seldom does a celebrated historian show Parkman's degree of indifference to archæology and his preference for nature over the works of man. At Naples he found that in the continual attacks of beggars and custodians "you have a sum of petty vexations enough to damp any man's zeal for exploring classical localities. Fortunately I never had much to lose. I would go farther for one look into the crater of Vesuvius than to see all the ruined temples in Italy."

He was fortunate enough to visit the volcano with Theodore Parker:

"Our guides went quite near to the base of the cone, dodging the falling lava with great activity. Some of these melted masses must have weighed a ton. As they fell, they spread out over a large surface. The guide would make a sudden rush at them, detach a small portion with a pole, which he carried to a safe distance and then stamped by pressing a copper coin into it. After a while Mr. Parker and I took our part in the exercise, and secured several trophies. The floor of the great crater on which we stood had been a sea of melted lava only three days before."

The memory of this scene possibly sprang up in his mind thirty years afterwards, when writing of the Missionaries, and suggested this telling comparison:

"Whether the foe was of earth or hell, the Jesuits were like those who tread the lava-crust that palpitates with the throes of the coming eruption, while the molten death beneath their feet glares white-hot through a thousand crevices." [1]

Of Lake Como he said:

"I have seen nothing at home or abroad more beautiful than this lake. It reminds me of Lake George — the same extent, the same figure, the same crystal purity of waters, the same wild and beautiful mountains on either side. But the comparison will not go farther. Here are

[1] *The Old Régime*, p. 81.

a hundred palaces and villages scattered along the water's edge, and up the declivities. There is none of that shaggy untamed aspect in the mountains — no piles of rocks, grown over with stunted bushes; or half decayed logs fallen along the shore. There are none of those little islands, covered with rough and moss-grown pine trees, which give a certain savage character to the beauties of Lake George. All here is like a finished picture; even the wildest rocks seem softened in the air of Italy. Give me Lake George, and the smell of the pine and fir!"

Crossing the Alps by the Splügen Pass, he found much that impressed him profoundly:

"I spent the day yesterday in the valley of Ferrera, one of the wildest and loneliest in the Alps, and accessible only by a bad foot-path. The river comes down at the bottom, which the sun scarcely ever touches. The mountains rise on each side many thousand feet, broken into crags and precipices, with streams falling down them in all directions, scattering into white mists before they reach the bottom. The spruce trees are sprinkled all over the cliffs, wherever there is a crevice to cling in; some gigantic pines stoop across the river and fairly seem to quiver with the tremendous roar of the water. All is solitary and still as death, excepting the noise of the river; yet you cannot sit on one of these rocks, and watch the green and furious water, glancing between the trunks and branches below, without fancying that you hear sounds and voices about you. I never knew a place so haunted by 'those airy tongues that syllable men's names.'"

The Alps, especially those wilder regions about Andeer, seem to have given him his deepest enjoyment of scenery on the continent. He wrote at this place:

"Nothing could surpass the utter savageness of the scenery that you find by tracing up some of the little streams that pour down on all sides to join the Rhine; not a trace of human hand — it is as wild as the back forest at home. The mountains, too, wear the same aspect. There is one valley where a large stream comes down to join the main river, a mile from Andeer. Last night I followed it for a mile or two, back into the mountains. Not Cooper himself could do it justice. The river was a hundred feet below, in a ravine, where it lashed from side to side, and bounded sometimes in a fall of fifty or sixty feet — the green headlong water, the white foam, and the spray just visible through the boughs of the distorted pines that leaned over the abyss. There was in one place a peasant's hut of logs, but it seemed only to increase the sublime effect of the wilderness. I got down to the bed of the river, and leaped out to some rocks near the centre. It was nearly dark — long after sunset. What with the deafening thunder of the stream — the gloom that began to involve the shaggy branches of the yellow pines, that leaned nearly across the gulf, and the stiff and upright spruces that sprung from every crevice of the rock — what with this and the savage aspect of the rocks, which were black and dripping with spray — there was something almost appalling in the place. Above the tops of the trees rose mountains like ours of New England, covered with fir trees, wherever one could cling in the crevices of the steep cliffs. And in another direction the more distant peaks were white with snow which retained its glistening brightness long after the moon had begun to cast a shadow. Here was a change with a vengeance, from the Italian beauties of the Lake of Como. I sat on the rock, fancying myself again in the American woods with an Indian companion; but as I rose to go away the hellish beating of my heart warned me that no more such expeditions were in store for me, for the present at least — but if I do not sleep by the camp fire again it shall be no fault of mine."

He added: "I never left any place with more regret than these mountains."

On reaching Scotland, he derived the keenest pleasure of his entire journey from the scenery connected with Scott and his works. He said:

"I like the Scotch — I like the country and everything in it. The Liverpool packet will not wait, or I should stay long here and take a trout from every 'burnie' in the Cheviot. The scenery has been grossly belied by Irving and others — it is wild and beautiful — I have seen none more so."

He regretted that he had not time to visit the Highlands. Edinburgh is the city he liked best of all: "The view from Calton Hill is, to my thinking, the only city view I ever saw that deserved to be called sublime."

His diaries of 1845 and of 1846, before he reached the prairies, contain very little relative to nature; but that little is not without interest, in showing a stronger tendency in his mind to study details. He wrote at Cahokia, near St. Louis, just before his departure on the Oregon Trail trip:

"I walked up the banks of the creek into the woods — it was nothing like our swift and clear mountain waters — all was teeming with life, animal and vegetable, just awakening in the warm spring sunshine. The creek was slow and sluggish — a haunt, in the season, for fever and ague — the luxuriant woods overshadowed it, interlaced with vines like snakes, and all bursting into leaf and flower — full, too, of birds, who would come down to splash and wash themselves in the water — and fragrant with the fresh smell of young leaves and blossoms. The pool was full of frogs and great turtles, sitting on logs, and among slime — now and then a water snake, with his head lifted high, would writhe his way across — and as you pass by some sheltered cove the whole water would be alive with minute fishes, skipping out of it in their terror."

As a final word on his love of nature may be given this passage from his diary in Sicily in 1843–44: "I never imagined that so much pleasure could be conveyed through the eye, a pleasure not inferior to and not unlike that of looking upon the face of a beautiful woman."

Unhappily his diaries came to an end with that of 1846, which was the basis of "The Oregon Trail." For this important and arduous journey he had prepared himself most thoroughly by the study of nature we have been following; by a systematic physical training in gymnastics, riding, and tramping; by the practice of shooting, trailing, camping, and woodcraft in general; by a long study of Indian character, life, history, and traditions. This book merits the reader's attention not only as a record of Indian life now no longer visible, but especially as a revelation of the writer's enthusiastic love of freedom, adventure, and activity; it shows with what absolute indifference he faced danger, with what fortitude he endured hardship, fatigue, and suffering, with what energy and persistence he pursued a most hazardous undertaking to a successful close. This trip and its record, so characteristic of the man, were a striking culmination of his study of nature in her wildest and grandest solitudes of prairie, desert, forest, and mountain, and in the company of the wildest tribes of men.

CHAPTER IV

PARKMAN'S education in books was from an early day governed by the same happy combination of wisdom, instinct, and good fortune that directed his relations to nature. In fact, with the exception of the study of chemistry, everything he did as boy and young man, — whether play, study, or travel — helped directly to prepare him for his future career. He attended his first school at Medford. In 1836 he entered the school of Mr. Gideon Thayer, in Chauncy Place, Boston. His teacher, the late Mr. Thomas Cushing, said of him:

"He was a quiet, gentle, and docile boy, who seemed to appreciate the fact that school meant an opportunity for improvement, and always gave an open and willing mind to instruction. He became, according to the ideas of the day, a good Latin and Greek scholar, and excelled in the rhetorical department. I think he early set his face in the direction of a literary life of some sort, though the idea of *historical* work was probably developed somewhat later. As a means to any sort of literary work, he no doubt saw the advantage and necessity of forming a good English style and acquiring correctness in the use of language, and took great pains with all exercises tending to bring about this result. His compositions were especially good, and he used sometimes as a voluntary exercise to versify descriptions of heroic achievements that occurred in his reading. I remember that he put into verse the whole description of the Tournament in Scott's "Ivanhoe," and then used it afterwards in declamation, and it was so much liked that other boys used it for the same purpose. I think he might have excelled in narrative and descriptive poetry (the poetry of action) had he not early imbibed the historical idea. He often expressed to me in after life the great advantage that he received from the instruction of one of the teachers at that time connected with Chauncy Hall school, in everything pertaining to the use of English and the formation of style, which he followed up at Harvard by diligent use of his opportunities with an excellent instructor, Prof. Edward T. Channing."[1]

Parkman gave this account of his study of writing:

"When fourteen or fifteen years old I had the good luck to be under the direction of Mr. William Russel, a teacher of excellent literary taste and acquirements. It was his constant care to teach the boys of his class to write good and easy English. One of his methods was to give us lists of words to which we were required to furnish as many synonyms as possible, distinguishing their various shades of meaning. He also encouraged us to write translations, in prose and verse, from Virgil and Homer, insisting on idiomatic English, and criticising in his gentle way anything flowery and bombastic. At this time I read a good deal of poetry, and much of it

[1] Wheelwright.

remains *verbatim* in my memory. As it included Milton and other classics, I am confident that it has been of service to me in the matter of style. Later on, when in college, and after leaving it, I read English prose classics for the express purpose of improving myself in the language.[1] These I take to be the chief sources of such success as I have had in this particular."[2]

He looked back with satisfaction upon his school days, and in after life it always gave him much pleasure to meet his old teachers and show them respect and kindness.

His college course brings to light his independence, strong practical turn of mind, and indifference to the spirit and theoretical aims of perfectionists. In opposition to the opinions and practice of his day, he was probably the first man in American colleges to follow an elective course and become a specialist. He was not led by ideality to desire the greatest breadth of culture; on the contrary, his instincts, tastes and judgment, all pointed to one field, and he confined himself to the straightest path thither. If we may judge by his reading, writing, and memorizing much poetry at school, and by the records of his reading at Harvard, poetry was the first aim of his literary ambition. He referred probably to this design in his autobiography:

"After the usual boyish phases of ambitious self-ignorance, he resolved to confine his homage to the Muse

[1] Burke is said to have been his chief model for style.

[2] *The Art of Authorship, personally contributed by leading authors of the day.* Compiled and edited by George Bainton, London, 1890.

of History, as being less apt than her wayward sisters to requite his devotion with a mortifying rebuff."

Not only did he early abandon his poetic illusion, but he also chose with great promptness the division of history to which he would devote himself. "At the age of eighteen the plan which he is still attempting to execute was, in its most essential features, formed."

Thus early in life did Parkman see his way and enter upon his course. He now changed his reading quite abruptly and completely from poetry to the accounts of border life, the Indians, the French and Indian War; directing his college labors chiefly to the study of history and of English composition. It was remarked that he always did with the greatest energy and persistence what he liked to do, and neglected other things in the same masterful fashion. He therefore attained to good scholarship in his chosen branches of history and rhetoric. He mastered also French, and Latin as far as was necessary for his future investigations. He described his own standing, as well as some of his college experiences with his chum, in an after-dinner speech in 1885:[1]

"Something more than forty years ago Mr. Benjamin Apthorp Gould, Master of the Latin School, and Dr. Parkman, Minister of the New North Church, took counsel together and agreed that their sons, who were just passing the freshman examination at Harvard, should be

[1] Speech at a dinner given in honor of Dr. Gould, May 7, 1885. *Boston Daily Advertiser.*

joined in bonds of chumship. This union, thus brought about by the parents between young persons who had never seen each other, was the foundation and beginning of a lifelong friendship. Its beginnings were a little breezy, I might say squally. On one occasion Mr. Gould came out to pour oil upon the troubled waters, and with a good humored seriousness he told us that chumship is like matrimony, — it requires a great deal of forbearance on both sides. Whether it was in consequence of this remark or not, I do not know, but certain it is that a most cordial harmony was soon restored between the parties, and has continued unbroken to this day. I remember an incident which took place on the evening of the day when we first occupied No. 9 Holworthy, which after it was over, gave us both a good deal of pleasure. It was a very hot night. We had opened our windows in search of air, when there was a knock at the door, and ten or twelve seniors came in. It was an immensely impressive circumstance. We regarded the seniors with awe and reverence. Still it was not above their dignity to haze a couple of harmless and callow freshmen. They closed the windows and took out cigars and began to smoke their cigars to smoke us out. We bore it for a while; then the air became thick, and we began to think we had had enough of it. Suddenly one of the seniors sprang up and rushed to the door and asked for the key. The door was open, he went out, left his supper on the doorstep and went to his room, followed by all the rest.

"The average scholarship of Holworthy was exceedingly creditable. As regards mathematics, it was particularly so — in spite of fate, I might say, for I always and invariably failed, and my chum came off with flying colors, making up all the difference. I remember the last examination when Professor Pierce in presence of a committee examined us, and I was required, according to the cruel custom of the times, to work out a problem on the blackboard. I had not opened my algebra for six months, having devoted to rifle-shooting the time which I was expected to devote to mathematics. A problem was proposed. I said 'Don't know it, sir.' Professor Pierce with great kindness then proposed another, to which I replied 'I cannot do it, sir.' He then tried a third. 'I don't know anything about it, sir.' 'Mr. Parkman, you may go.'"

But Parkman's standing must not be judged entirely by his jocose frankness as to his failure in mathematics. In the first term of the sophomore year he received a *detur*, a testimonial to deserving students "*pro insigni in studiis diligentia.*" In the second term of this year he was among the first eight; and at the exhibition he had doubtless a congenial topic in an English version of the "Speech of an Insurgent Plebeian" from Machiavelli's history of Florence. His diaries also show with what care he was training himself in composition, in phraseology, even in punctuation. By their simplicity, vigor and realism they rise considerably above the usual level of college productions. The next year he spoke again, his Dissertation being on the subject "Is a man in advance of his age fitted for his age."[1] His memory in his college days was not good, — a

[1] Wheelwright.

fact most interesting in view of the remarkable memory he developed later under the pressure of necessity.

But his practice in composition was not limited to the writing of academic themes; he made some mark likewise as a speaker and lecturer in the literary societies of the college. On one occasion he delivered as a lecture "a witty production, having for its subject 'The Puritans,' wherein he gave us in a very original and humorous style the front, flank, and rear of their offending."[1]

He often spoke in debates, once on the question "Whether the Republic of the United States is likely to continue." It is not known which side he defended. His contemporaries described him as a trenchant and forcible speaker; as one, indeed, who by the strength of his expressions and the vehemence of his manner, seemed ready to "knock his opponents down." His choice of topics, both in conversation and voluntary literary contributions, "even then showed symptoms of 'Injuns' on the brain. His tales of border life, wampum, scalps, and birch-bark were unsurpassed by anything in Cooper."[2] He graduated among the first twenty of his class, having attained "high distinction" in the department of history.

Parkman's record in school and college gives

[1] Report of the Secretary of the "Institute of 1770," quoted by Mr. Wheelwright.

[2] Horatio J. Perry's *Reminiscences*.

no evidence of genius in the proper sense of the word. While possessing more than the average ability in certain lines, he developed himself by long years of patient labor in a chosen field. The nature of his talents was unmistakable; but the extent of his subsequent success was apparently not anticipated even by his most intimate friends. On the other hand, neither did his achievements surprise his classmates. Professor Child, who was two or three years behind him, gave me what seems a very just report in saying that "Mr. Parkman's reputation in college spread downwards as a bright and original man." The shrewd grandmother of one of his classmates, whom he visited, said she considered him "a young man of remarkably quick parts and very correct."

His study of the law was another happy extension of education in the line of individual needs. Dr. Parkman, not approving of the literary and historical ambition of his son, naturally wished him to follow one of the liberal professions, and as the young man had no taste for either medicine or theology, he entered the Harvard Law School on graduating from college. The decision was quite acceptable to him, for he felt that the study of the law offered a mental training valuable to any man, and elements of knowledge especially useful to an historian. This course helped him in large ways, leading him to consider the rights of nations, the organization of governments, the principles and tendencies of national growth. Such a study of statesmanship was in fact necessary to one who would appreciate the opposing feudal and democratic systems of colonization on this continent. It had, moreover, a happy influence over his mental growth in cultivating the judicial spirit, — a much-needed restraint upon so impetuous a temperament, and a balance for a constitutional tendency to prejudice in certain matters. But the law was not allowed to interfere with his literary projects.

> "Here (writing in the Harvard Law School), while following the prescribed courses at a quiet pace, I entered in earnest on two other courses, one of general history, the other of Indian history and ethnology, and at the same time studied diligently the models of English style, which various pursuits were far from excluding the pleasures of society."[1]

He received his degree of Bachelor of Laws in 1846, but although fully qualified to enter the bar, he never did so. A question may be raised as to whether he ever intended to practise. There is some evidence that he did in the few letters referring to this project. He wrote to a classmate[2] in July, 1845: "I shall live in town (Boston) and come out (to Cambridge) every day, intending to study law in earnest, which I have not done, and did not mean to do this last year." Again in September, 1846, at the close of his Oregon

[1] Parkman's autobiographic letter to Mr. Brimmer.
[2] George S. Hale.

Trail trip, he showed respect for his father's wishes by an intention to do something in this direction: "The law has certain claims on me also, which will be fully answered now that I have returned from my last journey — the last I suppose it will be for the present, though not so if I consulted my inclination only." Both father and son still aimed at the law as late as 1847, but the pursuit of it was interrupted by Parkman's ill health and poor sight; and probably he soon dismissed the plan entirely. Dr. Parkman, though never in sympathy with his son's literary ambition, was always indulgent, generous, and helpful. In a kindly letter of August 7, 1847, he appreciates Francis's first success as a writer, and at the same time reflects probably a mutual understanding that the practice of law was only deferred. After describing some civilities shown to Eliot Parkman as the brother of the author of the "Oregon Trail" papers, which were then appearing in the "Knickerbocker," he goes on to say:

"I confess, my dear Frank, I was much gratified by this; but I should not be studious to write it out at length, did I not feel that under your trials and inability to do as much as you desire, you are entitled to know, that what you have done, and still can do, is fully appreciated. It is a consolation, when some of our plans are interrupted, to know that others have so well succeeded. And I congratulate you in having accomplished so much, and so successfully, amidst great discouragements."

It is clear from Parkman's own statements and his career that the law never had, and never could have, but a secondary place in his plans.

In assuming so early the direction of his own education Parkman was a self-made scholar to an unusual degree, despite his regular graduation from Harvard. With many a student such conduct would have endangered one of the most important aims of education, — the acquisition of methodical habits. But this student was saved by his centralizing ambition and his native earnestness and thoroughness.

CHAPTER V

PARKMAN'S study of man began at an early age and steadily grew in attraction and importance for him to the end of his life. It embraced ethnology, as far as that science was then developed, and the personal observation of the character and conduct of individual men.

His opportunities for studying ethnology while at college were very limited. The subject, at that time hardly more than named, had not yet grown into the modern complex science of races. Harvard then offered neither any course of instruction, nor books of much value, nor even the advice and encouragement of any professor having a special knowledge of the matter. In view of this deficiency Parkman used the term in a general sense, when he said in his autobiographic letter of 1886[1] that while at the Law School, 1844-46, he pursued a course of "Indian history and ethnology." He probably followed such an independent course of reading as was within his reach at the time; and judging by the books he took from the college library, this course was more an historical study of the life, man-

[1] To his friend the late Hon. Martin Brimmer.

ners, and customs of North American Indians than any attempt at a scientific understanding of races and the growth of civilizations. It is probable that he was then collecting the materials used in the introduction to "The Jesuits in North America," and in numerous notes in other volumes. He must have been one of the earliest to welcome the rapid development of ethnology that took place in the decade from 1850 to 1860. In "Vassall Morton,"[1] written in 1856, he thus recorded the hero's awakening to the larger interest in this science:

"Thierry's 'Norman Conquest' had fallen into his hands soon after he entered college. The whole delighted him; but he read and re-read the opening chapters, which exhibit the movements of the various races in their occupancy of the west of Europe. This first gave him an impulse towards ethnological inquiries. He soon began to find an absorbing interest in tracing the distinctions, moral, intellectual, and physical, of different races, as shown in their history, their mythologies, their languages, their legends, their primitive art, literature, and way of life. The idea grew upon him of devoting his life to such studies."

It is quite possible that Parkman here revealed his own experience and conceptions while in college; but if he thus early recognized the weightier topics included in ethnology as essential to his equipment as historian, it is somewhat surprising to find so little

[1] Page 37.

allusion to them in his diaries, and so few philosophical considerations in his books.

As we shall consider later his aversion for philosophizing, we must content ourselves at present with some further extracts from his diaries, showing the natural bent of his mind and the range of his observations. Here was a budding historian full of intelligence, self-confidence, and independence, making his first journey in the great world through countries offering the greatest range of interests in life, art, and history. Yet his diaries and letters are singularly free from sophomoric wisdom; — they reveal very little concern for the deeper lessons of human life, or for the broader interests of ethnology and history. The passages having any breadth of view in the study and comparison of races and civilizations are so few that we can give nearly all of them. In the mountains of Sicily for example, he came upon this scene:

"It was a dark and gloomy day. Down in the bottom of the valley a herd of oxen were grazing — there was a contadino's hut of reeds on one of the abrupt hills near by. It was like the lodge of an Indian — the cattle were like a herd of buffalo; I could have thought myself on the prairies. But as we passed by the herd, there stood the herdsman in his shaggy breeches of goatskin, leaning on his staff, gazing at us through his tangled hair and unshorn beard. His savage dogs, wild as himself, growled loudly as we rode by. The American frontier could show no such a group."

At Rome he thus contrasted Americans with Englishmen:

"Yesterday was the 22d of February — the birthday of Washington. The Americans here must needs get up a dinner, with speeches, toasts, etc. It was like a visit home. There they sat, slight, rather pale and thin men, not like beef-fed and ruddy Englishmen: very quiet and apparently timid; speaking low to the waiters instead of roaring in the imperative tone of John Bull. There was not a shadow of that boisterous and haughty confidence of manner that you see among Englishmen — in fact most of them seemed a little green."

Another passage in the same vein is not without interest, in view of his later critical attitude towards his own countrymen:

"There are numbers of American artists here, some of them fine fellows. In fact, it is some consolation after looking at the thin faces, narrow shoulders, and awkward attitudes of the 'Yankees,' to remember that in genius, enterprise, and courage — nay in bodily strength, they are a full match for the sneering Englishman. Would that they bore themselves more boldly and confidently. But a time will come when they may meet Europeans on an equal footing."

At Basle he wrote:

"Here in Basle you find none of the palaces and none of the dirt of an Italian city. No soldiers, except those of the garrison of the citadel and of the gendarmerie; no beggars; no spies in the cafés; no vexatious question-ings of suspicious officials; no anxious scrutiny into passports, or rummagings of baggage. The people walk about in the quiet streets with solemnity on their faces, and pipes in their mouths."

At Milan:

"Civility is almost universal among these Italians — farther south it is manifested in gesticulations, takings-off of the hat, bowings, and reiterated exclamations of 'padrone,' which is equivalent to 'your servant, sir.' Here it is shown rather in deeds than in words — thank a man for any favor, — he does not scrape and flourish, and say padrone; he only smiles quietly and replies 'niente fatto.'"

An entry at Piacenza is exceptional for him in the range of interests touched upon:

"Here again the striking difference between the towns of Northern and Southern Italy was manifested. The people looked as grave and solemn as the brick fronts of the palaces and churches. The town was just bestirring itself. Well-dressed men were thronging to the cafés for breakfast — the shops were being opened, and the market people coming in with their produce. Tall contadini were driving flocks of goats about the street, stopping and milking one into a little tin measure, whenever some housekeeper or the servant of some café came out to demand 'latte fresco.' There was an amusing concourse of market people in the public piazza, before the lofty front of the old government palace. Cheeses, meat, butter, eggs, and piles of live hens, tied neck and heels as you see them in Canada, were spread in every direction over the pavement, surrounded by sellers and purchasers, both apparently half asleep. At a little distance were two long lines of women and men, each with a basket of eggs in hand, standing immovable with an expression of patient resignation, waiting for a purchaser. The men were little shrivelled farmers, in breeches and broad hats, with staffs in their hands, and dickeys standing up erect, like diminutive Englishmen. High above this motley swarm of helpless humanity rose the statue of some great lord of the Farnese family, seated on horseback, holding his truncheon of command, as if at the head of an army, and looking as if one act of his single will, or one movement of his armed hand, would be enough to annihilate the whole swarm of poor devils below him."

He thus contrasted Paris and London, in his own graphic way, by stating without comment facts that present the philosophy of the situation:

"When I got to London, I thought I had been there before. There in flesh and blood, was the whole host of characters that figure in Pickwick. Every species of cockney was abroad in the dark and dingy looking streets, all walking with their heads stuck forward, their noses turned up, their chins pointing down, their knee joints shaking, as they shuffled along with a gait perfectly ludicrous, but indescribable. The hackney coachmen and cabmen, with their peculiar phraseology, the walking advertisements in the shape of a boy completely hidden between two placards, and a hundred others seemed so many incarnations of Dickens' characters. A strange contrast to Paris! The cities are no more alike than the 'dining rooms' of London, and the elegant restaurant of Paris — the one being a quiet dingy establishment where each guest is put into a box, and supplied with porter, beef, potatoes, and plum pudding. Red faced old gentlemen of three hundredweight mix their 'brandy go' and read the 'Times.' In Paris, the tables are set in elegant galleries and saloons and among the trees and flowers of a garden, and [here ?] resort coats cut by the first tailors and bonnets of the latest mode, whose occupants regale their delicate tastes on the lightest and most delicious viands. The waiters spring from table to table as noiselessly as shadows, prompt at the slightest sign; a lady, elegantly attired, sits within an arbor to preside over the whole. Dine at these places — then go to a London 'dining room' — swill porter and devour roast beef!"

His only reference to the effects of environment concern not a race or a class, but two individuals. The first is an English sailor who had lived many years in Sicily, — "the stubborn English temper was well nigh melted away with his long sojourn among the Gentiles." At home in 1845 he found a subject that called forth an exceptional amount of reflection:

"Where in America is to be found that spirit of sport and bluff hearty enjoyment that is seen in English country gentlemen and others? Business here absorbs everything, and renders people incapable of every other *pleasure*. Officers of the army and navy are sometimes an exception. There is an old retired navy surgeon at Medford, who lives with his dogs and his gun, like an English Squire, enjoying himself in the same hearty manner. Business, too, swallows much that is noble.

The somewhat chivalrous sentiments, the reference of all things to the standard of a gentleman's honor, a certain nobleness (though it may be joined with debauchery and blackguardism) is found among officers of armies. Our business men, on the other hand, have narrowed away all this. Thoughts bent on practical gains are not pleasant to contemplate, no matter how much virtue may accompany them."

Turning now from the philosophical division of ethnology, we find that Parkman was a much closer student of the more picturesque division, — life, manners, actions. On landing at Gibraltar he plunged with avidity into this study, and with rare vividness and vigor gave his first impressions of European civilization, gained from a visit to Algeciras.

"The middy and I passed the British line in a few moments, and found ourselves on genuine Spanish ground. Dirty scoundrels of soldiers, with rusty firelocks were lolling about some huts by way of guard. A long train of donkeys approached, each hidden under a pair of paniers full of charcoal. They all stopped before the guard-house where every panier was emptied, to see that no liquor was smuggled across the line. I was admiring the vigilance of the ragamuffin soldiery when we beheld a man mounted on a splendid horse advancing along the beach toward us. He was a noble-looking fellow, arrayed in a richly embroidered dress, wrapped in the huge Spanish cloak ; his horse's head, mane, and flanks were hung with tassels and spangled. He carried a carbine slung on his saddle behind him. He was a contrabandista — one who practised smuggling in open defiance of the law. A moment after, he was joking and laughing with the officers at the guard-house.

"After three or four hours' ride, we approached the town where more Spanish soldiers were lounging in a group by the roadside. 'Carracho! los Ingleses!' With that they set a dog on us; finding this of no avail, they blew their trumpets and shouted to scare our horses. We turned around, and sat laughing at them. 'Carracho! Carracho!' and one fellow not satisfied with this Spanish insult, made shift to exclaim 'Go to Hell!' Whereupon the whole took up the cry in chorus. As we rode through the narrow streets, similar maledictions were showered upon us. Boys followed us, first begging a cuarto, and then shouting Carracho. It is a beautiful town — the houses white as snow, with bright green lattices and porticos, the streets paved with square hewn stone and without sidewalks. But the noblest sight was the Plaza, or public square, round which stand the public buildings. It was paved with coarse marble; a large and beautiful column rose in the centre, in the midst of a space walled in from the public. All around, by the columns of the cathedral, about the porches of the houses, were stalls of merchants; and beggars in crowds roaring in the name of the Virgin for charity. We left this hospitable town behind, galloped at full speed round the beach, passing lepers by the wayside, soldiers, donkeys, black-eyed women, hedges of aloes, and groves of oranges, bare sun-burnt mountains, each crowned with its Moorish tower, — and long before the evening gun was fired were within the fortifications again.

". . . Here I had a specimen of every nation on earth, it seemed, around me. A dozen Moors with white turbans and slippered feet lolled one side; Jews by couples in their gabardines; the Spanish gentleman in his black cloak and sombrero — the Spanish laborer with his red cap hanging on one side of his head — the Spanish blackguard in bespangled tights and embroidered jacket. On benches among the trees officers and soldiers carried on successful love suits; on the parade [ground] below English captains were showing forth good horsemanship to the best advantage. The red coats of soldiers appeared everywhere among the trees, and in the crowd below. There were women in cloaks of red and black — ladies with the mantilla and followed by the duenna — no needless precaution — and the ten thousand more soldiers and civilians bond and free, man and woman and child. Not the least singular of the group were the little black slaves belonging to the Moors, who were arrayed in a very splendid and outlandish attire; following after their masters like dogs. Bands were stationed on the parade, and around a summer house among the trees. The evening gun dissolved the pageant — *God Save the Queen* rose on the air; the crowd poured through the gates into the town."

On his tour about Sicily he had a guide, Luigi, of artistic, antiquarian, and numismatic tastes. As the man seemed to know everybody of note along the way, Parkman had many opportunities for visiting the homes of many classes of people, and he never neglected such a chance for studying domestic life. At an inn at Sciacca he wrote:

"The baron brought us a melon and some fine nuts as a present, which he did not disdain to place on the table himself. While our mules were saddling I went with

Luigi to see the domestic establishment of his friend. It was a large and reasonably clean house — some women were spinning in a spacious outer room, where some hens were cackling about the floor. The baroness received me in the inner room — the bedroom. She was a stout, rosy damsel, with good physical womanhood about her, and much beauty, though not over refined. She blushed, as though not used to entertaining strangers. Five or six holy pictures, and little wax images with lamps burning before them were about the room. Luigi took down one of the pictures of Santa Maria, — the patroness of Sciacca, which he piously kissed and put into his hip pocket, observing that now we should have good weather till we got to Palermo. The baroness got me another, by way of making assurance doubly sure. Thus armed against fate we rode away."

Here is a passage that reflects well the distinctness of his impressions, and the occasional vigor of his language:

"The country inns of Sicily are notorious. This one of Castel Termini was a fair sample, though in point of dirt, fleas, etc., it fell far short of some others. A Sicilian albergo is an ancient gloomy building of stone, like all the rest; they usually have a little sign, or at least a branch of a tree stuck at the door, by the way of indicating their public character; but to look up at their half-decayed walls, and the small square windows thinly distributed over the front, you would take them for dungeons. Enter, and you stumble down a stone step into the kitchen — a spacious cavern, dark as Tartarus, with a floor of earth, and seldom any windows. Water jars, harness, and outlandish looking utensils are scattered about. Groups of idlers are crouching in the corner over a brazier of charcoal, and crucifixes and images with little lamps burning before them are hung about the walls. Close adjoining are large stone apartments for mules and asses, who have usually separate accommodations in the albergos, though in the private house a corner of the family room, usually the cleanest, is assigned them. Ask for 'apartamenti,' and a woman leads you up a broken flight of stone steps to a room floored with a kind of cement. There is one window — one strongly secured door — a holy picture on the wall, and a bed full of fleas. You can seldom get anything to eat unless it be macaroni. This is an inn of the interior. The others are better. I speak from the experience of three nights, and I solemnly aver that the picture is not over-colored. I have forgotten a prominent feature of the establishment — the beggars. A decrepit beast, covered with dirt, unshaven, with bleared, gummy eyes, and covered all but the face in a rotten capote, thrusts a rosary into your face, and whines out of his withered throat a petition for alms. All about the door stand groups of idlers, enveloped in the same capotes, staring and conversing listlessly. This capote covered the face exactly like the hoods of mail you see in the old editions of Tasso and Ariosto — but the face of a Sicilian is anything but martial or knightly."

Apropos of Messina we find this vivid sketch:

"I took my station outside one of the gates in the rear of the city, to look at the scum of humanity that came pouring out. All was filth, and age, and ruin — the walls, the tall gateway, with its images and inscriptions, the hovels at the top of the wall and in the ancient suburb, all seemed crumbling to decay. The orange and lemon groves in the ditch of the fortification were dingy and dirty — but away in the distance appeared the summit of the mountains almost as wild and beautiful as our mountains of New England. I thought of them, and in the revival of old feelings, half wished myself at home. I soon forgot, however, all but what was before my eyes, in watching the motley array that passed by me. Men and women literally hung with rags, half hid in dirt, hideous with every imaginable species of deformity, and bearing on their persons a population as numerous as that of Messina itself — these formed the bulk of the throng. Priests, with their black, broad-brimmed hats, and their long robes, fat and good-looking men — were the next numerous class. They draw life and sustenance from these dregs of humanity — just as tall pig-weed flourishes on a dunghill. Then there were mustachioed soldiers, very different from the stately and sedate soldiers of England. There were men bearing holy pictures and images — ladies in swarms, whose profession was stamped on their faces — musicians with a troop of vagabonds in their rear; all around the gateway were the tables of butchers, fruiterers, confectioners, money changers, bootblacks, and a throng of dirty men, women, and children — shouts, yells, and a universal hubbub."

Though enjoying many sights at Naples, he wrote little there that is significant. He took part in the carnival at Rome, driving with Theodore Parker and his wife. The King and his courtiers were the chief actors, while Parker and his wife seem to have been the chief victims, — Parker having his spectacles broken and Mrs. Parker receiving a hard blow on the nose from sugarplums. Parkman visited all the objects of interest, watched the scenes of the streets and markets, saw some funeral processions and military reviews, studied life in the humblest and most wretched quarters of the city, took walks in the country and drank his bottle of Falernian wine with peasants at a tavern in Baiæ.

This account of his visit to Virgil's tomb is too characteristic of him to be passed by:

"I met a laughable adventure here. Like a genuine tourist, I thought I would take away a memento of the poet, and seeing a bush which from its position had escaped the violating hand of former travellers, I determined to get a branch of it. The tomb stands at the edge of a rock about two hundred feet high above the street; this bush was on the side of the cliff just outside an opening in the back part of the tomb. There was a stout iron bar to hold on by — no man of ordinary nerve and muscular strength would have the slightest cause of apprehension. So I told the cicerone to hold my coat, grasped the bar, leaned from the opening, and got hold of the plant, which I was about to secure when I heard a simultaneous shout from both guides, who sprang upon me and seized me fast. I looked round at them. Both were pale as ghosts, with their mouths wide open, and eyes staring out of their heads. I asked them what the devil was the matter — they replied by seizing me by the arms and shoulders and pulling me away from the hole. I got free from them by a sudden effort, but they sprang at me again, and began to roar for help. 'Oh! come this way Signore! Come this way; you must not go there.' I was a good deal vexed, but could not help laughing at being mistaken for a madman. I thought I would try a little intimidation, so aimed a blow with my fist at the nearest fellow's face. They dodged off a moment, but returned to the charge with faces doubly earnest and anxious and pinioned me from behind. 'Oh! Signore!' they said, 'we don't want money; only come up with us to the gate.' I saw the folly of contending with the idea that had got possession of them, so told them I would go. Thus I went out from Virgil's tomb a prisoner. I thought my quiet compliance would have allayed their fears a little — no such thing: nothing would do but I must mount with them to the garden gate above. Half way up appeared a gang of men rushing in hot haste to secure the madman. They were soon about me, when, confiding in their numbers, they loosened my arms. I was resolved not to lose my relic of Virgil, so dispatched a boy to pluck a leaf from the door of the tomb, since the men would on no account suffer me to go myself. I got this memento of my adventure, and departed. I had some little suspicion that all this terror of my guides was counterfeited in order to give them a chance to pick my pockets; but all my money was safe."

Here are two scenes of the kind he liked to sketch, the first at an inn of Cara:

"In the corner [of the public room] crouched two or three old crones, like living skeletons. An unshaven countryman sat on one side — fat and silent loungers from the town, with infant moustache; shabby dandies in cloaks, children and dogs crouching together on the hearth. At a little distance two or three thin visaged and savage looking contadini stood erect and motionless in the glare of the fire. Our guide Giuseppe sat drinking wine at the long tables ranged around the barn-like room. He had a very pretty girl to wait on him, who would come from time to time and stoop over the fire so as to show to the best advantage her classic features and the enormous silver pin in her hair. Hunt[1] and I sat telling each other college stories and recalling college recollections till the people had withdrawn from the room, and left us almost alone, in front of a glowing pile of half consumed embers."

At Subiaco he wrote:

"We came suddenly upon Subiaco. It stood on the top of a detached rocky hill among the mountains. Goats, cattle, trains of mules and asses, women with jars of water on their heads, old woodmen with the heavy crooked chopping knife in their girdles, and a bundle of fagots on their shoulders, were coming down the different pathways from the mountains toward the gate of the town, for it was near sunset. The town was already in shadow, except the castle at the top.

"All this was very well: get within the gate and the scene changed. A crowded pile of high and crumbling stone houses — streets so steep that a horse cannot ascend them, and answering the purpose of a common sewer for all the filth of the inhabitants, so narrow, too, that a strip of the red sky could scarce be seen between the tottering roofs — here was Subiaco; and not Subiaco alone, but

[1] William M. Hunt, the artist.

Italian country towns in general, as far as my observation goes. The women, with water jars, were gathered around the town fountain, more were seated about the corners in a little public square spinning. More still were kneeling, singing vespers in the church. The men were lounging about in red breeches, smoking and staring."

Here is his first confession of the charms of vagabondizing in Europe, at Milan, — though he soon brought himself up with a very characteristic return to the rugged life of his beloved New England:

"This morning when the whole city was quiet, the shops shut in honor of Sunday, the people issuing from the Cathedral, gentlemen walking listlessly about, and porters and contadini sitting idle at the edge of the sidewalks, there was a group of gentlemen taking their coffee under awnings in front of each of the cafés in the piazza before the Cathedral. This vagabond way of breakfasting and seeing the world at the same time, is very agreeable. There is no place where you can be more independent than in one of these cities — when you are hungry there is always a restaurant and a dinner at a moment's notice — when you are thirsty there is always a café at hand. If you are sleepy, your room awaits you — a dozen sneaking waiters are ready at your bidding, and glide about like shadows to do what you may require in hope of your shilling when you go away. But give me Ethan Crawford or even Tom, in place of the whole race of waiters and garçons."

The democratic and wholesome atmosphere of Switzerland seems to have pleased him as much as the scenery:

"I never left any place with more regret than these mountains [about Andeer]. Descending into the wider valleys of the Grisons, the scenery was not less magnificent, though of a different character. At Coire, the capital of the Canton, I was reminded that I was no longer in Italy. A servant stood at the head of the stairs in the large inn there, welcoming each guest with a 'good evening,' and ushering him into a large low wooden apartment, where some thirty men and women were smoking, eating or lounging at the tables and benches. Boys stood ready to receive hats and cloaks; and waiters attended on each new comer to know what he would have. All was ease, good nature, and equality. The old Germans and Swiss grunted over their beer pots, and puffed at their pipes. The young ones laughed with the servant girls. A Frenchman gulped down his bowl full of soup — sprang to the window when he heard the postillon's horn, bounded back to finish one more tumbler of wine, and then, seizing his cane, dashed out in hot haste. A prim, strutting little German student, stalked to the window to watch him, pipe in hand and a complacent grin on his face; then turned to discourse in a half patronizing, half gallant way with the girls."

There is but one important passage concerning Paris, the place in all Europe that most concerned his future labors:

"I have been a fortnight in Paris and seen it as well as it can be seen in a fortnight. Under peculiarly favorable circumstances, too; for it was the great season of balls and gaieties, and I had a guide moreover who knows Paris from top to bottom — within and without. I like to see a thing done thoroughly. If a man has a mind to make a fool or a vagabond of himself, he can do it admirably in Paris; whereof I have seen many instances. If a man has a mind to amuse himself there is no place like it on earth; diversions of every character, form, and degree waiting for him at every step; let him taste them — then get into the diligence and ride away, or stay, and go to the devil."

Paris became more attractive to him later by reason of its close connection with his labors and its innumerable interests to any student of life. He thus wrote to his sister Mary in 1859 of the way in which he spent the most of his leisure time there, — not in society, galleries, or libraries, but in studying street life. The letter is characteristic of his habit of dismissing the subject of health in a few words; one would never suspect it was written in a period of the greatest mental and physical suffering.

"I am a little less lame. I get on well enough. The omnibuses of Paris — of which there are about seven hundred — are made with railings, etc., in such a way that, with a little science, I can swing myself to the top with the arms alone, and here I usually spend the better part of the day smoking cigarettes and surveying the crowds below. I have formed an extensive acquaintance among omnibus cads and the like, whom I find to be first-rate fellows in their way — also have learned pretty thoroughly the streets of Paris, where much may be seen from the top of an omnibus. When hungry or thirsty, I descend to any restaurant, café, or 'buffet' that happens to be near, whether of low or high degree if only clean.

In fair weather an hour or two may always be spent pleasantly enough between three and five o'clock, in the open air under the porches of the cafés on the boulevards, where all Paris passes by."

We may close these extracts concerning his study of manners and customs with the following sketch; the subject could hardly fail to appeal to his sense of humor after his experience of European martial scenes.

"'Cornwallis' at Brighton, October 18, 1844. I was there before the militia had gone off. Some had the large skirted coats of revolutionary officers, some wore battered helmets, some three-cornered hats, some nothing. They had every variety of weapon, from blunderbuss to rusty saw; and were of all ages and sizes. A more ragamuffin assemblage I never saw. 'Officers to the front,' exclaimed the general on his horse. The long line of ragamuffins who stood leaning on their rifles or muskets in every variety of outlandish costume, looked as if they had never an officer among them. But at the word, a number of fellows straddled out from the line, with yellow breeches and red coats; or with false beards, and dirty shirts, armed with axes, swords, or guns. These marched up to the front and faced gravely towards the general. 'Gentlemen officers,' he began, etc. The address over, the officers withdrew, and the music struck up, at which the whole line of ragamuffins got under way and marched straggling off the ground, just as the sun went down."

Parkman's study of character in individual men and women was an interest second only to his literary labors. It not only gratified an inherited taste and faculty for reading men, but also formed an important element of his preparation as historian. It was, besides, the chief means by which one of his reserved nature could be brought into intimate contact with humanity outside of a restricted circle of friends and relations; for his sympathies were not strong and broad enough by themselves to make him a lover of all men. It remained throughout his life a study of unflagging interest, being furthered by his tastes, faculties and opportunities. For his personal traits were fortunate; he attracted men by an unfeigned interest in them, thus inducing them to open their minds to him. He was singularly ready to listen to others, though he rarely if ever opened his own reserved nature in return for their confidences. Then his social propensities saved him from becoming a recluse, and counteracted the danger to manliness that lurks in the study. Again, circumstances brought him all the opportunities he could desire. At his father's hospitable board he met many men of distinction; at college he was always welcome among his classmates; he had a wide circle of family connections and friends; he was a member of various societies and clubs; and his travels at home and abroad brought him in contact with many national types, many classes, many interesting individuals. His maladies often necessitated a great deal of self-denial as to society; but he continued to the last, as far as his health allowed, to follow his social inclinations, saying that one should know as many people as possible. Throughout life the reading of fiction was an important element of his amusements, while historical researches and writing demanded a continual estimation of men from their words and actions; and his works show with what care he conceived and executed the strong outlines of his characters.

Parkman's skill in reading men came largely from persistent and careful practice. His first effort in this direction was another happy coincidence of boyish tastes with the subsequent needs of a historian. When about twelve years of age he with some equally youthful companions fitted up the loft of his father's unused coach house, and founded "The Star Theatre." The boys painted their own scenery and made most of their own "properties." The name, derived from the eminence of every member of the company, was duly signified by a tinsel star on a strip of green cambric crossing the stage above the curtain. Parkman displayed both energy and skill in this organization, — as mechanic in rigging up the curtain, as chemist in managing the colored lights for the scene, as artist wielding the whitewash brush, and finally as actor, chiefly in women's rôles, for which he is said to have been well fitted by the possession of a high voice; and if we may judge by the daguerreotype of him as a young man, reproduced in this volume, he must have had unusual charms of face and person. The company was successful. It seems to have given a performance nearly every Saturday afternoon, and sometimes on Wednesday also, during several months of 1835–36, and 1836–37. The audience consisted mostly of young relatives and friends, but it often contained others more critical and mature, and now and then a matron accompanied by her entire school. The first season opened with "The Dumb Boy of Genoa," in which young Parkman distinguished himself in the title rôle, played altogether in pantomime. Only a small part of the repertory can now be recalled, but it included "The Golden Farmer," "My Fellow Clerk," and "The Chicken" (translated from the French by F. Lee), also Shakspere's "Taming of the Shrew," in which Parkman played Katharina. Here is the bill announcing one of the most successful performances: —

Star Theatre.

BENEFIT OF MR. F. PARKMAN.

On Saturday, May 7th, will be performed the celebrated play of

Bombastes Furioso.

"Whoever dares these boots displace
Must meet Bombastes face to face."

Bombastes (a general)	J. C. Shaw.
Artaxomines (king of Eutophia) .	C. Shimmin.
Fusbos (Minister of State) . . .	G. Parkman.
Distafina	F. Parkman.

To conclude with the much admired play of

King's Bridge Cottage.

Mr. Richardson	S. Eliot.
Frederick	J. C. Shaw.
Percy	C. Shimmin.
Valmore	*F. Parkman.*
Cato	W. A. Marston.
Mary	F. Minot.
Maj. O'Bryan (a British officer in disguise),	G. Parkman.

Mr. C. F. Shimmin respectfully announces his benefit for Wednesday, May 18th.

F. Minot, Printer.

Parkman's Distafina is still remembered as a charming impersonation. These theatricals, continued for a considerable length of time and evidently developed with much study and pains for schoolboys, were of course undertaken solely for amusement. But as Parkman entered into them with the thoroughness and zeal that he brought to everything he did, they probably had some influence in awakening his love of the study of character — just as his boyhood adventures in the Middlesex Fells cultivated his love of nature.

His diaries contain some very significant bits of appreciation of character. They show this study to have been one of his deepest interests, probably deeper than any other outside of history. He began to record his observations as early as 1842, giving them increasing space and emphasis until they became the chief element of his note-books in 1844–45.

We may begin our extracts with the following account of the puppet shows of Naples, and then pass on from these rough sketches of strangers to his more finished portraits of familiar acquaintances.

"I went to-night to the teatro Sebeto — an establishment consisting of a pit, eight boxes, and a gallery where none but men sit. The piece was a deep tragedy, full of love, jealousy, and murder, dungeons, trap-doors, etc. Pulcinella here assumed the character of a pilgrim. He always wears a black vizard which covers his face as far as the end of his nose, leaving the lower part bare. His entrée, which was in the midst of the most tragic part, was greeted by a loud laugh. The father of the distressed lady was busy in bemoaning his afflictions on his knees, with hands clasped. Pulcinella kneels down a little behind him, and caricatured all his motions most ludicrously. In the next scene the distracted husband, whose lady has proved unfaithful, encounters the pilgrim and makes at him with drawn sword, taking him for the betrayer of his beloved. Pulcinella meets him with his pilgrim's staff, which he brandishes at him in a most laughable manner, turning into ridicule all his anger and distress. The audience roar with delight, but do not applaud. Pulcinella then has a scene to himself with two girls, each of whom falls in love with him, and treat him to sugarplums. Some of his evolutions were very particularly indecent. After this he did not appear again. Tragedy resumed her reign undisturbed . . . Pulcinella is a most original character. His ridicule does not spare the hero and the heroine themselves. In a terrific scene of incantation and sorcery which I saw to-day, Pulcinella pretended at first to be very much frightened, but seized an opportunity to knock over Death himself, who was rising out of a fiery pit to seize him. He kicked a Sultan in the face. He is always present in every tragic or pathetic scene, turning the whole to ridicule by his ludicrous caricatures, or his affected sympathy. He is always planning tricks to get his best friends into a scrape."

Here is one of his most graphic pages, written at Bologna:

"The diligence was full of Frenchmen. In one day and one night we got to Bologna. Here, in the yard of the office, among the soldiers and other officials who stood with folded arms listlessly staring at the strangers, was an animal nearly seven feet high, with a face like a large baboon. . . . His motions, too, exactly resembled a large monkey's. He bounded about, swinging himself up and down the diligence, tossing about heavy trunks and bales, as if they were feathers, with his long muscular arms. He kept his eyes rolling about in his head, glancing at everything in the yard, with an expression of infinite alacrity and anxiety, and whenever he saw anything that met his disapproval he would jump to rectify it with a sort of angry chattering in his throat. He was a deaf mute."

In London he found this subject for his pen:

"Walk out in the evening, and keep a yard or two behind some wretched clerk, who with nose elevated in the air, elbows stuck out at right angles, and the pewter knob of his cane playing upon his under lip, is straddling his bow-legs over the sidewalk with a most majestic air. Get behind him and you see his dignity greatly disturbed.

First he glances over one of his narrow shoulders — then over the other — then he edges off to the other side of the walk, and turns his vacant lobster eyes full upon you, then he passes his hand over his coat tail — and finally he draws forth from his pocket the object of all this solicitude in the shape of a venerable and ragged cotton handkerchief, which he holds in his hand, to keep it out of harm's way. I have been thus taken for a pickpocket more than a dozen times to-night — not the less so for being respectably dressed, for these gentry are the most dashy men on the Strand. There is an interesting mixture of vulgarity and helplessness in the swarm of ugly faces you see in the streets — meagre, feeble, ill-proportioned, or not proportioned at all, the blockheads must needs put on a game air and affect the 'man of the world' in their small way. I have not met one handsome woman yet, though I have certainly walked more than fifty miles since I have been here. Elsewhere Englishmen are tall, strong, and manly; here the crowd that swarms through the streets are like the outcasts of a hospital."

We shall discuss later the fact that Parkman rarely expresses sympathy or admiration for men, either as nations, classes, or individuals. For the present we offer the following three sketches as the only exceptions to this rule in his diary. While taking a drive in Sicily he met with this experience:

"At Giarri, a large place where we stopped to rest the horses, we were beset of course by beggars. One little rascal, about six years old — whose clothes, if they answered the purpose of warmth, answered no other purposes for which clothing is intended, followed me about for half an hour, like a little dog. I could not muster sternness enough to order him away with effect — and he was too small to kick into the gutter — so he went on, begging for a carlino. At last he began slyly to mock, for my edification, the grave countenance and stately air of Don Mateo, and did it so ludicrously that I stood laughing at him. At this he summoned a larger boy to his side, who hummed a tune, while he danced a sort of hornpipe on the pavement. I could forbear no longer, but gave him a grano — about the third part of a cent. A crowd of loungers had mustered to witness the performance of this manikin, who was about a foot and a half high. There they stood in their brown capotes, looking gravely from out of their hoods at the spectacle of my unparalleled generosity, which was a signal for action. I was half-stunned with supplications from men, women, and children, and glad, after cursing them a little, to escape into the carriage. Among the rest was a girl, most abominably ugly, who appeared to be a mute. I threw her a large copper coin — the young Spaniard added a couple more, which threw the girl into a perfect frenzy of delight. She danced about among the crowd flinging both hands into the air — then kissing the coins, and pressing them against her breast; tossing them on the ground before her, and gathering them up again; till her ugly face seemed absolutely good looking with the excess of her pleasure."

This sketch was taken on the steamer when leaving Palermo for Naples:

"An old monk was on board, among the crowd of nobles and exquisites, with the cord of St. Francis holding his tattered rags together. He had a little contribution box in his hand, and was gliding about in a crouching posture, with his cap in his hand, begging for his patron's benefit. He would look up into the faces of an inattentive group with an humble and supplicating countenance, just like a starved dog expecting a piece of meat at a dinner table. A pleasant voyage and perfect safety was to be the reward of all who dropped a grano into the box. My heart was moved with compassion toward the old fellow, he looked so humble and so miserable. I tried to catch his eye to give him something — but my unwonted feeling of benevolence toward a Sicilian beggar was destined to bear no fruit — for just then all visitors were warned off. The old monk tumbled himself over the side into the boat of a charitable facchino."

Another page reveals pleasantly his ready appreciation of manliness wherever it may be found:

"This morning as I got half asleep into the post carriage, at Colico [or Calico], I was saluted by a *bon giorno* by a small voice from a dark corner, where I discovered by groping about a fine boy of thirteen or fourteen with great promise of muscles yet undeveloped. He was a young Swiss, who spoke Italian; so I began to talk with him. He spoke in a frank and bold manner. I asked him if he did not mean to be a soldier. He said he should have to, for all the Swiss were obliged to serve from the age of eighteen to twenty-four. He was mistaken; the Swiss military system resembles ours. But he meant to be an officer because he was noble. The conductor at this moment brought a lantern to the window which showed a handsome Quentin Durward-like boy, but clothed in rough homespun, and clouted shoes that did not look much like nobility, and reminded me of Quentin's pretensions. He had not heard of America, and inquired with great curiosity how far it was, and how long the term of military service was. I told him the period that we are expected to be in readiness, which astonished him exceedingly. 'Corpo di Bacco! più di quarant' anni di militare! Ma quell' è bello! più di quarant' anni di militare!' He said he was a Calvinist and that all of his religion were considered as devils — *come diavoli* — by the people around. He fell asleep at last, and did not wake till we stopped at Chiavenna, when he jumped up, shook himself, took his stick, and walked off to the mountains."

Parkman's appreciation of the feminine character, which was both ardent and discriminating, found but few expressions in his diaries; women were not then the important element of his life and work that they subsequently became. Of Sicilian women he said:

"One passed me in the church of the Capuchin Convent, with the black eye, the warm rich cheek, and the bright glance that belong to southern climates and are beautiful beyond all else."

Of the women in Naples he observed:

"There is something particularly attractive about these women, who are seldom, however, handsome, properly speaking — but there is the devil in their bright faces and full rounded forms."

The charm and grace of Italian ladies evidently went to his youthful heart in the carnival at Rome:

"Few had any regular features, but there was an expression of heart and spirit, and a loftiness beside which did not shame their birth. They flung their flowers at you with the freest and most graceful action imaginable. To battle with flowers against a laughing and conscious face — showering your ammunition thick as the carriage slowly passes the balcony — then straining your eyes to catch the last glance of the black-eyed witch and the last wave of her hand as the crowd closes around her — all this is no contemptible amusement."

His aversion to certain types of women was as strong as his admiration for others; and his criticism was often expressed with a trenchant force that left no room for doubt. Thus in 1845 he made this observation of a noisy party in the cars in his own state of Massachusetts:

"Is not a *half educated* vulgar weak woman a disgusting animal? Where there is no education at all and no pretension, the matter is all very well — where high education and good sense are united it is very well indeed; but the half and half genteel — damn them!"

As against this we may put the following sketch of Mrs. General Riedesel, taken from his review of her memoirs. It seems by its sureness of touch as well as by its harmony with his known taste, to be the portrait of a woman he would have liked very much; in fact it seems to me to come nearer than any other writing of his to the expression of his ideal woman, hardly excepting the heroine of "Vassall Morton."

> "Her graceful and feminine character was braced by an admirable courage, and a spirit which must have made her a very piquant companion. She had resources for every emergency, made friends everywhere, and appears to have been equally mistress of the situation in the backwoods of Virginia, and in the family circle of King George III. . . . She was too sensible, natural, and pure to be a prude."

Parkman's memory of the eye, so remarkable for scenery, was equally good for faces. It is related that about 1885 he one day sat down to dine at a friend's house next to a lady whom he had not observed with much care. Presently she said: "I see, Mr. Parkman, that you do not recognize me." He then looked attentively at her face and at once replied: "The last time I talked with you was on your father's piazza at Palermo in 1843."

His more intimate study of men in friends and acquaintances shows him to have been free from class prejudice in personal relations. What he demanded first and last was manliness, character; the external circumstances of wealth, birth, education, set up no barriers between him and any man or woman; *hauteur* was never seen in his feeling or conduct. Any worthy individual, though from a class for which Parkman may have had no sympathy, became interesting to him as soon as personal relations were established. He showed interest in the history, character, plans, conduct, and welfare of all his acquaintances, and often of their children as well. He was catholic in taking into his friendship men of all kinds, — the grave and the gay, the exuberant and the reserved, the cool and the fiery. On the steamer going from Malta to Messina in 1843, he fell into pleasant, even friendly, relations with a Sicilian who had been a cook in Murdock's tavern in Boston, and some of his warmest expressions of regard and admiration are those concerning his guide on the Oregon Trail journey. Besides ending the book with praises of this illiterate man as a true gentleman, he says: "I have never, in the city or the wilderness, met a better man than my noble and true-hearted friend, Henry Chatillon."[1]

His diary on this journey through Europe in 1844 contains the longest of his sketches of character. He thus described his guide and muleteer in Sicily, Luigi Rannesi:

"Luigi, a diminutive Sicilian, with a thin brown face and an air of alertness about every inch of him, began to jabber Italian with such volubility that I could not understand a word. He must needs exhibit every article of the provisions he had got ready for the journey, extolling the qualities of each — and they deserved all his praises — always ended by pounding himself on the breast, rolling up his eyes and exclaiming 'Do you think Luigi loves

[1] *The Oregon Trail*, ed. 1849, p. 23.

money? No! Luigi loves honor!' and then launching forth into interminable eulogiums of the country we were going to see, and the adventures we should meet there. . . He talked and gesticulated half frenzied because he found I could not understand half he said; then seized my hand which he dutifully kissed and left me to my meditations."

On approaching Girgenti:

"One of his fits of enthusiasm had taken possession of Luigi. He began to lash his mule and drive him along over mud and rocks at such a rate that I thought him mad, till he told me that it was necessary —*fa bisogno* — to get to Girgenti before the Englishmen.

"'Corragio! my brave mule! Corragio, Signore,' he shouted. 'We shall be the victors!' At that he drove full speed up the steep hill towards the gate. Nothing would stop him. He leaped over ditches, — scrambled through mud and stones, shouting 'Corragio' at the top of his lungs. At last an insuperable gully brought him up short. He clapped his hand to his forehead exclaiming 'Santissima Maria' in a tone of wrath and despair — then recovered his spirits and dashed off in another direction. We succeeded. When we got to the top the carriage (containing the Englishmen) was a quarter of a mile off, and Luigi shouted 'Vittoria!' as he rode into the gate as much elated as if he had accomplished some great achievement.

"Luigi brings me pockets full of ancient money, and seems greatly astonished at my indifference. As for himself he is rabid [as a numismatic archæologist]. He dodges into every house and shop, inquiring for 'Antica moneta;' stops contadini at work with the same question; he has scraped together an enormous bag full for which he paid scarce anything, perfectly familiar as he is with its true value and the customs of the country. His enthusiasm embraces every object, far and wide. He raves of love on the road, tells how he eloped with his wife, sings love songs; then falls into the martial vein; shouts 'Corragio'; defies the wind, rain, and torrents. He enters into all my plans with a most fervid zeal, leaving me nothing to do. Every night he comes upstairs bringing all kinds of dresses and utensils of the people for me to look at. Sometimes he comes in with a handful of old coins, telling me with a chuckle that he had bought them for 'pochissimo'; kissing them repeatedly in the exultation of a good bargain. I have lived most sumptuously ever since I have been with him. He puts the whole inn into a ferment, rakes the town to find the best of everything and waits on table with an eulogium of every dish. 'Ah! Signore,' he repeats, 'do you think Luigi loves money? No! Luigi loves honor!' He has something to give to every beggar he meets. In short, the fellow is a jewel, and shall be my particular friend henceforth.

"I went with him to the house of a Signore Politi, who is fairly rampant with antiquarian zeal, and deeply enamoured moreover of the fine arts. The studio of this virtuoso presented a formidable display of old pictures, plaster casts, vases, fragments of statues, and a confused medley of indescribables. He was sitting at his easel copying a Madonna of Guido. Luigi pulled off his hat with great respect, advanced, and drawing an antique cameo from the multitudinous folds of his handkerchief presented it as 'Un piccolo complimento' to Signore. The virtuoso examined it through his spectacles, expressed his approval, and coolly pocketed it, leaving me in equal admiration at Luigi's making a 'complimento' of such value and at Politi's cavalier-like style of accepting it. The mystery was soon solved — it was like Turkish or Indian presents; Luigi expected as a matter of course a 'complimento' in return. In fact he retired with a handkerchief full of antiquities. He told me he always carried something with him, 'per fare un complimento' to the Signori who honored him with their acquaintance. He knows everybody, from princes to beggars.

"Luigi came up in the evening, to hold 'un discorso' with me according to his custom. He was in his usual state of excitement. He takes a glass of wine in his hand 'viva l' onora, signorino mio,' rolling up his eyes and flourishing his hands, 'viva Bacco; viva Dio; viva il consolo Americano!' and so on, the finale being a seizure and kissing of my hand, after which he inquires if I shall want him, looks about to see that all is right, kisses my hand again and goes off."

The following passage telling their nearest approach to robbery gives another touch to his sketch of Luigi:

"We were riding past an old house of contadini when Luigi suddenly reined back his mule upon mine, uttering in a whisper of consternation, '*Santissima Maria!*' I looked at him and saw that the natural muddy brown of his thin face was changed to a most cadaverous yellow. I asked him what was the matter. He made no answer, but shouted aloud for Michele — who was a little way behind among the trees — and then began to cross himself and mutter prayers. I could see nothing except a man with a gun walking away from the road toward a group of a dozen contadini who were standing in front of the shattered house. We had left them far behind, before Luigi was so far recovered as to tell me that a man had pointed a gun at him from the bushes, but had desisted when he saw Michele. He added that next to the mountains around Palermo this place was the most notorious for robbers in all Sicily. I do not for a moment imagine that the fellow intended us bodily harm."

Here is a note on Luigi's attendant muleteer:

"The way was enlivened by the edifying singularities of the muleteer Michele, who walked along talking without intermission for an hour together, though no one listened or replied. He interrupted his discourse only to belabor his mule and curse him in Sicilian. When we came to a steep place, he would take a firm hold of the beast's tail with one hand, while he belabored him with a rope's end that he held in the other, and thus they would scramble up together. Where the mud was more than a foot deep Michele would place both hands on the mule's rump and vault with a sort of grunt upon his back; wiggle himself about for a while to find a comfortable seat, and then burst forth with some holy canticle in praise of a Saint."

The study of life and character continues, after history, to be the most important element of his diaries all through 1844, 1845, and 1846, up to his departure from St. Louis for the Rocky Mountains, but his pages contain very few passages worthy of quotation. The fact of chief interest is that the historian devoted so much time and pains to the study of character and contemporary life. He sketched some of his classmates, his fellow students in the Law School; he attended public meetings, as those of the Millerites and Fourierites, not because he was interested in the causes, but to study men, both collectively and individually. The manners, the conversations, the traits of mind, the quality, the motives of men, all attracted his searching eye. His observation was directed impartially to the most diverse characters, — stage drivers, soldiers, Indians, sailors, priests, farmers, scholars, artists, the grave, the gay, the old and the young, — everybody was grist for his mill.

Here is a page written in 1845:

"J. — His vanity and love of display joined with energy combine to make a fool of him. He affects the man of the world — goes always in full dress, and though he has no sportsmanlike propensities keeps a breed of dogs about him, and affects the connoisseur, also a fine equipage. He is foolishly proud of money and his supposed rank in society, and lets drop no opportunity of showing his superiority. From constantly pushing himself into the foremost places and affecting to command everywhere, he has raised a host of enemies. His vanity impels him to lie enormously. I suspect him of not being remarkably brave, though I should never have made the remark but for some boastful lies he had lately been telling about a street battle with some fellows who insulted him. He is hospitable and bountiful, though ostentatious."

We may close these extracts concerning his study of character with this passage written at St. Louis, 1846, just before his departure on the Oregon Trail trip:

"How infinite is the diversity of human character! Old Mr. C. of nearly eighty, lively, bright, and active — the old man goes about rejoicing in his own superiority to age — wrapt up in himself, unobservant, impenetrable, impassive. His companion was the reverse — young, silent through bashfulness, observing all, feeling all, and constantly in hostility to external influences, — though resolute and determined, acting ever under the burden of constitutional diffidence. How hostile is such a quality to a *commanding* character. It is the mind as it stamps its character on the *bearing* and *manner* that carries weight; the bold, unhesitating, confident expression has authority — not the forced, sharp, painful expression of resolution struggling against diffidence. Some men have a sort of power from their very vanity — they are too dull, too impassive to feel a repressing influence from other minds — and, thinking themselves the greatest men on earth, they assume a port and voice that imposes a sort of respect. Others there are who, with many of the internal qualities of command, can never assume its outward features — and fail in consequence. How wide and deep and infinitely various is human nature! and how the contemplation of it grows more absorbing as its features disclose themselves to view!"

The unity of Parkman's life, the concentration of all his efforts from first to last on the writing of history, was not reached quite so early or so definitely as is generally supposed. In 1879, in an impersonal way, he described the wisdom of such a course; and the passage is too clearly a reflection of his convictions and conduct to escape a personal application:

"There is a universal law of growth and achievement. The man who knows himself, understands his own powers and aptitudes, forms purposes in accord with them, and pursues these purposes steadily, is the man of success. He who takes no account of his own nature, makes his will the father of his thought, shuts his eyes to unwelcome truths, places himself in false positions, and turns from the good within his reach to strain after the unattainable, is predestined to vexation and failure. Every one has his place in the world, and the wise and fortunate find it."

This passage may be a backward glance at some of his early struggles with his own nature. He confesses in his autobiographical letter that he was for a time divided between "the Muse of History . . . and her wayward sisters." We know that poetry commanded his attention up to the middle of his college course; and judging by his diaries, fiction shared his affections to a certain extent with the soberer muse at a much later epoch. The closing remark of the above quotation from his journal at St. Louis, stands out boldly by its emphasis and breadth as to his interest in the study of character. On the other hand it is noteworthy that neither letters nor diaries contain any expression of joy or interest in the pursuit of historical study. If this study had at that time become his sole aim and chief delight, his reserve was indeed extraordinary. His diaries are far more those of a novelist than a historian, being largely made up of sketches of character, manners, and customs, dialect, and other contemporaneous and realistic matters; but silent as to the deeper and broader questions of life that concern history.

He made "Vassall Morton" say (page 216):

> "When I was a boy I pleased myself with planning that I would study out the springs of human action, and trace human emotion up to its sources. It was a boy's idea — to fathom the unfathomable, to line and map out the shifting clouds and the ever moving winds. De Staël speaks the truth — 'man may learn to rule man, but only God can comprehend him.'"

Both Parkman and Motley felt the close relationship of history and fiction, and each yielded to the seduction of the latter in writing a novel early in their careers. Parkman wrote "Vassall Morton" after having tried his hand successfully as historian in "The Conspiracy of Pontiac." He seems to have deprecated being taken too seriously, and to have eased the launching of a maiden novel by putting on the titlepage this verse:

> "Écrive qui voudra! Chacun à ce metier
> Peut prendre impunément de l'encre et du papier."

It may be remarked in passing that each of the seventy-four chapters of "Vassall Morton," as well as those of the first edition of "The Oregon Trail," is headed by one or more quotations of poetry. The depth of Parkman's early interest in poetry stands revealed by the range of reading shown in these quotations, and it is equally remarkable that this interest never reappeared in either his writings or conversation after the publication of "Vassall Morton." His only use of verse in after life was a humorous one, — composing now and then a parody or quoting some stanza absurd for its illiteracy.

The facts of his life show very clearly that fiction never disturbed the essential unity of his career. Probably he wrote "Vassall Morton" chiefly as a recreation; enjoying work on this intermediate level of art between the heights of poetry he had relinquished and the plain of history he had accepted. Whatever his hopes may have been, they were abandoned after the publication and failure of the novel in 1856. His subsequent feeling towards the book might be taken as a reflection of some degree of secret disappointment, and of his strong love of dignity and consistency. He disliked to hear it mentioned, and never included it among his works. His aversion to it may have sprung in part from its autobiographic character, although this is well concealed from all but his intimate friends; certainly he need not have been ashamed of the hero as a personification of his own leading traits. Then again, his dislike may have sprung from a loftier feeling: coming as he did to have a legitimate pride in his own extraordinary fidelity to his chosen muse, in spite of all discouragements and dangers, he could hardly avoid displeasure at the rival that for a time led him a little astray.

On what kinds of expression did Mr. Parkman rely in his study of character? and what was the range of his impressions? His chief reliance seems to me to have been the external, matter-of-fact indications of words and deeds. While these are often a spontaneous and true expression of character, they are not always thus to be depended on. Words, even when used without the intention of hiding thought, are frequently quite inadequate to a sincere and full expression. Even the more substantial testimony of conduct is misleading without a full knowledge of the convictions, intentions, feelings, and circumstances from which it springs. The spirit, the essential character, lives and pursues its apparently contradictory play behind these masks of words, deeds, and material forms as perceived by the average eye and mind. The deeper and more essential revelations are made in subtile and unconscious modes of expression, which are visible only to him who possesses highly developed organs of sense and mental faculties capable of spiritual insight. He who has not an eye sensitive to the subtilities of form, line, color, and motion, will not see all the unconscious revelations made in face, attitude and gesture; without a fine ear he will not hear the significant delicacies of pronunciation, tones, and inflections of voice; or if he lack the intuitive and spiritual cast of mind, he will not duly appreciate the significance of the phenomena of the inner life that he may perceive. It must be said, however, that instinct often leads us to the truth beyond the line apparently drawn by the senses; and Mr. Parkman in this way may well have felt the nature of men in unexpected particulars. His sensitiveness to the influence of congenial and uncongenial persons lends some weight to this supposition. This impressibility, however, indicates an instinctive recognition of mutually congenial temperaments more than any deep penetration into the secrets of character. His reliance chiefly on words and deeds as the indication of character was very natural; for literature is the mode of expression that he mastered most thoroughly, and he was continually studying and writing the records of words and deeds of the past, and drawing portraits from these revelations.

CHAPTER VI

THE tragic element in Parkman's life is the probability that his sufferings were quite as much the result of ignorance as of inherited weakness. He himself said that with wiser management his diseases might have been cured and outgrown. As a boy he was delicate, though not sickly; his inherent forces and the activities of youth soon brought him out of the doubtful conditions of his childhood, making him as a collegian active and enduring beyond the average; while the abundance of his vitality and the strength of his constitution are fully attested by the entire course of his life, in resisting the depression of disease and in performing labor. The chief error was the not uncommon mistake of regarding exercise as the all-sufficient means of securing health. While developing his muscles, he failed in the larger duty of acquiring a thorough knowledge of the general laws of health.

His physical culture, as we have seen, had as close a connection with his personality as any other part of his education. His tastes and ruling traits pointed in advance to his course and the dangers he would be likely to meet. Early in his college life muscular development became his hobby; he desired to equal the

Indian in strength, agility, endurance, and skill in woodcraft; he also became convinced that a healthy mind could exist only in a healthy body. But in pursuing these laudable aims he was exposed to many risks. His self-discipline began when he was yet a boy at home; he would not permit himself habits or thoughts tending in the least to weaken the central virtue of manliness. He never could abide weakness, either physical, mental, or moral; men, women, opinions, emotions, to command his admiration must show strength and energy. Thus the ways of the prudent, complaining, and self-indulgent invalid were to him worthy only of contempt. He himself, going to the other extreme, drove his body to exercise with an excessive and destructive ambition. He treated his infirmities by the fatal method of "crushing them by force," attaining almost a savage's endurance of pain. If the strongest mind, bent on attaining health and ignoring illness, were able to cure disease by will-power, Parkman should have been the healthiest of men.

Although athletics had not then reached their present development in college life, he found sufficient means for attaining his ends. "It was in Parkman's junior year that a gymnasium was first provided by the faculty for the use of the students. It was in a wooden building of no great size, and was under the superintendence of a pugilist and popular teacher of the art of self-defence, but who knew little or nothing of scientific training as now understood.

It was provided with such apparatus as was then common, and the young men, with virtually no one to direct or guide them, were allowed to make such use as they pleased of the parallel bars, lifting machines, and other appliances. Parkman naturally availed himself with eagerness of this opportunity of increasing his muscular development, now become his favorite hobby. He was a constant attendant at the gymnasium, took boxing lessons, and emulated the foremost in trials of strength and endurance. The strain was too great for a constitution not naturally robust, and in the first term of his senior year he was obliged to suspend for a time his college studies, and seek relaxation and relief in a voyage to Europe."[1] Walking was one of his favorite exercises, and he connected it, as we have seen, with his literary purposes. "He was already training himself for expeditions into the wilderness, and preparing to make an exhaustive study of the aborigines by living among them in their native haunts. As a part of this preparation he was in the habit, while in college, of taking long walks, going always at so rapid a pace that it was difficult to keep up with him. This manner of walking became habitual to him, and he retained it to the last. Long years afterward, when crippled by disease and needing two canes to support his step, he might often be seen in the streets of Boston, walking rapidly for a short distance, then suddenly stopping, wheeling around, and propping

[1] Wheelwright.

himself against the wall of a house to give a moment's repose to his enfeebled knee. Whatever he did, he must do it with all his might. He could not saunter, he could not creep; he must move rapidly or stand still."[1] On these walks in the country he often carried his rifle, "Satan." He also did some rowing on Fresh Pond. Later, when a student in the Law School, he joined a class in riding under the instruction of a circus manager. With his chivalric and spirited temper he must have taken great pleasure in this knightly exercise. "He chose the hardest horses, practised riding in every form, with or without a saddle or stirrups; could run, leap, jump on a charger at full speed, — in short, perform feats which only a 'professional' could execute."[2] In this study he probably had in view his Oregon Trail trip, which occurred soon after. If our athletic games had then been in vogue, his skill, courage, coolness and activity would have made him a successful competitor.

Exercise was of exceptional importance to Parkman. His perpetual-motion energy of course could not be denied expenditure without repining and irritation; and his love of freedom and activity were too strong to be easily reconciled to canes and crutches in place of his youthful agility. But the matter was much more serious than this; whenever, as he said, confinement became unavoidable, "all the irritability of the system centred in the head." As

[1] Wheelwright. [2] Frothingham.

this tendency, of all things, had to be most carefully avoided, exercise was almost as necessary as food or air; and throughout his life he was faithful to this requirement. For many years his lameness did not prevent free walking at times, nor horseback exercise; he used also to do what digging and other work he could in his garden. Fortunately his arms remained serviceable till very near the close of his life, so that he could generally enjoy some form of exercise with them. Even when confined to his wheel-chair he would split wood, hoe in his garden, rake, or cut with a sickle the grass along the walks; he even did some carpenter work in making foot benches or other objects of utility. During much of his latter years he was obliged to use canes or crutches, and to carry a stool when working in his garden. Disliking eccentricity of all kinds, he was much annoyed at having to walk in the streets in his peculiar manner; yet he would not give up exercise and social intercourse so long as he could enjoy them by any means whatever. The pain and the loss of freedom caused by his lameness led him for a time to consider amputation of the leg; but the relief hoped for was too doubtful to justify the operation. When rheumatism finally came in the shoulders and stopped the last of his out-of-door exercises, he accepted massage, practised deep breathing and such other movements as could be executed in a chair.

The nature of the ailments that afflicted Parkman

and affected so much his life and character must be explained somewhat if we would fully understand his struggle for self-mastery. The causes of his early illnesses are enveloped in more or less mystery. Although in his autobiographic letter he touches on some of their relations to his literary labors, he nowhere enters into detail; nor do any of his friends seem able to tell much about them. He said that his childhood was neither "healthful nor buoyant," but with the help of free country life on his grandfather's farm, and the vital forces of youth, he soon outgrew this condition and acquired a good amount of health and strength. In college he was remarked for his physical powers and good condition, — so much so that his friends were surprised when, in his junior year, he had to give up his studies for a few months and go abroad for his health. Nothing very definite is known of the cause of this sudden change. Some think it was a trouble with his eyes, but there is no reference to this in his diaries and the few letters he wrote. It was probably as others intimate, with apparently better knowledge, a trouble of the heart resulting from overstrain in the gymnasium at Harvard. He wrote in his diary, on leaving Florence, in 1844:

> "After all I shall not see Grenada, — at least for some years; thanks to the cursed injury that brought me to Europe; for as I find no great improvement, I judge it best to see what a French doctor can do for me, instead of running about Spain."

Shortly afterward, when among the Alps, as already noted, he referred to the painful beating of his heart. This affection, however, does not seem to have been a persistent trouble; it did not prevent him, even at that time, from walking, climbing mountains, and ascending cathedral spires as only a vigorous man can do; and the malady does not figure among the chronic troubles of his after life. There is no subsequent mention in his diaries either of disease or medical treatment; but a previous writing, a letter to his mother from Rome, April 5, 1844, contains this passage:

"I find that though I am very well indeed in other respects, there has not been any great change in the difficulty that brought me out here. I am not alone in this, — there are several Americans in the same scrape, and having quite as little success in getting out of it. I have resolved to go to Paris to see Dr. Louis, the head of his profession in the world, and see if he can do anything for me. There is some satisfaction in having done the utmost, and left no stone unturned. I have been a perfect anchorite here, — have given up wine, etc., and live at present on forty cents a day for provisions. So if I do not thrash the enemy at last, it will not be my fault."

The first trouble of which we have any definite knowledge was the beginning of an affection of the eyes. During his first year at the Law School, 1844–45, he rose very early and studied by candle light, often without a fire. In the course of the next winter, when confined to the house by some sickness, he for the first time pursued his studies by listening to reading.

The Oregon Trail trip was undertaken partly to cure his eyes, partly to study Indian life. As an indication of his way of dealing with illness, we have the following account of his setting out from Fort Laramie:

"I had been slightly ill for several weeks, but on the third night after reaching Fort Laramie a violent pain awoke me, and I found myself attacked by the same disorder that occasioned such heavy losses to the army on the Rio Grande. In a day and a half I was reduced to extreme weakness, so that I could not walk without pain and effort. Having within that time taken six grains of opium without the least beneficial effect, and having no medical adviser, nor any choice of diet, I resolved to throw myself upon Providence for recovery, using without regard to the disorder any portion of strength that might remain to me. So on the 20th of June we set out from Fort Laramie to meet the Whirlwind's village. Though aided by the high bow 'Mountain Saddle' I could scarcely keep my seat on horseback."[1]

Once cast off from the last post of civilization, and launched in the wilderness among savages, the only thing to do was to keep up, and to wear a brave face. He speaks again of this experience in his autobiographic letter:

[1] *The Oregon Trail*, New Library Edition, p. 145.

"Joining the Indians, he followed their wanderings for several weeks. To have worn the airs of an invalid would certainly have been an indiscretion since in that case a horse, a rifle, a pair of pistols, and a red shirt might have offered temptations too strong for aboriginal virtue. Yet to hunt buffalo on horseback, over a broken country, when without the stimulant of the chase he could scarcely sit upright in the saddle, was not strictly necessary for maintaining the requisite prestige. The sport, however, was good, and the faith undoubting, that to tame the devil it is best to take him by the horns."

The chief trial on this trip was the lack of digestible food. He became worn to a skeleton, was often faint and dizzy, with lack of nourishment, having to be helped into the saddle; and his mind at times lost its clearness. The prolonged and excessive strain of this journey under these conditions permanently impaired his digestion, thus reducing his powers to resist the development of disease. In this way the Oregon trip was the immediate cause of his infirmities, though some of them may have had their source in heredity. Suffering as he did from troubles of digestion, he was unable to sleep during the night; when at dawn he dozed off, exhausted, his guide had to call him to depart. Thus began the insomnia that wearied him persistently all the rest of his days. From that time onward, during long periods of time, he would get but two or three hours of sleep out of the twenty-four; he often had less than this, or even none, and when four or five hours of unconsciousness came, he enjoyed an unusual blessing. His confidence in nature made him doubtful of physicians and drugs, and gave him most hope in the natural powers of the body. Insomnia so prolonged and persistent was one of the greatest of his physical trials; it indeed seemed that insanity must at last result from this exhausting and irritating form of suffering.

Inflammation and weakness of the eyes naturally increased with the decline of his general health on the Oregon trip. The disease never afterwards left him, though it fluctuated often, and diminished somewhat as he grew older. Still another physical misfortune was his to bear: rheumatic gout with effusion in one of the knees. Finally, the overstrain of his early life was most regrettable in helping to develop some inherited tendency to disorders of the brain and nervous system. His general troubles were believed by the doctors to "come from an abnormal state or partial paralysis of certain arteries of the brain."[1]

The Oregon Trail trip thus cost Parkman his health for life; but so predominant was his ambition, so much did he value his Indian studies, and so little compassion had he for his physical being, that he never regretted this costly but fruitful experience. From that time onward he was never free from illness of some sort. One or another of his maladies was always undermining his forces; making his per-

[1] Letter to Abbé H. R. Casgrain, Jan. 26, 1872.

sistent industry and fortitude one of the most impressive examples of human achievement and endurance. He used to call his infirmities "the enemy," with a quiet tone of humor and patience; the phrase covered many a solitary struggle of untold heroism.

The history of his health, like that of his life, offers few incidents of note. He passed through at least four severe crises of pain and disability within a period of twenty years. The extent of his sufferings is nowhere revealed, only hinted at in writing; he is remembered, however, by an intimate friend or two to have said that death would often have been a welcome end of his trials. Generally he passed acute attacks either in turning his thoughts and conversation to light and jocose topics, or in silent and patient endurance. Once, when his physician, during a bad attack, encouraged him by saying that he had a strong constitution, Parkman replied quaintly, "I 'm afraid I have." There is nothing to tell of these crises beyond the patience and fortitude with which he endured them. Sometimes, however, he felt so strongly that he had had more than his share of suffering, that a fresh attack would cause him to explode in a few very forcible expressions; then his quiet patience soon regained the mastery.

Parkman's pathological conditions and their relations to his work and his experience were altogether remarkable, and I regret not being able to go deeper into the many questions they open. His mysterious nervous disorder, his physical infirmities, his irrepressible mental energy, his remarkable powers of will and of mind contending for self-mastery and for the accomplishment of a vast amount of labor, — such a life and character offered to both physiologist and psychologist a study of exceptional complexity and interest.

Part II

PARKMAN AS SEEN IN HIS WORKS

CHAPTER VII

DESPITE his reserve, Parkman's individuality stands forth most impressively in his work. He should have been a knight of the Round Table; few men would have surpassed him in skill at arms, in courage, in doughty deeds, in gallant courtesy, in fidelity in friendship and service, or in winning favors from fair women. His chivalrous spirit, his martial bearing when on horseback, even his person seem to be embodied in the finest equestrian statue in Venice, that of Condottiere Colleoni. Parkman was much attracted to this work; when in Venice he often went to see it, and he had photographs of it on the walls of his study. He may have felt a certain degree of spiritual kinship with this celebrated soldier, and liked in fancy to return to the times when his own manly nature would have found free exercise in chivalrous accomplishments and martial achievements. His chivalrous turn of mind was shown in his school days, when he para·

phrased parts of the Æneid and turned into verse the tournament scene in "Ivanhoe." But, born in the nineteenth century, he had to content himself with choosing for a literary theme the most adventurous epoch of American history, and living by his imaginative sympathy in those experiences.

In considering Parkman as an historian I shall not depart from the principal aim of this memoir, which is to portray his personality. We shall therefore consider his books not as histories or literature, but rather as a mirror reflecting the author's own character. Nothing about him was more interesting and important than his intimate relations with his work. He enjoyed the rare blessing of harmony between his theme, his culture, his life, and his individuality. Loving his subject as he did, he truly lived in the writing of his books. His methods of working under immense disabilities were so characteristic of the man that the lesson of his perseverance and success cannot be too widely known. We shall do well to glance once more at his personal qualities, his education, his life, and his labors, the better to get a reflection of the man in his artistic products.

We have seen that from the start he directed his education so as to cover all needs and topics connected with his theme; as he said, writing of himself in the third person, he "entered upon a training well fitted to serve his purpose, slighted all college studies which could not promote it, and pursued with avidity such as had a bearing upon it however remote. His reliance, however, was less on books than on such personal experience as should in some sense identify him with his theme."[1]

Here we touch the most influential force in his preparation and method, — the very law of gravitation of his system. He early saw and obeyed the principle that the artist must seek the closest sympathy with his subject by knowledge, skill, and feeling. And he set out at once to attain this sympathy, both ideal and utilitarian, by two lines of effort — (1) by personal experience and observation of the elements of his subject; (2) by an exhaustive examination of documents.

1. His personal experiences, despite the fact that he had to do with times long past, brought him in contact with many objective elements of his theme. As we have seen, he began even as a child to become familiar with nature, and as years rolled on he increased this intimacy by some study of the natural sciences, by much observation in the pursuit of his recreations in the woods, and by travel, which cultivated his eye for the larger and more pictorial aspects of nature.

He visited all the important localities connected with his narratives, and this study of historic scenes did something more than fit him for describing military movements; it enabled him to give his work its remarkable realism. Genuine artist that he was, he

[1] *Autobiography*, pp. 351–352.

first seized the large features of a scene, its atmosphere, its light, thus getting his backgrounds; then added the details, of soil and rocks, trees and flowers, birds and beasts peculiar to the region. His love of the vivid, the strong, the effective, was always guided by the desire of accurate knowledge. He must have had a remarkable sureness of glance, of judgment in selection, and of memory; for a few meagre notes sufficed in subsequent years to recall the main features and details of scenes so accurately that they appear in his volumes as if drawn fresh from life. Knowing that his imagination depended on facts for its impetus, he gave free play to his tastes in studying his theme on its own ground, delighting in experiencing, as far as possible, the same hardships and adventures that were met by the discoverers, the war parties, the fur traders, and the missionaries of early times. The frontiersman interested him in his journeys about the wilds of New England and the West; the hardy pioneer in his log cabin in the stump-dotted field surrounded by the forest, made him realize the strenuous and pathetic struggle of the family there for a livelihood; and he had but to imagine Indians lurking under the trees to feel all the horrors of French and Indian massacres.

Unquestionably, the most important element of his objective study and experience was his observation of Indian life and character. Without an intimate knowledge of the red man he would have failed in some of the principal figures of his compositions.

His first contact with the Indian is mentioned in his "Half Century." In 1835 or 1836 a party of chiefs and warriors of the Sacs and Foxes visited Boston, and, as he says, "danced a war-dance on the Common in full costume, to the delight of the boy spectators, of whom I was one."[1] Soon after this his interest was more deeply stirred by reading Cooper; as early as 1841 he had become so identified with the novelist's red heroes that he dreamed of them, talked of them more than of anything else, emulated them in woodcraft when on his walks and his longer vacation journeys, often in the full flow of his enthusiasm whooping and jumping about and imitating the calls of wild animals. In his diary of that year occurs this first record of a working interest in the subject:

"Mr. Williams offered me the use of the notebook of his journies of last year in which he has preserved a considerable number of Indian legends taken from the lips of Anantz, who is well versed in the traditions of his tribe. I shall certainly avail myself of his offer."

On his vacation trip of 1842, while at supper in a tavern in Cambridge, Vermont, an old farmer seems to have had an intuition of his propensities:

"He turned to me and asked if I was not an Indian! I assured him that I was not, on which he coolly shook his head and said that he made it a principle never to contradict any man. He did not consider it any disgrace, for his part, to be an Indian; he had known Indians well

[1] *Half Century*, vol. i. p. 333.

edicated, afore now. He was very far from meaning to offend. He proved, after all, a fine old fellow; his sins being all of ignorance. Far from being offended, I favored his belief, for the joke's sake."

Again, in 1844, we find him entertaining his landlord at an Italian inn with tales of Indian life; and one of his friends of those days says: "His tales of border life, wampum, scalps, and birch-bark were unsurpassed by anything in Cooper."[1]

Once enlisted in the study, he pushed it on with his usual energy. He visited the remnants of tribes still lingering on the borders of civilization in New England, New York, Pennsylvania, Michigan, and Wisconsin; so that in 1845 he could write to a correspondent that, having read "almost all the works on the Indians, from Lafitau and the Jesuits down to the autobiography of Blackhawk," he had arrived at the conclusion "that their character will always remain more or less of a mystery to one who does not add practical observations to his closet studies. In fact, I am more than half resolved to devote a few months to visiting the distant tribes."

This resolution he carried into effect the next year, in his Oregon Trail journey. He was well prepared, both physically and mentally, for such an undertaking. A good shot with the rifle, and an accomplished horseman, fond of the experiences, adventures, and hardships of a wild life, he was ready even to follow the Indian on the war path. Moreover, his extensive

[1] Horatio J. Perry's *Reminiscences*.

Francis Parkman.

From a Daguerreotype taken about 1844.

Photogravure Goupil

reading, and observation of semi-civilized tribes, had given him what knowledge was then attainable, by which to appreciate what he should see. The wide scope of his interests is revealed in this passage:

"I had come into the country almost exclusively with a view of observing the Indian character. Having from childhood felt a curiosity on this subject, and having failed completely to gratify it by reading, I resolved to have recourse to observation. I wished to satisfy myself with regard to the position of the Indians among the races of men; the vices and the virtues that have sprung from their innate character and from their modes of life, their government, their superstitions and their domestic situation. To accomplish my purpose it was necessary to live in the midst of a village, and make myself an inmate of one of their lodges." [1]

The curiosity to which he alludes was but a small part of his motives in making this perilous journey; he had his life work chiefly in view, and felt that nothing short of this intimate objective knowledge could identify him with his theme. He secured by this course a unique position among American historians, for the disappearance or changed condition of these tribes now makes it impossible for any one to enjoy the advantages he seized with such wisdom.

2. The more one knows of Parkman's character the more interesting, as reflections of his strong personality, do his labors and productions become. His study of documents and books impresses one at once

[1] *The Oregon Trail*, p. 143.

with an idea of a just, thorough, and honest mind. From the time when he chose as his subject the "Old French War," he naturally gave much of his attention to history; and soon secured good standing in this department in Harvard. Then, as told us in his autobiographic letter, while attending the law school he "entered in earnest" on a course of general history. Although his labors had regard to a small fraction of the human race and a part of the earth of little value at that time, he very justly looked upon his theme as important, and prepared himself with characteristic thoroughness.

His originality and independence were evident in his college days, when he broke from the usual methods of historical work. In those times the discourse of the professor stood between the subject and the students; they were content to accept a second, or even third dilution of the truth. But Parkman soon started out on an independent course through the wilderness of American history, having his own ideas as to equipment, route, and destination, thus becoming one of the earliest pioneers in the modern scientific method of historical work — the study of comparative history, the search for original sources, and the continual comparison of history with contemporary life and character. Even in his earliest studies he rigorously demanded information at first hand. In a general way, as the various streams of his narrative began their course in England, France, or Spain, he traced them to their beginnings as he would a river in the wilderness; he familiarized himself with their history, especially with that of France under Louis XIV., as far as the scholarship of that day made it possible, often mastering details that were beyond the needs of his special theme. Then he soon drew upon these sources in more specific ways. We have already seen how carefully he studied the written history and ethnology of the North American Indians, gathering, besides, whatever could be learned of them by personal observation. He also ran through all the family papers he could find in New England, the West, and in Canada. His course of study in these lines is nowhere recorded; but we can see from his works that it must have included many of the deeper questions of civilization, of national policies, of racial peculiarities, of types of character, and of religious aims and organizations.

Romanism, as the central force in Canadian history, was soon recognized by Parkman as a subject of capital importance. As early as 1843 he saw that his literary undertaking "required clear impressions of monastic life, and of Roman Catholic ecclesiasticism in general." And he continued throughout his life to watch with great interest the effects of this religion on personal and national character. Born and bred a Unitarian, but early escaping from the broad limitations of even this belief, he was quite indifferent to sectarian distinctions; or, rather, he was antagonistic to religions of all kinds in proportion to their exaltation of doctrine and ritual above practical morality and the growth of character. The Roman Catholic Church repelled him by her moral code, her temporal and ecclesiastical ambition, her superstitions and supernaturalism, and her denial of freedom in mental growth. There can be no doubt that his long study of this mighty system had an influence over his own development. His most fundamental traits were absolutely opposed to many of the aims and methods of the church, though his love of truth and fair play never allowed him to ignore what was admirable in the character or conduct of her followers. He would have disliked with equal force any other church possessing equal power for enforcing similar aims; he had quite as much aversion for many features of Puritanism, from which he sprang; and he said that had he been writing the history of New England, he would have criticised the Puritans as severely as he did the Catholic Church in Canada.

Some interesting glimpses of his studies in this field are given in the diaries of his journey through Sicily and Italy, where he availed himself of every opportunity to visit churches, monasteries, and other religious institutions. He felt the need of understanding not the theological abstractions, but the principles and aims of Romanism in directing a civilization; the spirit and methods of education and monastic life by which she moulds the character of her followers; the kind of men that she turns out from her institutions. These questions were among the most important interests of his first journey to Europe; without this knowledge he would have lacked the key to many political events, and to the character and conduct of many of the most important personages in Canadian history. In this study he showed a keenness of perception and an impartiality of judgment very uncommon in a youth of twenty possessing strong adverse convictions.

At Messina he wrote this generous recognition of the good that may be derived from the church's artistic ritual:

"The church of the Benedictines is the noblest edifice I have seen. This and others not unlike it have impressed me with new ideas of the Catholic religion. Not exactly, for I reverenced it before as the religion of generations of brave and great men, — but now, I honor it for itself. They are mistaken who sneer at its ceremonies as a mere mechanical farce; they have a powerful and salutary effect on the mind. Those who have witnessed the services in the Benedictine church, and deny what I say, must either be singularly stupid and insensible by nature or rendered so by prejudice."

Another religious ceremony at Palermo served at least the purpose of stimulating the growth of his imagination:

"The next day I went to the Capuchin convent, where the holy fathers keep many thousand mummies, in vaulted apartments under ground. I was so edified by the interesting spectacle, that I bought a mass for fifty cents and appointed four o'clock the next morning to hear it performed in the sepulchres. Giuseppe waked me and we sallied forth. Though it wanted more than two hours of daylight, many people were abroad. Fires were burning outside the cafés and confectioners', with ragamuffins and *filles de joie* grouped around them for the sake of the warmth. The porter made his appearance at the gate of the convent, and conducted us in, where we found five or six of the fathers assembled with lamps awaiting the coming of the prior. When all was ready we descended into the tombs. The mummies, each from his niche in the wall, grinned at us diabolically as we passed along. Several large cats, kept there for the benefit of the rats, stared at us with their green eyes, and then tramped off. When we got to the little chapel, the prior put off his coarse Capuchin dress, and arrayed himself in white robes — the curtain was drawn aside from the image of the Virgin behind the altar, the lamps lighted, and the mass performed. When all was over one of the fathers lighted a torch to show the catacombs by its light. Coffins piled up below, — men shrunk to a mere nothing, but clothed as they used to be above ground, all ranged along the wall on either hand, — a row of skulls under the cornices — this made up the spectacle, which was rather disgusting. There were one or two children, just dead, and a few men, flung down in a corner, waiting for the drying-up process."

Here is the account of a more pleasing experience in a convent near the same city:

"We turned off to the left, and after a long ride, came to the monastery of San Martino, in a wild and sublime situation among mountains. The Benedictines here are all of noble blood. Everything is on a scale of magnificence and luxury, pictures, fountains, the church, the chapels, the library, the interminable galleries of the enormous building. There are no tawdry ornaments; everything is in good taste; but for ascetic privations and mortification of the flesh, look elsewhere than at San Martino. The fathers were at the table. I was served with a dinner of lampreys and other delicacies, which a prince might have envied. There is a preserve of wild game, a formidable establishment of cooks and scullions, a beautiful conversazione, and billiard rooms, for the diversion of the pious devotees. In a palace-like hall, below the surface of the ground, sustained by columns and arches of the rich marbles of Sicily, and lighted from above, is a noble statue of San Martino. He is a young soldier on horseback, with as little savor of the saint about him as any of his votaries in this luxurious monastery."

In Rome he continued his observations, visited various religious institutions, got himself presented to the Pope, and attended all the ceremonies of Holy Week. He wrote of the last: "These ceremonies of Holy Week, about which so much is said, would not be worth seeing, were it not for the crowd of people they draw together." Outside of his reading and continual observation of the effects of Romanism on character and conduct, his most intimate study of the system was made while spending some days in a Passionist convent in Rome, an account of which was published in "Harper's Magazine" for August, 1890. In it he refers to the efforts made by the Jesuits and others to convert him. One is struck by his fearlessness, in voluntarily facing their heaviest guns, and even putting himself into their hands for the sake of study. He wrote this frank acknowledgment of the learning that was brought to bear on his heresy:

> "It is as startling to a 'son of Harvard' to see the astounding learning of these Jesuit Fathers, and the appalling readiness and rapidity with which they pour forth their interminable streams of argument, as it would be to a Yankee parson to witness his whole congregation, with church, pulpit and all, shut up within one of the great columns which support the dome of St. Peter's — a thing which might assuredly be done."

He continued his study and observation of Romanism to the last, with increasing aversion for many of its effects on personal and national character. While in camp in Canada, in 1886, we read together Paul Bert's translation of Gury's Moral Theology, in which the wonderful moral code of the church is set forth as a practical handbook and guide for confessors. I see him now get up from his stool and stride about, giving vent in the most forcible terms to his wrath at such an organized system of pardoning everything. Yet no one was more ready in acknowledging the worth of Catholic men and women, wherever they showed themselves as faithful followers of the larger Christian principles of that religion, or as strong enough in native manliness and virtue to resist its demoralizing ecclesiastical influences. His own moral earnestness and deep interest in all that helps to elevate mankind forbade him to ignore the good side of Romanism or to treat it in a flippant way. The result is that while some Roman Catholic writers complain of his severe criticisms and exposures, others admit his fairness. And certainly in view of his knowledge of the system, and of his deep-seated temperamental antipathy to much of it, he shows in his writings a remarkable degree of moderation and self-control.

His study of documents presents the further interest of bringing to light a part of his long moral discipline and many evidences of the power of his elemental will. Having "no natural inclinations" for historical research, he found it "abundantly irksome and laborious." His instincts pointed to freedom and activity out of doors, — a kind of life needed by him on account of his delicate health. Moreover, being financially independent, he might have excused himself for enjoying an existence of idle ease, and also for shirking extreme demands for accuracy, because of the almost insurmountable obstacles to research presented by his weakness of eyes and brain. There was yet another invitation to superficiality in his strong imagination and his great love of the picturesque. It would have been easy for him to give rein to his fancy, and to paint most effective pictures out of little knowledge. But his ambition, energy, and sincerity were more than sufficient against any such temptations; in fact, none of these circumstances tempted him in the least. His highest satisfaction was in doing work well; he lived for this end. Yet the success he attained sprang from something deeper than the writer's ambition; — his persistent industry was a necessity to his inborn energy and force of will, while his scholarship and accuracy were the natural result of deep sincerity.

He developed very early, as we have said, the historian's passion and skill for getting at original documents. It is told of him that when he was beginning his investigations for the writing of "Pontiac," he went to a relative to borrow some money for purchasing a MS. he needed, — his father being at the time in Europe. This lady refused to gratify what she called the whim of a boy; but he said that he should get it elsewhere, and so he did, and thus began his collection of historical documents. When possible he penetrated into the monasteries of Canada for a sight of their hidden records, or obtained copies of documents referring to his subjects. In his Preface to the first edition of "Pontiac" he gives a very short statement of his long labors, an account that applies in a general way to his researches for the entire series of volumes:

"The most troublesome part of the task was the collection of the necessary documents. These consisted of letters, journals, reports, and despatches, scattered among numerous public offices and private families in Europe and America. Contemporary newspapers, magazines, and pamphlets have also been examined, and careful search made for every book which, directly or indirectly, might throw light upon the subject. I have visited the sites of all the principal events recorded in the narrative, and gathered such local traditions as seemed worthy of confidence."

Parkman's personal address was not an insignificant part of his equipment. In spite of his reserve, his frankness and good breeding inspired confidence and won friendly assistance in quarters not easy of access; while his knowledge of men was often most serviceable, even indispensable, in ranging the wide field of his investigations. He fitted himself and his correspondence to the personal temperament and the national customs of the people with whom he had dealings. His letters to Frenchmen were written in excellent French, and in the polite forms usual with that people. In all of them there is found a courteous and generous recognition of services rendered, and a readiness to reciprocate favors. Thus he was generally very successful in approaching both public and private sources of information on both continents. It is unfortunate that the few letters he wrote refer so seldom to topics of general interest; they deal almost exclusively with the details of the researches he directed; nevertheless, they contain some passages sufficiently interesting and characteristic for reproduction.

The only serious obstacle met with in his researches was the refusal of M. Pierre Margry, director of the

Archives of the Marine and Colonies at Paris, to let him use a large collection of documents concerning La Salle and other explorers of the West. This affair is related in the prefaces to "La Salle," at least as far as Parkman cared to publish it. His account is extremely charitable; for experts censured M. Margry very severely for regarding as private property a collection of papers obtained largely from the documents of which he was the official keeper; and also for the mercenary and "intractable" spirit with which he kept the truth under lock and key. Parkman was obliged to publish his volume on La Salle without a sight of these papers, and knowing that he would probably have to rewrite portions of the book. Yet his tact and patience never failed him through years of effort to see those documents, which he at last got published actually for M. Margry's profit by means of an appropriation from Congress. Parkman in a letter[1] thus refers to his efforts in this matter:

> "Petitions were sent in [to Congress] from the principal historical societies east and west, from professors of Harvard College, and other persons of literary prominence to whom I explained the nature of the proposed publication. During the winter I wrote some forty letters to congressmen and others and made personal applications to various persons whose influence would have weight."

When this effort had reached a successful issue, after so much trouble that should never have arisen,

[1] To Mr. Harrisse.

he was capable of writing the following letter to M. Margry, characteristically making light of his own services:

"MON CHER AMI, — Enfin nous avons de quoi nous féliciter. La galère commence à vaguer. Votre dernière lettre (sans date, suivant votre blâmable habitude) m'a réjoui le cœur. Je vous crie grâce de vos taquineries; vous m'en avez fait de belles. N'importe; soyez gai et gaillard ; riez, plaisantez, quand vos documents seront publiés nous aurons, vous et moi, de quoi nous réjouir ensemble. Cependant, écoutez le cerf agile,[1] qui vous parle du fond de ses forêts. Courage, dit-il, par ce collier je chasse de la rivière les canots ennemis qui pourraient troubler la navigation; je donne une grande bonace au lac qu'il faut traverser, j'apaise les vents et je tempère la colère des eaux; je dissipe tous les nuages; je vous nettoie les oreilles afin que vous entendiez la voix de ma sagesse; je rends les chemins unis pour vous faire courir heureusement à la fin de votre grande entreprise." [2]

As another example of his keenness of scent and perseverance in hunting down historical materials,

[1] Margry's name for Parkman, on account of his rapid step.

[2] "DEAR FRIEND, — At last we may congratulate ourselves. Our troubles begin to take wing. Your last letter (without date, according to your unfortunate custom) did my heart good. Enough of your teasing! You have given it to me heavy. But no matter; make merry as you like, laugh and joke, — when your documents are published we shall have good reason to rejoice together. And yet, listen to the agile deer, who speaks to you from the depths of his forest. Courage, he says, by this necklace, I drive from the river the enemy's canoes, which might interfere with navigation; I calm the lake that is to be crossed, I quiet the winds and soothe the anger of the waters; I blow away all clouds; I clear your ears

read this account of his discovering Montcalm's letters to Bourlamaque:

"Many years ago I was informed that an important collection of autograph letters of the Marquis de Montcalm was in the possession of a person in Paris who wished to sell them, but I was unable to find the slightest clue to the person in question. At length I was told that the papers were sold, and that the purchaser was said to be an Englishman. Beyond this I could learn nothing. The descendants of the Marquis de Montcalm had heard of the existence of the papers, but were totally ignorant into what hands they had passed. As the late Sir Thomas Philipps was the greatest collector of manuscripts in England, I examined the catalogue of his vast collection, but made no discovery. It was about fifteen years since I had heard of the existence of the papers, and all my attempts to view them had completely failed, when a gentleman connected with the British Museum kindly offered his aid in making the inquiry, and, in a few months, sent me the welcome announcement that the custodian of Sir Thomas Philipps's collection had informed him that the Montcalm letters were in his keeping, having been purchased by Sir Thomas, but not catalogued. I at once went to Cheltenham, where this wonderful collection was preserved, and obtained a copy of all the Montcalm letters. They proved to be written to Bourlamaque, one of his chief officers, and are doubly interesting because they were meant for no eye but his, and often contain the injunction, *brûlez cette lettre*, or *brûlez toutes mes lettres*, which, fortunately for us, Bourlamaque did not do. The handwriting of Mont-

that you may hear the voice of my wisdom; I smooth the roads that you may run easily to the end of your great enterprise."

calm is never very clear, and these letters being hastily written, are unusually difficult examples of it. The copyist, though he took great pains, was now and then at a loss to decipher some intricate passage; yet it is believed that every essential part has been successfully transcribed."

Imagination, judgment, sincerity, industry, scholarship, and the faculty of identification with his pursuits were thus happily united in Parkman, — partly by the constitution of his temperament, and partly by his distinct purpose to balance the studies of the closet by observation and experience. He managed to see and feel nearly everything he had to describe. For much of his work related to primitive and unchanged elements, — the forest, the main features of historic scenes, the experiences of woodcraft, the border life of pioneers, the fundamental elements of human nature, the life and character of the Indian then still untamed. Gathering together these still present objective remnants of the past, Parkman, with his imagination and his constructive skill, composed historical pictures of extraordinary vividness and realism. He identified himself with his theme so completely that he was possessed by the one desire to tell his story. To this aim he consecrated his time, strength, and fortune. And this purpose, with some help, it is true, from his philosophy of historical writing, was so absorbing that it almost buried his own personality in his pages; he rarely showed any consciousness of his own thoughts, feelings, experiences or philosophy; he gave the story, and that only.

In looking at the great mass of manuscript he collected and digested, one partially realizes by the material evidence of mere bulk how much he did for the sake of thoroughness, but fully only when one remembers the weakness of eyes and brain that increased his labors tenfold. In the preface to "A Half Century of Conflict," he thus referred to his collection at the close of his labors:

> "The manuscript material, collected for the preparation of the series now complete, forms about seventy volumes, most of them folios. These have been given by me from time to time to the Massachusetts Historical Society, in whose library they now are, open to the examination of those interested in the subjects of which they treat. The collection was begun forty-five years ago, and its formation has been exceedingly slow, having been retarded by difficulties which seemed insurmountable, and for years were so in fact. Hence the completion of the series has required twice the time that would have sufficed under less unfavorable conditions."

He spoke in detail in other prefaces of the materials used in the preparation of each volume.

A collection standing for so much money and labor was, naturally, to him an object worthy of great care. Moreover, it was his witness that he had fairly and thoroughly dealt with all the evidence then attainable. In the interest of historical truth, and in the consciousness of a duty well done, he wished his papers to be kept together in a place of safety that should be easily accessible to students. They were accordingly given to the Massachusetts Historical Society, of Boston.[1]

[1] See the Society's *Transactions*, 2nd series, I. 360–362; III. 152, 153; VI. 165, 391, 392; VII. 348, 349; VIII. 171.

CHAPTER VIII

The history of literature can hardly show another writer who made his work so predominant an interest throughout his life, who overcame so many serious obstacles, or who worked with so much apparent independence of hindering physical conditions. One naturally asks, How did Parkman manage, with poor sight, to conduct his researches? How did he make his notes? How did he write or dictate his books? What kind of assistance did he find it possible to employ? Then there is the larger interest of his intellectual processes. What were his methods of planning and constructing his books? What was his philosophy of writing history?

The mechanical means by which he overcame the difficulties besetting all writers having defective vision are easily explained; his means of economizing and directing the precarious and abnormal energies of his brain are not so readily stated, though they will be considered in treating of his daily life and social habits. His intellectual steps and processes of composition are still less within our grasp, for he left very meagre records of them.

Parkman needed all his money, ability, and will-power to face the difficulties of his career. His diseases gave him a much deeper trial than physical suffering; they continually threatened him with an ineffectual life, and a denial of his innermost longings. No one can estimate the power he must have lost in the mere strain of enduring imperfect digestion, insomnia, rheumatism, arthritis, nervous troubles. These, with pains in the head, were one or the other, and often all together, continually sapping his force. He never saw a perfectly well day during his entire literary career. Still less can we appreciate how much power was lost by the innumerable interruptions, the frittering away of force in continually starting and stopping his intellectual machinery, and by the self-control needed for the preservation of his mental balance. To these difficulties must be added some specific disorders that of all things were the most discouraging to a historian, — weakness of sight and frequent incapacity for consecutive and prolonged thought.

While never losing either sight or sanity, he used his eyes and his brain always with the understanding that any excess of labor or pleasure would lead to increased suffering and possibly to total disability. His autobiographic letter states in simple terms an experience not matched by any other that I know in literature:

"During the past eighteen years (1847–1865), the state of his health has exacted throughout an extreme caution in regard to mental application, reducing it at best within narrow and precarious limits, and often precluding it. Indeed, for two periods, each of several years, any attempt at bookish occupation would have been merely suicidal. A condition of sight arising from kindred sources has also retarded the work, since it has never permitted reading or writing continuously for much more than five minutes, and often has not permitted them at all."

He could not endure even ordinarily rapid reading, and at his best could work only two hours a day, with many short periods of repose. About ten years of his life were thus lost from work, not counting short interruptions of days, weeks, and months. Writing of this matter in 1886 he said:

"Taking the last forty years as a whole, the capacity of literary work which during that time has fallen to my share has, I am confident, been considerably less than a fourth part of what it would have been under normal conditions."

In the face of all these difficulties he took up a labor of exceptional magnitude, one that he estimated at the outset would require, with good health, about twenty years. Moreover, he resolved that nothing should be an excuse for stopping short of the nearest possible approach to finality in research, or in exactness and fulness of statement. The task took him fifty years instead of twenty, and the thoroughness and extent of his work under such conditions make his achievement certainly one of the wonders of literature.

In trying to see the conditions that made this labor possible, we find one mystery among some very plain facts of character and culture. We have already had a hint of the helpful harmony that existed between his theme and his temperament; we have seen how good sense, pecuniary independence, and breadth of view as to the historian's duties presided over his education and guided his experience; how comparative freedom from family cares and distractions favored the concentration of his strength upon one end; how independent means, an elemental force of will, a happy balance between the driving power of impetuous energy and courage, and the regulating power of caution and method, — how all these, combined with great self-knowledge, enabled him to pursue his course close along the very verge of disaster.

Yet all these favorable traits and circumstances would have been unavailing had his physical infirmities produced their usual effects on the nervous system and the brain. For the conditions of the physical organism cannot be long ignored, no matter what amount of moral force may drive it for a time. Parkman's case was altogether exceptional. Putting aside the drudge who turns out his daily pages of mediocrity, writers generally find their greatest difficulty and their rarest success in keeping up the enthusiasm and sensibility that alone can attune their faculties to harmonious creation. But Parkman's difficulty was not in arousing but in restraining his faculties. His most intimate literary companion wrote that his "maladies intensified his impulses to exertion and mental application, while they limited the hours he could wisely give to reading and writing."[1] Though an invalid, he was blessed with a very remarkable exemption from an invalid's lassitude. He had an "inborn irritability of constitution" as he said, which made "labor a passion and rest intolerable." His mysterious affection of the brain seems to have consisted in good part of this spurring force. He aptly described his condition as "that of a rider whose horse runs headlong, the bit between his teeth, or of a locomotive built of indifferent material, under a head of steam too great for its strength, hissing at a score of crevices, yet rushing on with accelerating speed to the inevitable smash." He said: "The exclusion of thought demanded an effort more severe than the writer ever put forth in any other cause." Thus his inability to work during many periods longer or shorter, was not due to mental inertia; it sprang from the nervous conditions that made it often imprudent or at times even impossible to exercise the brain. During half a century he thus led a life of repressed activity, with spaces of complete idleness, at the best allowing himself but a brief play of his powers. His self-control was nowhere more noteworthy than in this restraint of the mind. His ability to work at all depended on the repression of an impetuous temperament and a surplus of energy.

[1] Dr. George E. Ellis.

The reasonableness of his nature is shown by his success. After actual illness came upon him, and he saw that the "crushing out" policy was a mistake in dealing with his maladies, he always showed great common sense and docility in regulating his habits according to medical advice. But in one particular he persistently refused obedience — he would not give up his literary labor wholly, even when the doctors forbade it under threats of the most serious consequences; and when they told him to prepare for death, he straightway prepared to write books. With this supernormal energy continually furnishing a high pressure of nervous force to his ambition and imagination, and with good sense controlling and concentrating his powers on one purpose, he was, in a measure, independent of a surplus of health for creative power.

His relations to his work were thus far from unfortunate; they enabled him to wring many advantages and compensations from his restrictions. One may say even that his disabilities constrained him to reach a standard not wholly in accord with his natural tendencies. The predominance of the utilitarian over the spiritual in his temperament, his eagerness, his love of the tangible and effective, all made him dislike the scholastic idea of perfection. In his own special field he worked under a driving desire to tell his story and the whole of it, and under a fear that his strength might not hold out even from one volume to the next. It would seem, therefore, that his dominant qualities and defects, and many of his circumstances forbade much lingering over his work in the love of artistic perfection. But fate in some measure forced him to build better than he would. Able when in medium health to visit historic localities, examine documents, direct researches and transcriptions, plan his books, digest and arrange materials, thus pushing forward the easier and more clerical parts of his labors, he was compelled by his infirmities to compose only when in his best condition. Thus he followed the plainest requirements of all who expect to do their best, whether prize-fighter or poet. It is doubtful that with his temperament he would have shown this professional conscientiousness had health left him perfect freedom. In one respect, however, he commended himself to the perfectionist's pains though not to his spirit. In regard to accuracy he was a worker of inexhaustible patience and thoroughness. Here no delay, no trouble, no minutiæ appeared to him fastidious. In the preface to "Pontiac" he thus acknowledged his indebtedness to his misfortunes:

> "I am well convinced that the authorities have been even more minutely examined, more scrupulously collated, and more thoroughly digested, than they would have been under more ordinary circumstances."[1]

And so it was that he wrung the greatest compensation from adversity. One day in 1886, in talking

[1] *Pontiac*, p. xii.

of his books, I expressed, in a few words, my admiration for them, and my hope that he would be able to complete the series. To my surprise he replied, with a tone of firmness and some reserved meaning quite mysterious to me: "That does n't matter much." I felt that I ought not to question him; and in recalling the remark often since then, I have not been able to find a place for it in his character or his strenuous efforts, so long continued. Possibly he felt that he had already done enough work under such trials to prove his valor. And although nothing would have got from him any expression of the thought, self-justification under a life so burdened with inactivities must have been exceptionally dear to one with such a passionate love of energy and honor.

Did Parkman succeed in keeping his weakness out of his work? Composing as he did, very slowly, and only in his best hours, he almost accomplished this impossibility. The first twenty years of his labors — from 1847 to 1868 — contained the most of suffering and interruption; then during the next twenty years his brain and his eyes slowly improved a little, so that he enjoyed his best powers of thinking and seeing in his last decade of life. Yet as regards the greater number of its component elements, the work went on with remarkable independence of these fluctuations. The large lines of construction for unity and dramatic effect; the thoroughness of research; the digestion of material; the selection and condensation of matter for rapidity of movement;

the accuracy and fulness of statement — in all these points no weakness is shown, even in the volumes written during his worst epochs. Such qualities could be reached by slow and patient labor. But the subtle matter of style springs too much from moods and conditions to be wholly under the guidance of skill and industry; and it seems to me that some reflection of his condition may be seen in his books. "Pontiac," for example, is fascinating not only by its vigorous picturesqueness, but also for the color, flow, and fervor of its diction. Although produced under great difficulties, it was written before he had been permanently affected by his hard experience. His mental habits and creative faculties had not then suffered from the effects of physical infirmities, continual interruptions, remouldings of self to meet new conditions, and the strain of prolonged efforts for self-control. The wonder is that he escaped so well in subsequent volumes the inevitable effects of his condition.

The mechanical and clerical details of his method of working may be easily described. Extreme sensitiveness of sight obliged him to employ the eyes of others for almost all his reading and writing. In his researches abroad he would take some educated man with him to a library, spending as many hours a day as his strength allowed in listening to the reading of documents, and in noting what he should need for subsequent and more thorough study of a subject. These labors of the book-worm, "abundantly irksome," as he acknowledged them to be under any circumstances, were especially wearisome when using other men's eyes for hunting through historical haystacks for possible needles. With his own eyes he could have gleaned with a glance, but now he must listen to every paragraph for fear of losing in some unimportant and tedious paper a desirable item or reference. Then to avoid continually crossing the sea he must examine with care a large range of subjects in each visit; he must consider not only all the points concerning a given epoch, but also the bearing of these details on the larger interests of his whole series. But whatever his condition or the severity of the task might be, he never shirked the pursuit of every clue and the examination of every original source of information, nor depended on another's judgment in any important matter. He always held his subject in the firmest grasp, and directed his assistants with a clear knowledge and a firm hand.

Under such disabilities for writing he naturally took as few notes as possible, and developed a very retentive memory. As the sensitiveness of his eyes often made it impossible for him to look at paper while writing, he caused to be constructed what he called his "gridiron." This simple invention was an indispensable companion in all his labor up to the completion of "La Salle" in 1869. After these first and worst twenty years, he was able to use his eyes enough to make notes, at least, without such a guide.

Copying and collecting documents formed an important division of his labors. It was impracticable for him to compose away from home. His working power depended on the most careful hygiene, and on the help of assistants far more devoted and considerate than any that could be hired. As he based his works on original sources, the most of which had not been printed, he had to have copies made of a vast number of papers. This expensive process cost him a considerable part of his fortune; and he used to say that the income from his books would never give him much more than the cost of his preparatory labors. Having in hand the lists and calendars made in his own researches, he could safely direct the collection of his materials. He engaged responsible and experienced students and collectors in Canada, Paris, London, to employ copyists, verify the accuracy of their transcriptions, and ship the manuscripts to him at Boston. Having thus collected all his material in his study, he felt himself master of the situation. He could work whenever he was able, and when unable, wait for health to return.

Parkman's characteristic reserve was especially noticeable in regard to his work. He kept his inner workshop locked, and a sign of "no admittance" on the door. The more literary and intellectual steps of his labors are therefore not so easily traced as the clerical and mechanical details. There were among his diaries, letters, notes, papers, no skeletons or guides for the construction of his works. This is the more remarkable from his knowledge of the precariousness of his working powers, and his experience of frequent and long interruptions. Fourteen years passed between the production of "Pontiac" and of "The Pioneers," — ten of them in absolute separation from his labor; while other interruptions, long or short, continually broke up the course of his thought. His progress at best was made by short steps under such distracting conditions that a detailed chart of his course would seem to have been indispensable. Yet there is no evidence that he ever had such guides on paper. Once, however, he communicated to a friend [1] at least a general intention concerning "Montcalm and Wolfe":

"Le plan de mon ouvrage sur la guerre de 1755–63 n'est pas encore arrêté, mais en vue des dangers qui menacent toujours les monuments historiques dans ce beau volcan qu'on appelle Paris, je voudrais bien avoir entre les mains la partie la plus essentielle des documents qui regardent ces événements. J'essayerai peut-être d'écrire l'histoire de la guerre depuis son commencement; peut-être je me bornerai à la période comprise entre l'arrivée de Montcalm et sa mort, faisant du grand marquis la figure centrale de la pièce, et groupant les événements autour de lui. Ce plan me semble être le plus simple et le plus dramatique, mais il demande des renseignements les plus étendus et les plus intimes sur les années dont il est question." [2]

[1] M. Pierre Margry, no date.

[2] Translation: "The plan of my work on the war of 1755–63 is not yet determined, but in view of the dangers that always threaten

Despite the absence of much that we fain would know, we can give a few of the external facts concerning his method of examining documents and composing his books. In beginning a volume he had all the documents concerning it read to him, the first time for the chief features of the subject. While this reading was in progress he made, now and then, a short note, or walked over from his shady corner to where the reader sat in the light, to mark a passage for future reference. The margins of his volumes of documents contain almost no writing, — merely crosses, double crosses, and vertical lines in red pencil. He could not listen to this reading for more than an hour or two per day in even his best health, and with the help of frequent rests, requiring in the reader a quiet manner, a low voice, and a slow pace. Having very rarely sight and strength enough to work at stated times, he seldom kept a salaried amanuensis. His assistant was generally some member of his household; at other times he employed a pupil from the public school. As most of his material was in French, of which the pupil was ignorant, and in old French at that, the reading often seemed

historical monuments in the splendid volcano named Paris, I should like to have in hand the most essential portion of the documents concerning those events. Perhaps I shall try to write the history of the war from its beginning; perhaps I shall confine myself to the period comprised between the arrival of Montcalm and his death, making the great marquis the central figure of the composition, and grouping events about him. This plan seems to me the simplest and the most dramatic, but it demands the most intimate and extensive knowledge of that epoch."

Mr. Parkman's Study, Jamaica Plain, Mass.

anything but the accurate and serious information required by a historian. Then came a second reading, during which he noted accessory matters and details of the story; and sometimes a third examination was needed of portions of his great mass of documents. By this slow method he acquired perfect possession of the materials needed for a volume. He then set to work at composition, always finishing one volume before touching another. His inability to compose rapidly, as we have already seen, offered some very valuable compensations for difficulties and delays. It forced him to consider well his plan, to digest his material thoroughly; and by keeping him living for some time in each part of his subject as he went along, secured freedom and leisure for the exercise of both imagination and judgment.

In the long hours of enforced solitude and idleness in the subdued light of his study, or during his sleepless nights, his subject pressed upon him with the insistence of an absorbing interest. It is easy to understand that his hardest effort was to keep his mind at rest. Few men could have sustained their interest and power under such tedious delays; but he had precisely the faculties needed to meet the situation, — breadth and firmness of grasp for details and general lines, a retentive memory, great constructive skill, and a vivid imagination, — the whole driven by supernormal energy. When it came to writing or dictating the book, he had each day's production already arranged, probably some of it composed and memorized. He dictated at a moderate pace — sometimes holding a few notes in his hand — without hesitation and with a degree of finish seldom requiring any correction. At the close of the morning he would listen to what had been written down, and make necessary changes. During the day he would look over the composition, for he never failed to verify his citations and authorities himself, or to paste with his own hand his notes on the bottom of the pages. The only record of his methodical habits of working is the orderly arrangement of his papers in bound volumes, and the presence of the word "used" written on each paper when he had taken its substance. But although methodical, he was never fastidious or finical. He marched on as well as he could, with his mind on large, practical, and tangible results more than on niceties of method or execution.

His amanuenses still speak of their wonder in witnessing the creation of his books. It must have been, indeed, interesting to watch the transformation operated by the magic of his imagination, — the living characters and real scenes suddenly brought forth from dry and disconnected facts read to him in bits for months, or even years. One could hardly get a more intimate contact with the artistic faculty, at least in its activities of preparation and execution. During the last few years of his life his eyes allowed him to write quite freely for very short periods of time. Thus he was able to write out by himself, with pencil on orange colored paper, the greater part of his "Half Century" and "Montcalm and Wolfe." This manuscript shows very few corrections. He had become master of a fluent, chaste, and simple diction.

His method cannot be dismissed without referring to his exceptional efforts for accuracy, though we can say but little concerning his special means of attaining this marked characteristic of his work. Proofs enough of his efforts are seen in his pages and in the collection of documents he accumulated. The few letters which he wrote and received show what pains he took to examine every possible source, both public and private, in America and Europe. He was averse, however, to the overloading of pages with citations, especially those referring to collateral and illustrative matter, which must necessarily predominate "where," as he said, "one adhering to facts tries to animate them with the life of the past." One of his letters reveals his pursuit and careful verification of detail. He wrote to an eminent astronomer:[1]

"I believe there is a difference between the way of estimating latitude in the seventeenth century and now. Can you without much trouble tell me how this is? In 1685 La Salle calculated a certain point on the Gulf of Mexico at 28° 18′. What would this correspond to on a modern map? How can I ascertain if a comet — a somewhat remarkable one — was visible from the site of

[1] His classmate, Dr. B. A. Gould, June 26, 1868.

12

Peoria, Illinois, in January, 1681? Also, how can I ascertain on what day of the month Easter Monday, 1680, occurred? I want the information to test the accuracy of certain journals in my possession."

His pursuit of the truth was shown by his sagacity and persistence in ferreting out documents, such as the letters of Montcalm to Bourlamaque, for which he hunted fifteen years. His care and judgment in weighing evidence are displayed on every page. Finally, his love of accuracy carried him cheerfully through the historian's most trying experience, — the revision of his works. In writing to a friend apropos of "La Salle," he stated the feeling that animated him from the beginning to the end of his career: "Should evidence turn up showing me to be anywhere in error, in fact or in judgment, I shall recant at once, as I care for nothing but to get the truth of the story."[1] When at last the materials that had been unjustly refused him were published through Parkman's own efforts, he rewrote considerable parts of "La Salle" without complaint. The revision of his works was still going on at the time of his death; and he proposed a still more important revision after the publication of "A Half Century." Possibly it was the uncertainty of his life and working power that led him to cast his subject in monographs, enabling him to finish the work in pieces as he went along; it is certain that he did not regard his history as complete. While

[1] Letter to J. G. Shea, Dec. 14, 1867.

each volume is a whole in itself, one notes a deficiency in the larger lines of connection with the Franco-English struggles, and with the history of the American colonies. He intended to make this connection closer and more apparent by remoulding his monographs into a continuous narrative. Unfortunately he was not spared to put these harmonizing touches to his work.

Professor Fiske, in speaking of Parkman's perseverance under difficulties, says:

> "The heroism shown year after year in contending with physical ailments was the index of a character fit to be mated, for its pertinacious courage, with the heroes that live in his shining pages."[1]

[1] John Fiske. Introductory Essay (1897).

CHAPTER IX

ART being the inevitable revelation of the soul producing it, the artist's character and productions serve each to the other as a revealing light. A study of Parkman made from either his books or his life alone would be deficient in some essential feature. For his Puritan blood barred him from freedom in feeling and utterance, while in writing, his philosophy of historical composition and his identification with his theme ruled out any explicit expressions of personal thoughts and emotions. But no man's work is impersonal, if the analysis be pushed far enough. We shall see that under the shelter of Parkman's reserve and his philosophy of art, he yet found more or less free play in a theme suited to his temperament.

Parkman's philosophy of historical writing is a clear illustration of the practicalness and simplicity of his character. In this as in other things, he knew his own nature, and formed his aims and methods accordingly. He seems, indeed, to have formed his philosophy as early as he chose his topic; or else following from the start his natural tendencies, he perhaps worked according to his philosophy before it was formulated. His writings cannot be divided into epochs or manners; for although his style developed with the gradual improvement of his taste and skill, his work is a unit as to aims and method.

His philosophy is nowhere stated in clear terms. He had no inclination to reveal his creed; and his theme rarely demanded more than simple narration and description. As every artist, however, derives his working formula from his tastes and beliefs, so Parkman's philosophy of writing necessarily sprang from his philosophy of life. We can judge, therefore, of the invisible foundations of his historical structure both from his general attitude towards civilization and the incidental revelations of his pages. From these data it seems to me that his deepest interest in history was embodied in the question: What kind of men and women did a given civilization produce? Surely no interest can be compared for importance to this study of the growth of individual and national character.

But his edifice rests also on desires and purposes that are more evident and above-ground. He built on these four cornerstones: (1) Sincerity; never stopping short of the utmost thoroughness and impartiality. (2) Industry; which must not fail before any amount of labor and hindrances. (3) Scholarship; which must embrace a knowledge of topics that are even remotely connected with his theme. (4) Identification with his theme. The general spirit in which he worked is clearly set forth in these golden words:

"Faithfulness to the truth of history involves far more than a research, however patient and scrupulous, into special facts. Such facts may be detailed with the most minute exactness, and yet the narrative, taken as a whole, may be unmeaning or untrue. The narrator must seek to imbue himself with the life and spirit of the time. He must study events in their bearings near and remote; in the character, habits, and manners of those who took part in them. He must be, as it were, a sharer or spectator of the action he describes." [1]

Coming now to still more tangible aims, the working force of his method was the desire to tell his story with the utmost simplicity, accuracy, and vividness. The various merits of his work flowed from these aims as a stream from its sources. He believed that a history should be an artistic creation, having due regard to unity, and with large purposes sweeping on to an effective climax. But he never regarded artistic aims as an excuse for neglecting prosaic or adverse facts, or for twisting history into drama. In striving to exclude all that could be spared, he was not led to neglect details, even the most minute. It is told of him that he criticised Bancroft for making history too dignified. With his frequent vigor of language he said, "Damn the dignity of history; straws are often the best materials." His objective and practical mind made him desire a very realistic method of treatment: he had no taste for sentiment or theories.

[1] *Pioneers*, p. xiv.

One of the most important features of his method was a demand for original sources. He was one of the first to elevate this need and that of individual research to their modern importance, holding that the historian had not done his duty until he had examined every known or discoverable document relating to his theme. Parkman not only desired the original record of an event, and if possible one that was made by an eye-witness while memory and feeling were still vivid, but he wished this record to be given in its first state. "In mending the style and orthography, or even the grammar," he said, "one may rob a passage of its characteristic expression, till it ceases to mark the individuality of the man, or the nature of his antecedents and surroundings." Speaking of the editorial glosses of the letters of Dinwiddie, he referred to their "good English without character, while as written they were bad English with a great deal of character. The blunders themselves have meaning, for Dinwiddie was a blunderer, and should appear as such if he is to appear truly." [1]

His method of historical writing included another aim that was purely a personal matter and very influential over the nature of his works. His history has been criticised as deficient in philosophic depth; and to the casual reader who gives himself up to the charm of his picturesque narration and description, this criticism may seem well founded. His pages are made up of facts, without either

[1] Winsor, *The Atlantic Monthly*, May, 1894, p. 662.

generalizations, sermons, sentiments, or personal opinions. In explanation of this unusual reserve, it has been suggested that as generalizations cost a deal of hard thinking, he was deterred by his disorders of the nervous system from formulating his wisdom. This guess may have some truth, but it seems to be contradicted by all we know of his mental habits, character, and culture. His reverence for hard truth, and his matter-of-fact and practical turn of mind would have made him at least shy of generalizations. The facts of experience and observation rather than the ideal elements, were his natural material. We have seen that at college he neglected philosophical studies and acquired a very special rather than a broad and general culture, and he was remarkable for early crystallization of aims, opinions, and methods. Again his inability to read much would probably have curtailed his subsequent excursions in philosophy had he looked in these directions. It seems, therefore, improbable that he would ever have written otherwise under any circumstances of health. Philosophizing on life may have seemed a too intimate self-revelation for his reserve, even when directed to impersonal or historical topics.

In spite, however, of this evidence, Parkman really had a philosophical side, and a strongly marked one too. We have seen that he always studied individual and national life and character with the interest of the keenest observer. He was distinctly a serious student; he always impressed people as a man of wisdom. The facts are that with his moral earnestness, his keen perceptions, and his capable mind, he was of necessity a man of depth and ability in those directions that were opened to him by his organization. With little interest in spiritual, abstract, and metaphysical lines of thought, he possessed exceptional strength and clearness in other directions. His intimates were continually discovering new veins of knowledge in him, especially in regard to history, nature, and human nature. It is difficult to determine his limitations in these fields: the records of his schooling and subsequent reading are too inadequate: and even if they were full, they would hardly serve to gauge such a memory and such readiness of acquisition. The principal element of his wisdom was perhaps his strong common sense; he studied life and history with the intelligence of an intensely practical man of scholarly interests.

There were thus two opposing forces in him, — a philosophic interest in life, and a detestation of theorizing and moralizing. Parkman wrote as a non-philosophizing philosopher. As it happened, I heard from him one day a statement that seems authoritative as to both his general method and his practice. In discussing a book on French-Canadian life and character, he said to the author, "Describe them just as they are, and let the reader philosophize as much as he likes." "The Old Régime in Canada" reveals most clearly this rule of his method. The volume is full of political philosophy and object lessons of the clearest import, though without either sermons or theories. While weighing causes and effects, he seldom mentions them, or formulates any theories of growth. His pages are built up exclusively of facts; but he presents these in such a way as to carry their own lesson. His work is just the opposite of Garneau's, which he said has the manner, but not the matter, of a philosophical history.

Parkman's theme was the deepest joy of his life. It was at once the attraction and the means that led him onward through his trials to his intellectual and moral development. His practical relations to it are as interesting and characteristic as his philosophy of historical writing. Lowell says that "one of the convincing tests of genius is the choice of a theme . . . In the instinct that led him straight to subjects that seemed waiting for him so long, Mr. Parkman gave no uncertain proof of his fitness for an adequate treatment of them." Some have considered that the direction of his life was providential; he himself said that it was governed by his tastes and a clear perception, when still a mere youth, of his capacities and limitations. He thus told the story, looking back from 1878[1]:

"Vous demandez pourquoi j'ai conçu le dessein d'écrire l'histoire des Français en Amérique? C'est tout simple. Dans ma jeunesse j'avais le goût des lettres; et j'avais en même temps ce des forêts, de la chasse, des sauvages. Je fréquentais (leurs) camps, je parcourais les

[1] Letter to M. Pierre Margry, Dec. 6, 1878.

bois avec eux, j'y voyageais à pied et en canot. C'était ainsi que je passais mes vacances. Eh bien, je compris de bonne heure que ces deux goûts, des livres et des forêts, pourraient se réconcilier, pourraient même s'aider réciproquement, dans le champ d'histoire Franco-Américain." [1]

He said again, in his autobiography (p. 351):

"Before the end of the sophomore year my various schemes had crystallized into a plan of writing the story of what was then known as the 'Old French War,' that is, the war that ended in the conquest of Canada, for here, as it seemed to me, the forest drama was more stirring and the forest stage more thronged with appropriate actors than in any other passage of our history. It was not till some years later that I enlarged the plan to include the whole course of the American conflict between France and England, or, in other words, the history of the American forest: for this was the light in which I regarded it. My theme fascinated me, and I was haunted with wilderness images day and night."

His selection at that time did not seem so wise as it appeared when subsequent success had justified it. American history was not popular, and he had

[1] Translation:
"You ask why I conceived the purpose of writing the history of the French in America? The answer is very simple. In my youth I was fond of letters, and I also liked the forest, shooting, and the Indians. I frequented their camps, I roamed the woods with them, I went shooting, I journeyed on foot and in canoes. I passed my vacations in this way. Well, at an early day I saw that these two tastes, for books and for the forest, could be reconciled, could be made even mutually helpful, in the field of Franco-American history."

to create a taste for his subject. His father, in common with many others, took little interest in the old French Wars, — a contest of bushrangers for the possession of a wilderness. Parkman pointed out that this conflict was a very important event in the history of the world, since it decided the destiny of a continent. But his father continually ignored or forgot these excellent reasons, and called upon his son again and again to defend his selection. To most minds the subject was barren, "with spaces too vast, heroes too few, and savages too many."[1] His undertaking was all the more uncertain because of the unknown nature of his materials. As he said of these:

> "The field of the history was uncultured and unreclaimed, and the labor that awaited me was like that of the border settler, who, before he builds his rugged dwelling, must fell the forest trees, burn the undergrowth, clear the ground, and hew the fallen trunks in due proportion."

While the topic, however, presented one great source of possible success — that of novelty, — his style was not considered sufficiently artistic to draw readers to an unpopular subject. Even that remarkable volume "The Conspiracy of Pontiac" was declined by one of the principal publishers of New York in obedience to his reader's opinion that "both the subject and the style" would deny the work

[1] Judge John Lowell.

any profitable success; and the first reception of the book justified this opinion. The next work, "Vassall Morton," was a failure. Then, after the appearance of "Pontiac," which met with but a modicum of success, Parkman's state of health kept him for ten years unable to do any literary labor whatever. He thus began his career with what seemed only moderate talents and achievements, and an outlook that was far from encouraging. But he had a true estimate of the possibilities contained in his theme, and a still stronger faith in his own relations to it. When his wife, in her affectionate interest, asked him why he did not write on some European historical topic, which would interest the public, he answered that he "must write what he was made for." His mind indeed moved as gladly and freely in his chosen literary world as he had moved through the forest or over the prairie in his youth. The Franco-English contest was the last great struggle in which personal valor and address triumphed as they did in the days of chivalry. War had not then become a game played with long-range guns. Parkman could throw himself body and soul into this congenial subject; and he found in it many interests not restricted to time and place. He had to offer the world a study of the last remains of primitive society in the stone age, — a picture of the life of the ancestors of every civilized nation of to-day; he had to record the struggle and fall of the savage races before the civilized powers of Europe.

He had also to tell the longer story of the three-handed conflict between France, England, and the Indians for dominion in the new world.

At first sight his history seems to be merely a chronicle of the contest; and Parkman says in his autobiography that in his earlier years he regarded his subject as the history of the American forest. Thanks to the scenery, the variety of races and characters, the nature of events and experiences, few epochs in history excel his in romance, picturesqueness, heroism, and adventure. The subject indeed might easily have demoralized a man of his nature and tastes, and seduced him to an undue expansion of these alluring elements. But fortunately his theme contained also many deeper problems, and called for self-control, judgment, scholarship, and caution. He had in hand two opposing systems of civilization — that of feudal, militant, Catholic France in conflict with democratic, industrial, and Protestant England. He made this comparison from all points of view, — religious, political, military, social, industrial, educational; he omitted nothing essential. He enjoyed a rare happiness — that of a new theme, perfectly fitted to the artist's hand.

CHAPTER X

We come now to Parkman's works; or rather we are still approaching them through questions that probe to the centre of his character. 1. How much of the artistic temperament had he? 2. How far did his works answer the innermost, generative impulse of the artist to express and justify his personality? 3. What are the sources of the powerful effect of his books?

1. Speaking with certain reservations, Parkman cannot be called an artist born. The love of beauty which springs from keen sense-perceptions acting on a mind gifted with spiritual insight, though influential in some directions, was not a general force pervading his personality. Yet nature in denying him a keen appreciation of the more delicate and poetic elements of beauty, or much interest in the fine arts, for their own sake, gave him the fullest enjoyment of what is virile, bold, and effective in the physical world and in literature.

Nothing could have been more fortunate for him than the cultivation of his taste by his journeys to Europe. He thus recorded his own sense of this in 1843–44:

"I have now been three or four weeks in Rome — have been presented to his Holiness the Pope, have visited churches, convents, cemeteries, catacombs, common sewers, including the Cloaca Maxima, and ten thousand works of art. This will I say of Rome, — that a place on every account more interesting, and which has a more vivifying and quickening influence on the faculties, could not be found on the face of the earth, — or at least I should not wish to go to it if it could."

But in spite of the interest revealed by this one passage, the only one reflecting much enthusiasm for the creations of man, the beautiful in nature was far more to him. He scarcely mentioned works of art in his leisurely journey through Italy; but he described at length scenery, men, life, manners and customs.

His artistic sensibilities should be judged chiefly in connection with his own art of writing, as we shall do presently; yet his relations to the other arts are not without interest. Architecture, judging by his diaries, must have interested him most of all, though his references to it do not show any critical enjoyment of its beauties. Here are the only passages that seem of any importance, and the first one, by its emphasis, shows plainly that his tastes lay in a different direction:

"A weary week of lionizing. I would not give a damn for all the churches and ruins in Rome, — at least such are my sentiments at present. There is unbounded sublimity in the Coliseum by moonlight, — that cannot be denied; St. Peter's too, is a miracle in its way, — but I would give them all for one ride on horseback among the Apennines." "The Milan Cathedral is worthy of Rome, — I like it as well as St. Peter's."

After visiting it from vault to roof, he said further:

"With every visit the beauty and majesty of its hundred and sixty marble columns, of its rich tombs, its carvings, the rich fretwork of the roof and dome, and of the windows painted [with] the histories of saints, strike you with a stronger effect."

Of painting and sculpture also he said very little. Their chief attraction was their worth as human documents and historical data; painted landscapes, even of the wilderness, were still less important. The gallery of all Europe that interested him most was that of Versailles, with its pictures and statues of historic scenes and persons. When surrounded by the treasures of Rome, he found it worth while to make only this entry concerning art:

"There is an artist here, Overbeck, from Germany, who is a man of wonderful genius. I visited his studio to-day. His works are scarce more than sketches with a pencil, — but every face may be an hour's study, and speaks plainer than words the character of its author's mind, mild, earnest, and devout to enthusiasm. All his subjects are scriptural."

When in Milan, he found no more to say of Leonardo's "Last Supper," a work that by its extraordinary force and distinctness of characterization should have impressed him as a student of men than this:

> "Leonardo da Vinci's 'Last Supper' is here — in the refectory of a suppressed convent, — but miserably injured, or rather destroyed by the dampness of three centuries and a half. An old man, who has charge of the place, told me that he was at the bridge of Lodi and was a sergeant at Marengo."

The stage had no deep interest for him. Aside from the little people's theatres at Naples, he mentions none in his diaries, not even the Français when he was at Paris. Yet as a schoolboy we have seen him an eager and successful actor; and at the time of this journey he was very much given to the study of men. He seems early to have abandoned the histrionic art as completely as he did chemistry. Perhaps in common with many keen observers of character, he was repelled by the artificialities of theatrical presentation. It may be said, however, that although he was not a lover of the theatre, he would probably have gone oftener than he did to see a first-rate actor or play, if his eyes could have endured bright lights.

Music was an unknown world to him; it never attracted him at any time of his life. Yet he liked the Fifth Symphony, and he had one favorite song in his last years, "Sam Hall," whose dramatic force, grim humor, virility, and anti-clerical sentiments delighted him.

His appreciation of painting and the other fine arts

grew somewhat with the greater development of his spiritual nature. In the later part of his life he spent much of his enforced idleness in looking at illustrations and photographs; he enjoyed the perfection of Japanese pictures of birds, fishes, monkeys, and flowers; and had in his study some of Barye's statuettes of animals; also many engravings — chiefly portraits of historic persons. Undoubtedly a part of his failure to develop taste in these directions was due to his sensitive eyes; but the root of the matter lay in his physical and mental organization.

A glance at Parkman's relations to nature will not be devoid of interest, to show how happily they conformed to his sensuous and mental sensibilities, to the aims of his ambition, and to the nature of his productions. We have seen that though his senses were not very highly developed, his sight was in many ways keen, as in woodcraft and the study of the natural sciences. In spite of this, he had little appreciation of the more spiritual elements of beauty; he seldom remarked the charm of colors, forms, or lines in graceful composition. Even in his favorite pastime of horticulture, his attraction to flowers sprang largely from other things than their beauty. The processes of hybridization and growth, the wonder of new varieties, the vigor and perfection of a well grown specimen, — these things held his interest. But he showed no taste or care in the laying out of his garden to secure pleasing effects, and seldom remarked the beauty of a flower or an autumn leaf.

He lacked also the poet's gift of sympathy that connects nature with humanity, and the poet-naturalist's eye for the inner life and spirit of living creatures. Two of his strongest characteristics were love of the real and aversion to the visionary and spiritual; and such a nature can hardly include the poet's capacity for contemplation and revery. He loved nature, but not as a lover who sits down quietly for intimate communion. He could not abide Wordsworth and his followers. Although admitting that Thoreau was a notable man, he had little sympathy with him; he felt repelled by what he considered Thoreau's eccentricities, transcendentalism, self-consciousness, and affectation of being natural. Parkman's interest in nature lay in quite a different direction. Were we to confine our attention to the externality of his appreciation, and his need of a knowledge of her for literary reasons, we should commit the error of saying that he was more an observer than a lover of nature. It naturally follows that he cared not at all for highly humanized landscapes. The charms of rural England are not mentioned in his diaries, neither does he record anywhere the sight of picturesque compositions in New England, where with the simplest means man has unconsciously made some of the most charming pictures. Judged by his diaries and conversation, he saw no beauty in these rough yet not wild scenes; much less did he feel the subtle connection between this beauty and the pathetic, passionate human experiences which it framed. He saw only the objectionable effects of meddling with nature, the destruction of his beloved wilderness. He acknowledged in a way his limitations, when descending the Mohawk Valley in 1845: "I am getting a stronger relish for quiet beauties." We cannot but respect his perfect freedom from sentimentality, and from the slightest pretence of admiring what he did not feel.

Along the lines opened to him by his organization and his literary projects, his love of nature was very strong indeed. These were the lines that gratified his love of adventure and the picturesque. The wilderness with its free life was perhaps more to him than the softer charms of nature. As his diaries frequently show, he took great pleasure in what is vast, powerful, savage; often noting the large effects of light and atmosphere over a landscape, breathing most freely on a mountain top surrounded by limitless plains, responding best to the roaring life and irrepressible activity of cataracts, to the wild energy of a storm sweeping over the prairie or the ocean. In spite of the silence of the diaries on this point, we know that his love of thoroughness and realism were gratified in the natural sciences. He enjoyed the firmer grasp of nature to be had in the details of rocks, soils, trees, plants, and animals; — these things gave him close contact with the actual life of the wilderness. He noted the elements that affect life there, especially the means of subsistence and the exigencies of travel. Lakes, streams, swamps, ranges of mountains, windfalls, tangled undergrowth, laurel thickets, game, and fish, the trails of animals and men — he delighted in all such features, both for themselves and for their practical connection with the ever present object of his ambition.

It has been said that the love of the wilderness was his ruling passion. He himself refers to it in his autobiographic paper, saying that it "gained full control of the literary pursuit to which he was also addicted." This was undoubtedly true of him as a young man, but it seems equally true that his deepest interest in life and his greatest enjoyment soon came to be centred in the writing of history. It is surprising that he should never once have sought the wilderness during forty years after his trip to the Rocky Mountains. His lameness naturally made travel in the woods difficult; yet he often journeyed far to collect historic material. But it is probable that he loved the adventures of a wild life more than the wilderness itself; and therefore neither the woods nor the prairies had of themselves power to attract him after his infirmities denied him perfect freedom in physical activity. Certainly he drove on his literary labors in spite of obstacles, with a persistence, courage, and energy that would have enabled him frequently to visit the wilderness had the love of nature been his dominant passion.

We who to-day read his books are interested to

see how admirably his relations to nature served his needs as a historian. His scientific knowledge would not be called profound in these days of specialists — it was chiefly the knowledge of an intelligent and keen-eyed observer. Yet it was more than sufficient for his purposes, enabling him to give reality to the scenes of his history, by specifying the fauna, the flora, the rocks and earth of which they were composed. No less than this exactness and realism would have satisfied his standard of thoroughness. The very externality of his relations to nature was fortunate. The poet's dreamland, the poet-naturalist's humanized scenes, and the scientific minutiæ of the naturalist would each have been more or less dangerous interests. What he needed was just what he had, a ready feeling for large natural forces and effects, a keen perception of the picturesque elements of a scene, and a moderately scientific knowledge of the geologic and botanic make-up of a landscape.

But to return to his relations to art. A definite ambition was very early mingled with taste in his pursuit of poetry; but as his favorite authors were Scott, Byron, and Cooper, it seems probable that this kind of reading was chosen to gratify his love of activity and chivalry quite as much as his love of art. At all events, this line was soon abandoned, and the love of mere beauty in writing never again showed itself as a notable element in either his literary studies or recreation. Oratory interested him much for its importance in directing public opinion in our democracy, and we have seen him an active member of the debating societies in Harvard College and the Law School; but there is no evidence that he felt any special pleasure in it as an art. He seldom went to hear noted speakers or actors.

His skill in writing appears most clearly in the structural elements of composition. He was always bent on large lines and proportions, in spite of the abundance of details that he compelled to contribute to the general effect, using them so as to secure great rapidity of movement. Perhaps the only interruptions of his admirable dramatic march are some of the more lengthy descriptions of nature. It was here that he expressed beauty the most clearly. These passages show how beguiling to his imagination were the beloved woodland scenes, now to be recalled only in the shadow of his study. He also possessed a fine instinct for choosing the centre of interest and getting the right perspective. Thus, chiefly through the possession of strong common sense, he became truly an artist, even at times a poet; but he dealt so little with the purely æsthetic and spiritual elements that he cannot be classed with poets in general. This non-philosophizing philosopher wrote profound history without generalizing; this unpoetical poet, by a singular union of realism and picturesqueness, painted scenes and told stories full of imaginative effect.

Coming now to a consideration of his style, we

find it everywhere well fitted to his sincerity of thought, to his dominant desire for vividness, strength, and clearness, though lacking in the more sensuous charms of diction. In talking with him one day of the gifts needed for the literary profession, he regretted his unmusical ear; he seldom would listen to authors whose chief merit lay in the charm of their diction; and, indeed, he had a distinct aversion for the professed *littérateur.*

There would seem to be a close connection between Parkman's comparative deficiency in sensuous sensibilities and his frequent use of high coloring and strong language. In his pronounced taste for what is well emphasized in nature and in writing, there was a strong contrast to his love of quietness and simplicity in life, and hatred for what is showy or theatrical. This tendency is most evident in his earlier works; and it is an interesting fact in his growth that several decades were required to reach the simplicity and gentleness in style that distinguished his maturer character. Native impetuosity and love of action being denied their scope, he clothed the vivid conceptions of his mental world with forceful terms. In his diaries of "The Oregon Trail" the style is natural, simple, sometimes plain almost to baldness. But when with "Pontiac" he formally entered the lists as historian, something of his native simplicity disappeared — perhaps under the high pressure of youthful exuberance and self-confidence, or the recollection of his rhetorical masters. He himself came to consider this work as turgid and too highly colored. Yet here is shown in its highest development the chief excellence of his writing: its picture-painting quality.

There is another curious opposition between the exuberance of his style and his extreme reserve. With a sensuous organization which naturally inclined him to forcible expression, his Puritan reserve held in check all excess of sentiment and feeling. Thus caution modified his impetuosity, making him a man of under- rather than over-statement.

Parkman's love of strong language, however, sometimes got free play in the intimacy of friendly intercourse. Nothing could be more unexpected from this dignified and reserved gentleman than his outbursts of jocose exaggeration and ridicule, touched off with a bit of profanity; such outbursts were generally fired at contemporary men or measures that he did not approve. His swearing was ruled by its definition as "superfluous profanity;" it never reflected either vulgarity or any degree of the sacrilegious spirit. So far as I know, his swearing was limited to an occasional but emphatic *damn*, and this expletive often arose from nervous irritability more than from any other cause. The following extract from his diary, written in 1844 at Edinburgh, shows how he regarded the matter:

"In the castle are the regalia of Scotland, the crown, sword, scepter, and jewels, the first worn by Robert Bruce and all who succeeded him till Charles II.'s time. They were hidden from the light for many years. The soldier pointed out the heavy oaken chest where they lay concealed, until the Scottish nation should have forgotten its ancient independence and become content under its 'annexation' to England. I remembered the scene just after the opening of the chest, when a party of literati and ladies were looking at these insignia of ancient glory, and one frivolous fellow lifted the crown to place it on the head of a simpering young lady. 'No! By God,' exclaimed Scott, who stood by. The man blushed like scarlet and laid the crown down. There is a power in a little profanity when it comes from a moved spirit."

It may be added that his love of strength for its own sake sometimes led him to indulge in humorous exaggeration. Moreover, his rules of damnation were not rigid, for he would now and then damn a thing for which he had not the most utter contempt.

In the progress of his literary career his prudential traits, together with prolonged infirmities, imposed beneficial restraints on his style. While the necessary slowness of composition, much meditation, and continual practice naturally improved his taste and skill, the fashion of the times also moulded him here, by changing from scholastic formality of expression to greater freedom and naturalness. But after all, his best powers came directly from his spiritual growth, under both suffering and success. Self-control, serenity, and the more delicate powers of sympathy had to come to him, before his style could reflect them in the chastened diction of "Montcalm and

Wolfe." He regarded this volume as his best work; and certainly it represents him at his ripest, after the sunshine of success had permeated his strong nature with its mellowing rays.

2. It is manifest from what precedes that Parkman's books bear a very close relation to his character. Indeed the inexorable revelations of every form of art make it impossible for the artist to elude his autobiography; the question is not as to the reality of the revelation, but who has the eye to read it. Having as a key our personal knowledge of him, we may hope to see at least something of him in his works, and find out how far they reveal and justify his personality.

Parkman's love of truth was almost a religion, and his work might be taken as the altar of his self-sacrifice. In this cult he knew no limit of pains, no fluctuations of feeling. "When you credit me with loyalty and honor," he writes, "you give me praise that I value most of all." [1] The honesty of citation that has been remarked in his pages, is only a small part of the sincerity of his work. His Puritan conscience was ever on the watch against the strong temptations offered by the picturesqueness of his theme and his own love of striking effects; and anticipating that these dangers would be felt by the reader of his graphic pages, he gave this assurance of his exactness:

"If at times it may seem that range has been allowed to fancy, it is so in appearance only; since the minutest

[1] To Abbé Casgrain, Jan. 26, 1872.

details of narrative or description rest on authentic documents or on personal observation."[1]

But his work shows that love of truth did not stop at this primary need of accuracy, of which we have spoken in previous pages. Sincerity with him rose to impartiality in all historical questions, despite the strongest prejudices in relation to contemporary men and movements. This apparent inconsistency is easily explained by the obvious difference between historical and contemporary studies, also by his strong conservatism as regards modern civilization. It is rarely possible to collect all the evidence in a contemporary matter, or to free it from the distortions of passion, prejudice, and a too near point of view. But in writing history Parkman collected all the authorities, weighed the evidence with exceptional care, coolness, and wisdom, and finally gave his opinion, entirely independent of feeling. His conservatism met in his themes little to call it forth in the expression of prejudices; but even if it had been aroused, the completeness of the evidence and his love of scholarship and fairness would still have made him impartial. The following extracts from a letter in reply to a French Canadian critic[2] are of interest here:

"I am an abonné of the 'Revue Canadienne,' and have just read your article on 'The Old Régime,' with attention and interest. It is very much what I had expected,

[1] *Pioneers*, p. xiv.
[2] To Abbé Casgrain, May 9, 1875.

knowing your views and the ardor with which you embrace them, as well as the warmth and kindliness of your feelings. I could take issue squarely on the principal points you make, but it would make this letter too long, and I do not care to enter into discussions with a personal friend on matters which he has so much at heart. Moreover, I wish to preserve an entirely judicial, and not controversial frame of mind on all that relates to Canadian matters. . . . I have also always declared a very cordial dislike of Puritanism. I recognize some most respectable and valuable qualities in the settlers of New England, but do not think them or their system to be praised without great qualifications; and I would not spare criticism if I had to write about them. . . . If you have mistaken my views, I could also point out a good many other mistakes in your article. You say that I see Canadian defects through a microscope, and merits through a diminishing glass. The truth is, I have suppressed a considerable number of statements and observations because I thought that, while they would give pain, they were not absolutely necessary to the illustration of the subject; but I have invariably given every favorable testimony I could find in any authentic quarter; and after I had finished the volume I made careful search in Ferland and Garneau to see if they had discovered anything which had escaped me. The materials of Canadian history, it is true, proceed almost entirely from the pens of persons born and bred in France — for the Canadians themselves wrote very little indeed, but only a very few of these persons wrote in an adverse spirit. Wherever it was possible, I have used their own language. . . . In exhibiting the different workings of two political systems, it was necessary to make comparisons which seem invidious; but these comparisons are not, as you say, continual; for they are confined to three or four pages at the end of the book, and the points of military efficiency on which the system of authority had advantages are fully exhibited. . . . I am well on in the story of Frontenac, whose good and bad traits I shall endeavor, after my custom, to exhibit clearly. Perhaps, when you read what I have written, you will not think me so partial after all."

This passage enables us to put our finger on one of the most important qualities of Parkman's character and work. Although by nature more given to strictures than laudation, he was most distinctly a kindly spirit in his life and his writings. Despite the absence of sentiment from his pages, which yet deal so much with experiences calling for pity, this guide lays on the reader a silent hand that is humane and gentle. Then again, his humor, though critical and incisive, is always kind, having generally a moral aim, as against a lack of manliness, common-sense, freedom, or honesty. And in spite of their long lists of hardships and tortures, his books are all cheerful in tone.

But to return to his love of truth, Parkman's impartiality in historical work is shown in two broad topics that of necessity run through many of his volumes: Catholicism and Feudalism. Romanism in particular, taking it simply as a system of practical morality, roused his strongest antipathy by many of its fundamental principles in education and daily conduct; but however little Parkman cared about the religious life, he esteemed too highly deep feeling of some kind as the motive force of character, to treat lightly the sincere practice of any religion. He never failed to appreciate devotion to duty, and victories of the conscience. It was a lofty view of life and character, quite as much as the impartiality of the historian, that led him to set forth the heroic labors and martyrdoms of the early Missionaries of Canada. He said:

"But when we see them, in the gloomy February of 1637, and the gloomier months that followed, toiling on foot from one infected town to another, wading through the sodden snow, under the bare and dripping forests, drenched with incessant rains, till they descried at length through the storm the clustered dwellings of some barbarous hamlet, — when we see them entering, one after another, these wretched abodes of misery and darkness, and all for one sole end, the baptism of the sick and dying, we may smile at the futility of the object, but we must needs admire the self-sacrificing zeal with which it was pursued.

"Yet withal a fervor more intense, a self-abnegation more complete, a self-devotion more constant and enduring, will scarcely find its record on the page of human history."[1]

His work reflects his equipoise in another matter. Although exceedingly fond of New England, he

[1] *The Jesuits*, Chapter VIII.

did not spare the lethargy and factiousness of the English colonists; and it is noticeable that he seldom went a step out of his way to show the redeeming virtues of his own people.

His work is characteristic also by the naturalness and simplicity of his conceptions. His elemental temperament led him to keep the reader as much as possible out-of-doors, amid the space, air, and freedom of primeval nature. He conducted his narratives with the same quick, firm step he had in walking; his keen perceptions and good memory enabled him to seize a multitude of details along the way; but he never lost the trail, or failed to subordinate details to the general effect. Such rapidity of movement is impossible to a mind unable to see things in broad masses.

The same is true of his treatment of character. He cared little for the underhand elements of history — the complexities of diplomacy, petty personal matters, meanness of motives and conduct received small development under his hand. Whatever men and events may have been in their depths, his conception and presentation of them were frank, strong, and simple. Truly fortunate was he to find in his theme so much that was simple and manly. Probably he would not have done so well in writing a history of Europe, entangled in a complex web of many lines of interest and jostled at every turn by crowding peoples of diverse origins and destinies. He needed just what he had, — the stories of a few single-minded heroes leading small bodies of men through the wide spaces of the wilderness, and the deeper, though still simple history of two opposing systems of colonization and national growth.

As the production of a "passionate Puritan,"[1] his work bears in itself the fire and the reserve of his dual nature. He often wished to get rid of the repressive force that held him down. In this subterranean warfare of his nature, Puritanism was nearly always the victor. While willing to expand considerably a description of the scenic setting of an incident, he was entirely unable to express his sym-

[1] This happy phrase comes from the following poem by his daughter, Mrs. J. T. Coolidge, Jr.

To F. P.

Stoic and warrior, through the din of strife
Thy path was hewn with strength of iron will.
No fear could stay thy dauntless course through life,
Nor destiny's decrees thy purpose kill.
Straight to the mark with head erect and free,
Enduring all, determined to attain,
Nor count the cost ; thy strong vitality
Transfigured pain to power, and loss to gain.
When the long fight was fought, the laurel wreath
Of high success was thine, — faithful to death.

Passionate Puritan, master of thy might,
The faint of heart grew strong in seeing thee ;
A dominant idea the leading light
And talisman that gave thee victory.
Deep in thyself was force of burning fire
That nerve must hold until the prize be won;
Fearlessly guiding it to thy desire
Thy hand drove on the chariot of the sun
Until the gates flew wide, and on thy vision
Burst light of conqueror's calm in Fields Elysian.

pathy for a victim tortured to death, or to cast over an event the halo of a poetic or moral sentiment. This reserve showed itself so strongly in "Pontiac," written in the exuberant and expansive period of life, as to call forth the following letter from his mentor, Professor Sparks. After referring to the atrocious acts of the Paxton men he says:

> "Altho you relate events in the true spirit of calmness and justice, yet I am not sure but a word or two of indignation, now and then, at such unnatural and inhuman developments of the inner man would be expected from an historian who enters deeply into the merits of his subject." [1]

Parkman was inevitably in his work what he was in his temperament, — Puritan, Spartan, and Stoic all in one. We are constantly impressed by his Puritan economy of praise. Few achievements or characters call out any expression of admiration, although his pages glow with their strong diction and rapid movement. Although as a man he suffered under the strain of these opposite qualities, as a historian he found in them a large part of his success.

His manner under criticism was naturally that of a strong and independent soul standing on solid ground, and loving a fight. He wrote: "I believe that, when I feel confident in my position, I am not very sensitive to criticism." [2] But he had no fond-

[1] Letter written in 1850.
[2] To Abbé Casgrain, May 23, 1873.

ness for polemical and metaphysical contentions; he was decisive rather than argumentative. Early in life he formed his opinions on nearly all the topics he afterwards had occasion to handle, and he held to these views with great firmness. His self-defences consisted chiefly of a presentation of facts, rather than any consideration of principles and theories. Once he had given his opinion he was apt to drop the subject, or listen to his opponent in silence. Thanks to thoroughness and the need of economizing his strength and sight, he seldom felt obliged to take up his pen in self-defence; but when he did, he left nothing to be desired in the way of firm thought and incisive expression. In a few papers he has given us a glimpse or two of this side of his nature.

For what Parkman thought of other historians we have very little data. It is said that he admired Prescott when in college, yet no record of this influence or of any other is extant. Later his reading was for the most part determined by the need of relaxation; so that he knew little history outside his own special field. Unfortunately, but few of his passing remarks on historians have been preserved. We have already given his opinion of Garneau, as having the philosophical manner without the matter, also his vigorous censure of Bancroft for estimating too highly the dignity of history, and avoiding the use of homely and trifling incidents. He considered De Gaspé's "Anciens Canadiens" an "admirable picture of life and manners, one of the chief attractions of which is its manifest truth."[1] Occasionally he wrote a short review of historical works concerning the Indians, such as Stone's "Red Jacket." Rameau, however, in presenting the Roman Catholic view of the old régime in Canada, called forth a review that contains several characteristic passages.

> "He is the bravest of generalizers; snatches at a detached fact and spreads it over as much ground as his theories require. . . . His book is a curious example of the manner in which a man of confused brain and weak judgment, eager to see things in his own way, will distort some facts, overlook others, magnify others that are trifling into gigantic proportion, and all with no apparent intention to deceive anybody."[2]

But these papers are a very inadequate gratification of the general desire to know the opinions of an expert. Parkman's inability to read much is perhaps to be regretted here more than anywhere else; since his originality and independence would have made his criticism most valuable.

Despite the fact that a Puritanic economy of praise held a mask before his sympathies, we may yet learn something personal from a view of his gallery of historical portraits. His self-revelations, however, must be looked for more in his style and treatment than in any evident signs of sympathy. At most we can now and then catch a confidential word to some of his heroes as they march along.

[1] Letter to Abbé Casgrain, June 3, 1871.
[2] Review of *Une Colonie Féodale.* — *The Nation*, No. 652.

The strong and effective, in character as well as in nature and language, attracted him. He adhered conscientiously to facts in portraiture, indulging in no hazardous or imaginative touches, however inviting they might be for the sake of artistic symmetry and completeness. His energy and imagination, concentrated on the ideal world of his solitary study, brought him to look upon his characters as real people; he thus attained much of the novelist's or dramatist's vividness of conception. The range of his knowledge of men and life is shown by the variety of classes handled. He seized with certainty the salient traits of men and women, courtiers and savages, priests and politicians, seigniors and peasants, nuns and *coureurs de bois*. Here by sympathy, there by antipathy, more often still by simply a keen intellectual comprehension, he reached in the long years of slow work and solitary meditation very close relations with his characters. The chief wonder is that in this prolonged intimacy he should have given so little of himself.

Parkman's methods in portraiture were happily varied according to his materials and in view of the literary contrasts and effects he wished to produce. Now the chief traits of a man would be given in a few lines; then built up by successive touches brought in as the course of events required; or again the antecedents and education of a person would be set forth in a more or less biographical sketch. Or perhaps a man's own contemporaries were allowed to testify on all sides as to his character and conduct, thus reassuring the reader by the most unquestionable impartiality. Parkman's love of unity and effectiveness received the highest gratification whenever he found a figure that could be justly used as the centre of interest for grouping the men and events of an epoch. La Salle and Frontenac were thus favorite subjects with him, while "A Half Century" repelled him by its lack of a hero and a controlling purpose. His love of action made him fond of the dramatic in history: he liked a character to portray himself by his acts. This method, I think, was his first choice whenever proportion and material allowed of its employment.

Parkman's portraits are further interesting as a record of his growth. In the earlier works their firmness of treatment is not free from a certain hardness. Though living and effective, these portraits generally give only the external forces that are made manifest in a public career: they show keenness of perception more than sympathy. But suffering, friendships, years of hard work, and success at last, could not fail to mellow a nature so capable of culture. In his later volumes Parkman shows more interest in the emotional and spiritual forces of character — as may be seen in his describing the meanness of Braddock towards women, Montcalm's affectionate and domestic qualities, and the filial and poetic sentiment that graced the pathetic figure of Wolfe.

If I were restricted to one word that should describe both the life and the character of Parkman, that word would be *heroic*. In following out the harmony of his character with his theme, and seeking for reflections of that character in his works, I was therefore delighted to meet with the following passage in Professor Fiske's "Introductory Essay" (p. xxxv):

"In all the history of the American continent, no names stand higher than some of the French names. For courage, for fortitude and high resolve, for sagacious leadership, statesmanlike wisdom, unswerving integrity, devoted loyalty, for all the qualities which make life heroic, we may learn lessons innumerable from the noble Frenchmen who throng in Mr. Parkman's pages."

If ever an artist was blessed with a congenial subject, it was Parkman. And this harmony was especially close in the most central and important element — the humanity, the life and character connected with his theme. He was continually meeting some trait or experience of his own in following his people; and in one or two cases he stood singularly close to his heroes.

Parkman's imaginative sympathy, the very heart of the artist, deserves a word for its relations to his portraits. Inevitably allied to the human sympathy from which it springs, it followed the same growth, from its externality in youth and middle life to a deeper insight in his maturity. True, frank, and persistent though he was in friendship, his faculties and sympathies were unable to reach the spiritual elements of life and character. In his humanities as in his relations with nature, he was true to himself, — never affecting sentiments not clearly felt by him. In his diaries, for example, he seems to have viewed life as a pageant, men and women not within the circle of his friendship being mere persons in a procession. In training himself for observation and description, he was satisfied with noting only the external, material facts of the show, not even attempting to read the story of intimate experience in any person, class, or nation, nor to penetrate into the recesses of character. But those things that his organization enabled him to perceive he saw very clearly, and devoted his attention to them with his usual concentration and energy. We shall see other effects of his specialized sympathy in his miscellaneous papers on public questions.

His treatment of the Indian is another illustration of this point. It is so exceedingly graphic and impressive as to carry the general reader along in complete absorption. Yet it has found critics among philanthropic students of to-day who have the advantages of more recent discoveries and methods. They say that his treatment lacks sympathy, as well as a knowledge of the deeper interests connected with that peculiar race of men. While they admire his work for its thoroughness and for its remarkable charm of picturesqueness, they are inclined to treat lightly opinions formed from the superficial works of the Jesuits and other early writers, or on the traditions of New England derived from the political economy of Miles Standish, and on the experience of border settlers who had suffered from Indian cruelty and revenge. These critics say that when Parkman went west to see for himself, he confirmed these opinions by a sojourn of only a few months with a band of Sioux, during which time suspicion rather than sympathy ruled the intercourse, rendering it impossible for him to penetrate beneath the surface; and that as his infirmities prevented him from closely following subsequent studies, his work must be regarded as the most accurate and graphic picture of the pageantry alone, the bare external life and character of men in the stone age. On the other hand, many people, especially frontiersmen, who consider modern philosophic lines of appreciation as visionary, hold to the simpler conceptions of Parkman as the true, practical, and sufficient portrayal of the Indian.

The only point that concerns us here is the significance of his study as a revelation of his own personality. At the time of his investigations the science of ethnology had not yet been even named; much less had the doctrine of evolution been applied to the study of it. No one then dreamed of studying the tribal life of Indians as a connecting link between the prehistoric epoch and the earliest recorded period of civilization. But even had these ideas been in force, it seems doubtful that Parkman would have followed them, having no taste for such philosophical studies, or for psychological phenomena in traditions, ceremonies, and language. He described just what he most liked to observe — the pageantry of wild life and the manifest, effective traits of Indian character. He could not decorate his accurate work with visionary savages; he could use neither the romance of Cooper nor the abstractions of ethnological speculation. He followed his own bent for realism.

In his solitary study Parkman dwelt with a company very real to his imagination. Some of them he obviously hated; he treated others in his reserved way as friends; and one he seems to have regarded almost as a brother. In looking at his gallery of portraits, it would seem as if fate had selected the leaders of New France with special reference to her future historian. Except a few men and women of the soft and saintly type, the persons in that history were generally of heroic temper; and even the exceptions often came within the range of his feeling by their heroic labors and hardships. The men who left luxurious France to face the savagery of early America, had to have a certain measure of manliness. But Parkman presents his heroes as he spoke of his friends in real life — without praise in even the soberest terms. A sense of sympathy and comprehension are conveyed by the simple noting of facts; or some close, forcible phrase, giving the motive or quality of character or conduct, serves for explicit appreciation. Thus when Daulac took Parkman with him on his heroic expedition to the Long Sault, the latter opened his own heart in saying: "The enthusiasm of honor, the enthusiasm of adventure, and the enthusiasm of faith were its motive forces."[1]

I do not ignore the slightness of the evidence contained in such historical facts and obvious appreciations taken as autobiographic confessions, and I am aware that to those who have never known Parkman personally, this evidence will have little value. But to those who knew the man, these slight signs may be not unwelcome additions to the interest felt in his works. The chivalrous Champlain, the brave and loyal Tonty, the lion-hearted Brébœuf, and many others, appealed to his own natural parts; and he unconsciously responded in his treatment. His antipathies were equally stimulated by Menendez, Marie de Médicis, and Pompadour. Nothing struck fire from his steel more quickly than the assumptions of the church in temporal affairs. His animation of feeling on this point is frequently met in Frontenac's contests with the Jesuits and with Bishops Laval and Saint-Vallier. Dearly did he love a fight, and a good fighter; witness his lengthy account of Frederick the Great's single-handed struggle with all Europe, — a struggle not closely related to the war in America. As a minor figure that appealed to the same martial taste, take Rogers the Ranger, who captured Parkman's youthful enthusiasm and led him to follow the Ranger's trails about Lake George and Lake Champlain, and to write the only poem he ever published.[2]

His detestation of duplicity may be seen in his

[1] *Old Régime*, p. 123. [2] See Appendix.

treatment of Laloutre and other Indian-agent missionaries, as well as of many ecclesiastical politicians. Another example is his presentation of that curious compound of feminine wiles and Roman Catholic morality, Madame de la Peltrie.[1] On the other hand, he gave himself out with equal distinctness in dealing with the admirable personalities of his group. The portrait of that strong woman, Marie de l'Incarnation, shows his ready appreciation of power and native nobility. Perhaps his nearest approach to sentiment and pathos is the account of Jogues mourning for his murdered companion Garnier; yet this impression is conveyed only by the facts of the incident. An exceptional estimation of poetic beauty in character is shown in the portrait of Marquette:[2]

"He was a devout votary of the Virgin Mary, who, imaged to his mind in shapes of the most transcendent loveliness with which the pencil of human genius has ever informed the canvas, was to him the object of an adoration not unmingled with a sentiment of chivalrous devotion. The longings of a sensitive heart, divorced from earth, sought solace in the skies. A subtile element of romance was blended with the fervor of his worship, and hung like an illumined cloud over the harsh and hard realities of his daily lot. Kindled by the smile of his celestial mistress, his gentle and noble nature knew no fear. For her he burned to dare and to suffer, discover new lands, and conquer new realms to her sway."

[1] P. 316. [2] *La Salle*, p. 50.

But within the wide circle of these friends of second degree, there was a small group of men who drew him into still closer sympathy. Lord Howe, the cultured gentleman and "complete model of military virtue," was a figure that Parkman took by the hand. Under similar circumstances he himself would have shown the same earnestness and practical wisdom that Howe displayed in serving under Rogers to study the needs of men fighting in the wilderness, and in reorganizing the service to suit these conditions. Pitt, in spite of certain weaknesses, also drew forth some sympathetic words; Parkman could not stand aloof from the gifted, ambitious, incorruptible patriot, the commanding and inspiring statesman who was leading England to success in all quarters of the globe.

Wolfe was another of his affinities. Wolfe's portrait contains many touches that are surprisingly true of Parkman in his early manhood; and these resemblances would have been still more striking had the historian's martial instincts been brought to light by a military career. For example: [1]

"Wolfe was a delicate and sensitive child, but an impetuous and somewhat headstrong youth who from childhood had dreamed of the army and the wars, and who had showed along with a painstaking assiduity a precocious faculty for commanding men. . . . Always ardent, always diligent, and constant in military duty. He made friends readily and kept them, and was usually a pleasant

[1] *Montcalm and Wolfe,* vol. ii. p. 184.

companion, though subject to sallies of imperious irritability, which occasionally broke through his strong sense of good breeding. For this his susceptible constitution was largely answerable. . . . In spite of his impatient outbursts, the officers whom he had commanded remained attached to him for life, and in spite of his rigorous discipline, he was beloved by his soldiers. Frankness, directness, essential good feeling, and a high integrity atoned for all his faults. In his own view, as expressed to his mother, he was a person of very moderate abilities, aided by more than usual diligence ; but this modest judgment of himself by no means deprived him of self-confidence, nor, in time of need, of self-assertion. He delighted in every kind of hardihood : and in his contempt for effeminacy, once said to his mother : 'Better be a savage of some use than a gentle, amorous puppy, obnoxious to all the world.' He was far from despising fame, but the controlling principles of his life were duty to his country and his profession, loyalty to the King, and fidelity to his own ideal of the perfect soldier. To the parent who was the confidant of his most intimate thoughts, he said : 'All that I wish for myself is that I may at all times be ready and firm to meet that fate we cannot shun, and to die gracefully and properly when the hour comes.' Never was wish more signally fulfilled. And again he tells her : 'My utmost desire and ambition is to look steadily upon danger.' And his desire was accomplished. His intrepidity was complete. No form of death had power to daunt him. Once and again when bound on some deadly enterprise of war, he calmly counts the chances whether or not he can compel his feeble body to bear him on till the work is done. A frame so deli cately strung could not have been insensible to danger; but forgetfulness of self, and the absorption of every faculty in the object before him, shut out the sense of fear. He seems always to have been at his best in the thick of battle; most complete in his mastery over himself and over others."

Parkman in his darkened study, combating his infirmities and difficulties, bore himself as Wolfe did in sailing for Quebec:

"In a few hours the whole squadron was at sea, the transports, the frigates, and the great line of battleships with their ponderous armament and their freight of rude humanity, armed and trained for destruction; while on the heaving deck of the 'Neptune,' wretched with seasickness and racked with pain, stood the gallant invalid who was master of it all."

Frontenac is another member of his inner circle of friends, but one whose closeness did not depend chiefly on resemblances to Parkman. While some of their most fundamental traits were found in both, many of the Frenchman's peculiarities were quite foreign to the self-restrained Puritan. Frontenac held his place by a variety of circumstances. Parkman said:[1] "The history of New France is a great and significant drama, enacted among untamed forests, with a distant gleam of courtly splendors and the regal pomp of Versailles." The volume "Frontenac and New France under Louis XIV." is the climax of this drama, and its dénouement is "Montcalm and

[1] Preface to *Frontenac.*

Wolfe." Count Frontenac was thus a most fortunate find for the historian, being in true perspective the central figure of the whole work. They were closely related by several personal traits, — a frank manner, clear and decisive speech, martial tastes, independence, keenness and fire, love of action, masterful energy, and strength of will. Even Frontenac's violent outbursts in connection with the Jesuits were in accord with Parkman's controlled impetuosity. The historian could not but enjoy such a man in such surroundings, a man of whom he said: "A more remarkable figure in its bold and salient individuality and sharply marked light and shade is nowhere seen in American history."[1] Then again Frontenac gathered about him topics that enlisted his liveliest interest, — such as the conflicts of church and state, and the vast plans that Frontenac imposed as the future policy of France in America. Frontenac may be regarded as Parkman's masterpiece in portraiture.

But he had a still more intimate friend. La Salle, whose character and labors appealed with exceptional force to his sympathies, and drew out of him autobiographic touches of the most intimate kind, was almost a brother. In La Salle he found his own manly character matched, and inevitably warmed to the man who had shown such courage, hardihood, and strength in the wilderness, who pursued with so much determination and energy plans of the greatest importance.

[1] *Frontenac*, p. 436.

Through the sympathy born of these and other essential similarities, Parkman seems often to have spoken of himself in describing La Salle; and this opinion is further sustained both by our knowledge of the former's traits and by the fervor, insight, and sureness of touch shown in his chapter on the explorer's character. Take, for example, these temperamental traits of the young La Salle:

> "The cravings of a deep ambition, the hunger of an insatiable intellect, the intense longing for action and achievement, subdued in him all other passions. . . . A youth whose calm exterior hid an inexhaustible fund of pride, whose inflexible purposes, nursed in secret, the confessional and the 'manifestations of conscience' could hardly drag to light; whose strong personality would not yield to the shaping hand, and who by a necessity of his nature, could obey no initiative but his own, was not after the model that Loyola had commended to his followers. A young man in whom the fire of youth glowed not the less ardently for the veil of reserve that covered it; who would shrink from no danger, but would not court it in bravado; and who would cling with an invincible tenacity of grip to any purpose which he might espouse."[1]

Nor could Parkman be more autobiographic than in saying:

> "The staple of La Salle's character, as his life will attest, was an invincible determination of purpose, which set at naught all risks and all sufferings."[2]

Aside from the difference of Parkman's ultimate success and La Salle's failure, the following passage

[1] *La Salle*, p. 3. [2] *Ibid.*, p. 17.

again is true of Parkman, not only as to his personal history in regard to labor, risk, and fortitude, but also as regards his spirit, at least in the early and middle epochs of his career:

"He had staked all, and all had seemingly been lost. In stern and relentless effort, he had touched the limits of human endurance, and the harvest of his toil was disappointment, disaster, impending ruin. The shattered fabric of his enterprise was prostrate in the dust. His friends desponded; his foes were blatant and exultant. Did he bend before the storm? No human eye could pierce the depths of his reserved and haughty nature; but the surface was calm, and no sign betrayed a shaken resolve or an altered purpose. Where weaker men would have abandoned all in despairing apathy, he turned anew to his work with the same vigor and the same apparent confidence as if borne on the full tide of success." [1]

And later:

"He had no thought but to grapple with adversity, and out of the fragments of his ruin to build up the fabric of success."

Even La Salle's reserve and pride, marred by coldness and irritating hauteur, were well within Parkman's comprehension; for, possessing the former traits, he escaped the latter only through the opposing force of frankness and geniality. He felt keenly for La Salle in the isolation that must always result from such a temperament:

[1] *La Salle*, p. 188.

"We have seen La Salle in his acts. Few men knew him, even of those who saw him most. Reserved and self-contained . . . he was a sealed book to those about him. His daring energy and endurance were patent to all; but the motive forces that urged him, and the influences that wrought beneath the surface of his character, were hidden where few eyes could pierce."[1]

Parkman also appears to say a word in his own defence when recognizing in La Salle "an incapacity to express, and much more to simulate feeling, — a trait sometimes seen in those with whom feeling is most deep."[2] Still other passages are both biographic and autobiographic:

"He was the hero, not of a principle nor of a faith, but simply of a fixed idea and a determined purpose. As often happens with concentrated and energetic natures, his purpose was to him a passion and an inspiration; and he clung to it with a certain fanaticism of devotion."[3]

Again:

"Such was the indomitable nature of this man, whom no peril could deter, and no failure discourage. So he remained to the end, battling against destiny with the same unflinching mettle. Fate hounded him to death, but could not shake his courage . . . La Salle was a grand type of incarnate energy and will."[4]

These words also would seem to spring from Parkman's own experience:

[1] *La Salle*, p. 307.
[2] *Ibid.*, p. 319.
[3] *Ibid.*, p. 406.
[4] *Ibid.*, p. 446.

"All that appears to the eye is his intrepid conflict with obstacles without, but this, perhaps, was no more arduous than the invisible and silent strife of a nature at war with itself; the pride, aspiration and bold energy that lay at the base of his character battling against the superficial weakness that mortified and angered him. In such a man, the effect of such an infirmity is to concentrate and intensify the force within."[1]

He recognized in La Salle his own central fire, — a "deep enthusiasm of character which may be read in his life, but to which he rarely allowed the faintest expression."[2] And finally, he could not have painted himself with more striking veracity, in at least the harder periods of his life, than in this summary:

"Cavalier de la Salle stands in history like a statue cast in iron; but his own unwilling pen betrays the man and reveals in the stern, sad figure an object of human interest and pity."[3]

Parkman's success in dealing with many of his personages thus sprang from intimate personal sympathy with them and a knowledge of himself. It is very doubtful that any other historical writings present such versatility of acute interest and clear comprehension of character.

3. The sources of Parkman's power are deeply interesting to the student of literature and history. First of all, there is the richness of the theme itself,

[1] *La Salle*, p. 320. [2] *Ibid.*, p. 314.
[3] *Ibid.*, p. 320.

freely offering vivid pictures, dramatic events, and striking characters. Also it has the freshness of originality, in the strictest sense: no other epoch of history takes us so far back towards our origin, by furnishing such graphic accounts of the life and character of man in the stone age, or by the experiences of civilized men in the wilderness. But the broadest material distinction that marks his work is its realism. Both the man and his books are felt to be solid. His work is built of facts as a palace of dressed stones, which, without mortar, hold themselves together and form a fair edifice. In portraiture his sincerity forbade him to pass beyond appreciations that were natural to his organization, or to put in any touches not justified by good evidence. Keeping his eye on the actual, and on broad, positive, effective traits and motives, he avoided the weakness of possible contradictions in details, and made his men and women consistent, vital, and full of action. But in this exceptional devotion to the matter, he never lost sight of the spirit and general effect. A fact was simply a stone in his edifice, and as such, kept subordinate to the general plan. The singular combination of an eye for the picturesque with a practical, matter-of-fact mind enabled him to appreciate both detail and mass. Thus he enjoyed an advantage that subsequent historians can hardly hope to have, — even when the sciences of ethnology and psychology shall have made clearer the permanent and the transient in history, and connected more closely the present with the past. Professor Fiske in his "Introductory Essay" (p. xxiii) presents this excellent summary of the effectiveness of Mr. Parkman's realism:

"This elaborateness of preparation had its share in producing the intense vividness of Mr. Parkman's descriptions. Profusion of detail makes them seem like the accounts of an eye-witness. The realism is so strong that the author seems to have come in person fresh from the scenes he described, with the smoke of the battle hovering about him, and its fierce light glowing in his eyes. Such realism is usually the prerogative of the novelist rather than of the historian."

But all these basic realistic elements were merely the body that needed the breath of life; we must penetrate to the more intimate elements of personality if we would understand the sources of his power. We meet at once his ardent nature and the supernormal energy by which his work profited and his body suffered. He ran his race on a fiery steed, revelling in the freedom and swiftness of motion over solid ground. This energy, felt everywhere in his work, despite the moderation and dignity necessary to historical writing, animates the reader much as music does, independently of specific aims; being keenly alive, the bare facts give him vivid impressions, which may be largely determined by his own knowledge and powers of sympathy.

Another central and permeating force, perhaps the

very soul of all this body of facts and fire, was his chivalrous spirit. What we might call a matter-of-fact imagination was exalted by intense love of romance. In possessing these traits, each in a high degree, he was blessed with two of the most effective forces of the historian. Although his histories are peculiarly American, largely scientific in method, and modern in interests, their power over the reader depends very much on the mediæval spirit of the theme and of the writer. Parkman's romantic turn was not towards the mystical and ideal, but towards the adventurous, the courageous, the picturesque. Take for example his description of the founding of Montreal:[1]

"Maisonneuve sprang ashore, and fell on his knees. His followers imitated his example; and all joined their voices in enthusiastic songs of thanksgiving. Tents, baggage, arms, and stores were landed. An altar was raised on a pleasant spot near at hand; and Mademoiselle Mance, with Madame de la Peltrie, aided by her servant, Charlotte Barré, decorated it with a taste which was the admiration of the beholders. Now all the company gathered before the shrine. Here stood Vimont, in the rich vestments of his office. Here were the two ladies with their servant Montmagny, no very willing spectator; and Maisonneuve, a warlike figure, erect and tall, his men clustering around him, — soldiers, sailors, artisans, and laborers, — all alike soldiers at need. They kneeled in reverent silence as the Host was raised aloft; and when the rite was over, the priest turned and addressed them:

[1] *The Jesuits*, p. 208.

"'You are a grain of mustard seed that shall rise and grow till its branches overshadow the earth. You are few, but your work is the work of God. His smile is on you, and your children shall fill the land.'

"The afternoon waned; the sun sank behind the western forest, and twilight came on. Fireflies were twinkling over the darkened meadow. They caught them, tied them with thread into shining festoons, and hung them before the altar where the Host remained exposed. Then they pitched their tents, lighted their bivouac fires, stationed their guards, and lay down to rest. Such was the birth-night of Montreal."

This passage closes with the question: "Is this true history, or a romance of Christian chivalry? It is both."

As a summary of his entire work and its intimate relation to himself, this remarkable picture may stand alone:

"The French Dominion is a memory of the past; and when we evoke its departed shades, they rise upon us from their graves in strange romantic guise. Again their ghostly campfires seem to burn, and the fitful light is cast around on lord and vassal, and black-robed priest, mingled with wild forms of savage warriors, knit in close fellowship on the same stern errand. A boundless vision grows upon us; an untamed continent; vast wastes of forest verdure; mountains silent in primeval sleep; river, lake, and glimmering pool; wilderness oceans mingling with the sky. Such was the domain which France conquered for civilization. Plumed helmets gleamed in the shade of its forests, priestly vestments in its dens and fastnesses of ancient barbarism. Men steeped in antique learning, pale with the close breath of the cloister, here spent the noon and evening of their lives, ruled savage hordes with a mild, parental sway, and stood serene before the direst shapes of death. Men of courtly nurture, heirs to the polish of a far-reaching ancestry, here, with their dauntless hardihood, put to shame the boldest sons of toil."[1]

We have been looking into Parkman's books not so much with the purpose of discussing them as literature or history, as aiming to find in his pages reflections of his nature. As the exactness of these reflections depends on the accordance of the artist's inmost being with his subject, training, and experience, we have incidentally searched for these harmonies. But this study, of fundamental importance in the biography of any creator, has been too superficial to give much satisfaction. We are still a long way from any real knowledge of the psychological facts and principles required for good biography.

Yet in glancing back at his career we cannot fail to get some valuable lessons. Nature had endowed him with good though not wonderful intellectual powers; but she had been lavish in the manly gifts of energy, common sense, will, persistence, and courage. Ambition drove his mind and body — strangely compounded of weakness and strength — through the most beneficial intellectual and moral discipline, and

[1] *Pioneers*, p. xii.

pushed on his growth to full maturity. Unavowedly he has described his own career in the passage placed on the title-page of this memoir. Even among artists who have been financially as independent as he, few if any, have directed their lives and labors so closely in accord with their interior forces. He allowed none of the usual distractions of life to interfere with him. Neither physical weakness, personal tastes or habits, outward pleasures, domestic cares, counsel of friends, changes of aim or method, nor the influence of criticism and public opinion, had any effect on this man of clear vision and iron will.

Parkman's highest wisdom lay in his perception of the dangers lurking in the pursuit of technique. He knew how readily the mind becomes enamoured of the hand; how rarely the artist possesses breadth and strength enough to resist the fascination, so that only the very greatest escape blindness to the fundamental human interests of art; he saw that the most painful aberrations of judgment, the worst of mistakes in subject and treatment as related to vital interests, are to be found in works of great technical excellence. Thus he feared the atmosphere of the study, warned students against "emasculate scholarship," and desired to keep himself broad and sane by all possible contact with the world.

It was a great pleasure to observe his quiet but profound happiness in his own success, as an offset to the unfortunate side of his life. If this Spartan at times wished for death as a relief from suffering, he received at last a double crown, — one for his heroic endurance and another for his productions.

External success answered generously to his sacrifices. It is true that for a long time his financial profits were far short of a reasonable recompense for his heavy outlays of money and labor; but in other ways his reward was great. The most prudent and competent critics recognized him as a writer of accuracy, vivid imagination, cautious temper, and independent judgment; one who in his pages united sound scholarship and a wide interest in life with literary charm; who had cast a halo of genuine romance over the whole of North America; and whose achievement was only the better assured by the passage of time, which would deny to his successors personal contact with the Indian and the frontiersman. He could not have asked for a more substantial reputation in his specialty. Those who looked beyond immediate accomplishment to the farther reach of spiritual aims, looked upon him as one of the most important figures in American literature, not only by the brilliancy of his productions, but also by the exaltation he gave to thoroughness and discretion in scholarship. He had the further satisfaction of never feeling his work or his fame on the decline, for his last books were the best. Many degrees and honors came to him from institutions and societies of learning in America and Europe; but the reception now and then of a letter from some live boy who wrote to express his enjoyment of "La Salle" or

"Pontiac" delighted him quite as much as these public marks of appreciation. This brings to light another of the oppositions in his make-up. In describing Vassall Morton as "ambitious and fond of applause," and in referring more than once in his other writings to these traits, he surely gave an autobiographic touch. Nothing short of the greatest ambition could have carried him through such difficult labors; and to value commendation of the right kind was perfectly in keeping with his nature. But reserve, dignity, good breeding, and hatred of all forms of self-aggrandizement made it impossible for him to bid for applause in any way. He was noticeable for never doing anything to make himself personally prominent, or even to advertise his literary productions. Yet so inextricably is one's life and character interwoven with his artistic aims and works, that Parkman's heroism became known abroad and attended his books around the world. No man had a more sovereign scorn than he for physical or mental weakness, or for the pity and sympathy that is apt to come so annoyingly close to the victim of them. One day, in talking over a biographical notice in which a friend had dwelt on the historian's feebleness, he exclaimed: "Damn it, I'm not feeble!" But although his peculiar temper and habit of stoical endurance always kept him personally somewhat aloof from pity and tenderness, his sensitive nature accepted gratefully a straightforward expression of sympathy, especially if offered with a certain reserve.

The world thus offered him its highest tribute in recognizing the merit of his work and the personal worth for which it stands. He must have had, too, the inward happiness of feeling — though he never would have uttered it — that what he had done perfectly satisfied the artist's need of self-expression.

CHAPTER XI

THE picturesqueness of Parkman's character appears vividly in his citizenship. The making of history was fully as interesting to him as the writing of it. Such an eager student of life and character could not be indifferent to the lines of our national growth. He regarded "the direction of affairs of State as the noblest field of human effort;" saying also: "That greatest and most difficult of sciences, the science of government, dealing with interests so delicate, complicated, and antagonistic, becomes a perilous guide when it deserts the ways of temperance." He took his civic duties to heart and, considering his disabilities, fulfilled them generously. Indeed, these impersonal topics were sometimes a welcome outlet for feelings that could hardly break through the barrier of his reserve in personal matters, or get suitable opportunity for outlet in historical writing. There was a certain grandeur in the impersonality of his relations to life. If his sympathies were limited on the spiritual side, they were strong and quick on the side of culture and public interests. Nowhere else did he experience so much emotion, or give such forcible expression to his individuality.

His miscellaneous papers, therefore, although few in number and limited in range, are important documents in studying him. His intimate conversation was exceedingly characteristic, vigorous, and racy when dealing with public men and measures; but it was not recorded at the time, and it cannot be recalled with any accuracy of detail. Parkman showed himself a ready and acceptable speaker on the few occasions when he accepted invitations to speak at dinners or other meetings. Although only occasionally allowing himself to write or talk of current events, his opinions on many topics were highly valued by conservatives, and the country lost much by the infrequency of the warnings from this keen-eyed student of life. Feeling so much concern as to the lines of our national development and such alarm at the gigantic evils growing up under the shelter of our political system, it is quite certain that he would have written much more on public affairs had his health permitted.

The miscellaneous papers left by Parkman admit us to some of the innermost courts of his character; for they were written under the impulsion of strong feeling and without the restraints necessary in historical composition. They reveal, therefore, many of the qualities and defects that were structural in his nature as opposed to those acquired by experience, culture, and force of will. This distinction was less easily perceived in his latter years, when many of his native tendencies had been subdued to an uncommon degree. How should one suspect that this man of quiet manners and patient, gentle spirit was fundamentally remarkable for exactly the opposite qualities? Yet one of his classmates said that Parkman's manner in the college debating club was almost pugilistic in its vehemence. Even in old age, talking of certain national tendencies, he would become hot with indignation, speaking in unmeasured terms, and clenching his fist with the desire to fight injustice and corruption. Two other structural elements of his character are displayed in these papers, — conservatism and prejudice. Both sprang from his inmost constitution; yet, as we shall see, their lines were happily softened by liberality and the judicial spirit. Whatever court of his character we visit in these unrestrained, unstudied pages, we encounter solidity, practicality, objectivity, hatred of theories; yet we also find these materialistic elements infused with noble ambitions for honesty and culture. Finely compounded were the contradictions of this non-philosophizing philosopher, this unpoetical poet, this utilitarian idealist.

The deepest and broadest question that history has to answer is: What kind of men and women does a given civilization produce? Parkman held truly that the level of a civilization depends on the worth of its units, and that a democracy cannot pursue a successful career without placing the direction of public affairs in the hands of worthy, capable, and educated leaders. This was the very corner-stone of his political edifice.

As a friend of learning and a patriot, he felt the scholar's debt to civilization in return for the blessings of culture and protection. Education, especially the higher education of leaders or statesmen, was consequently the civic subject that most fully commanded his sympathies and as much time and strength as could be spared from literary labors. He expressed his hopes and fears for education and its relations to our national life, in the following article:[1]

"The Tale of the 'Ripe Scholar.'

"Not many years ago, a certain traditional prestige, independent of all considerations of practical utility, attached to the scholastic character, at least in New England where the clergy long held a monopoly of what passed for learning. New England colleges were once little more than schools for making ministers. As the clergy has lost in influence, so the scholar has lost in repute, and the reasons are not hard to find. The really good scholars were exceptions, and very rare ones. In the matter of theology some notable results were produced, but secular scholarship was simply an exotic, and a sickly one. It never recovered from its transplantation, and drew no vital juices from the soil. The climate was hostile to it. All the vigor of the country drifted into practical pursuits, and the New England man of letters, when

[1] *The Nation*, Dec. 23, 1869.

he happened not to be a minister, was usually some person whom constitutional defects, bodily or mental, had unsuited for politics or business. He was apt to be a recluse, ignorant of the world, bleached by a close room and an iron stove, never breathing the outer air when he could help it, and resembling a mediæval monk in his scorn of the body, or rather in his utter disregard of it. Sometimes he was reputed a scholar merely because he was nothing else. The products of his mind were as pallid as the hue of his face, and, like their parent, void of blood, bone, sinew, muscle, and marrow. That he should be provincial was, for a long time, inevitable, but that he was emasculate was chiefly his own fault. As his scholarship was not fruitful of any very valuable results, as it did not make itself felt in the living world that ranged round it, as, in short, it showed no vital force, it began at length to be regarded as a superfluous excrescence. Nevertheless, like the monkish learning of the middle ages, it served a good purpose in keeping alive the traditions of liberal culture against a future renaissance. We shall be told that we exaggerate, and, in one sense, this is true, for we describe not an individual, but a type, from which, however, the reality was rarely very remote, and with which it was sometimes identified. The most finished and altogether favorable example of this devitalized scholarship, with many graceful additions, was Edward Everett, and its echoes may still be heard in the halls of Congress, perplexing Western members with Latin quotations, profuse, if not always correct.

"As the nation grew in importance and in sensitiveness, the want of intellectual productiveness began to trouble the popular pride, and an impatient public called on its authors to be 'original.' Spasmodic efforts were made to respond, and the results were such as may be supposed. The mountain went into convulsions of labor and produced a mouse, or something as ridiculous. After an analogous fashion some of the successors of our pallid clerical scholars raise the cry, 'Let us be strong,' and fall into the moral and physical gymnastics of muscular Christianity. This, certainly, is no bad sign, in so far as it indicates the consciousness of a want; but neither originality nor force can be got up to order. They must spring from a deeper root and grow by laws of their own. Happily our soil has begun to put forth such a growth, promising in quality, but as yet in quantity and in maturity, wholly inadequate to the exigent need.

"In times of agitation, alive with engrossing questions of pressing moment, when all is astir with pursuit and controversy, when some are mad for gold, and some are earnest, and some rabid for this cause or for that, the scholarship of the past is naturally pronounced not up with the times. Despite his manifold failings, 'the self-made man,' with his palatial mansion, his exploits in the gold-room, in the caucus, on the stump, in Congress, and in the presidential chair, flatters popular self-love and fills the public eye. Only a slight reason is wanted for depreciating the scholar, and a strong one is offered. Because the culture which our colleges supplied, and which too many of them still supply, was weak, thin, and unsuitable, it was easy to depreciate all culture. By culture we mean development, not polish or adornment, though these are its natural and by no means useless belongings. Using the word, then, in this sense, culture is with us a supreme necessity, not for the benefit of a few, but of all. The presence of minds highly and vigorously developed is the most powerful aid to popular education, and the necessary condition of its best success. In a country where the ruling power is public opinion, it is above all things necessary that the best and maturest thought should have a fair share in forming it. Such thought cannot exist in any force in the community without propagating its own image, and a class of strong thinkers is the palladium of democracy. They are the natural enemies of ignorant, ostentatious, and aggressive wealth, and the natural friends of all that is best in the popular heart. They are sure of the hatred of charlatans, demagogues, and political sharpers. They are the only hope of our civilization; without them it is a failure, a mere platitude of mediocrity, stagnant or turbid, as the case may be. The vastest aggregate of average intelligences can do nothing to supply their place, and even material growth is impeded by an ignorance of its conditions and laws. If we may be forgiven the metaphor, our civilization is at present a creature with a small and feeble head, a large, muscular and active body, and a tail growing at such a rate that it threatens to become unmanageable and shake the balance of the vital powers.

"The tendency of a partial education, such as the best popular education must of necessity be, is to produce an excess of self-confidence; and one of its results in this country is a prodigious number of persons who think, and persuade others to think, that they know everything necessary to be known, and are fully competent to form opinions and make speeches upon all questions whatever. As these are precisely the persons who make the most noise on the most momentous questions of the day, who have the most listeners and admirers, and who hold each other up as shining examples for imitation, their incompetency becomes a public evil of the first magnitude. If rash and ignorant theorizing, impulsive outcries, and social and political charlatanry of all sorts are to have the guiding of our craft, then farewell to the hope that her voyage will be a success. The remedy is to infuse into the disordered system the sedative and the tonic of a broad knowledge and a vigorous reason. This means to invigorate and extend the higher education; to substitute for the effete and futile scholarship which the popular mind justly holds in slight account, an energetic and manly development, trained to grapple with the vast questions of the present, and strong enough in members to temper with its mature thought the rashness of popular speculation. Our best colleges are moving hopefully in this direction; none of them with more life and vigor than the oldest of them all. The present generation will see an increase in the number of our really efficient thinkers, but it is a positive, not a relative increase and is far behind the fast increasing need. Powerful causes are at work against it, and we will try to explain what, to our thinking, some of these causes are.

"Perhaps the most obvious of them is the ascendency of material interests among us. To the great mass of our population, the clearing of lands, the acquiring of new territory, the building of cities, the multiplication of railroads, steamboats, and telegraph lines, the growth of trade and manufactures, the opening of mines, with the resulting fine houses, fine clothes, and sumptuous fare, constitute the real sum and substance of progress and civilization. Art, literature, philosophy, and science —

so far as science has no direct bearing on material interests — are regarded as decorations, agreeable and creditable, but not essential. In other words, the material basis of civilization is accepted for the entire structure. A prodigious number of persons think that money-making is the only serious business of life, and there is no corresponding number who hold a different faith. There are not a few among us who would 'improve' our colleges into schools of technology, where young men may be trained with a view mainly to the production of more steamboats, railroads, and telegraphs; more breadstuffs; more iron, copper, silver, and gold; more cottons and woollens; and, consequently, more fine houses and fine clothes. All this is very well, but it does not answer the crying need of the time. The truth is, our material growth so greatly exceeds our other growth that the body politic suffers from diseases of repletion. A patient bloated with generous living, and marked already with the eruptions of a perverted, diseased blood, is not to be cured solely by providing him with more food.

"The drift towards material activity is so powerful among us that it is very difficult for a young man to resist it; and the difficulty increases in proportion as his nature is active and energetic. Patient and devoted study is rarely long continued in the vortex of American life. The dusty arena of competition and strife has fascinations almost irresistible to one conscious of his own vigor. Intellectual tastes may, however, make a compromise. Journalism and the lecture-room offer them a field midway between the solitude of the study and the bustle of the world of business; but the journal and the lecture-room have influences powerfully adverse to solid, mature, and independent thinking. There, too, is the pulpit, for those who have a vocation that way; but in this, also, a mighty and increasing temptation besets the conscientious student. As for politics, they have fallen to such a pass that the men are rare who can mingle in them without deteriorating.

"Paradoxical as it may seem, the diffusion of education and intelligence is at present acting against the free development of the highest education and intelligence. Many have hoped and still hope that by giving a partial teaching to great numbers of persons, a stimulus would be applied to the best minds among them, and a thirst for knowledge awakened which would lead to high results; but thus far these results have not equalled the expectation. There has been a vast expenditure of brick and mortar for educational purposes, and, what is more to the purpose, many excellent and faithful teachers of both sexes have labored diligently in their vocation; but the system of competitive cramming in our public schools has not borne fruits on which we have much cause to congratulate ourselves. It has produced an immense number of readers; but what thinkers are to be found may be said to exist in spite of it. The public school has put money in abundance in the pockets of the dealers in sensation stories, sensation newspapers, and all the swarm of trivial, sickly, and rascally literature. From this and cheap newspapers thousands, nay, millions, draw all their mental improvement, and pamper their mental stomachs with adulterated, not to say poisoned, sweetmeats, till they have neither desire nor digestion for strong and wholesome food. But we would speak rather of that truly intelligent and respectable public which forms the auditories of popular preachers and popular lecturers, which is the lavish patron of popular periodical literature, which interests itself in the questions of the day, and has keen mental appetites of a certain kind. This public is strong in numbers and very strong in collective wealth. Its voice can confer celebrity, if not reputation; and it can enrich those who have its favor. In truth, it is the American people. Now, what does this great public want? It is, in the main, busied with the active work of life, and though it thinks a little and feels a great deal on matters which ought to engage the attention of every self-governing people, yet it is impatient of continuous and cool attention to anything but its daily business, and sometimes even to that. Indeed, the exciting events of the last ten years, joined to the morbid stimulus applied to all departments of business, have greatly increased this tendency; and to-day there are fewer serious and thoughtful readers than in the last decade. More than ever before the public demands elocution rather than reason of those who address it; something to excite the feelings and captivate the fancy rather than something to instruct the understanding. It rejoices in sweeping statements, confident assertions, bright lights and black shadows alternating with something funny. Neither does it care much for a terse, idiomatic, and pointed diction, but generally prefers the flatulent periods of the ready writers. On matters of the gravest interest it craves to be excited or amused. Lectures professing to instruct are turned to a tissue of jokes, and the pulpit itself is sometimes enlivened after a similar fashion. The pill must be sugared and the food highly seasoned, for the public mind is in a state of laxity and needs a tonic. But the public taste is very exacting, and it offers great and tempting rewards to those who please it.

"That which pleases it pays so much better in money and notoriety, and is so much cheaper of production, than the better article which does not please it, that the temptation to accept light work and high wages in place of hard work and low wages is difficult to resist. Nothing but a deep love of truth or of art can stand unmoved against it. In our literary markets, educated tastes are completely outridden by uneducated or half-educated tastes, and the commodity is debased accordingly. Thus, the editor of a magazine may be a man of taste and talents; but his interests as a man of letters and his interests as a man of business are not the same. 'Why don't you make your magazine what it ought to be?' we once asked a well-known editor. 'Because,' he replied, 'if we did we should lose four-fifths of our circulation.' A noted preacher not long ago confessed to us that the temptation to give his audience the sort of preaching which they liked to hear, instead of that which it was best that they should hear, was almost irresistible.

"The amount of what we have been saying is, that the public which demands a second-rate article is so enormously large in comparison with the public which demands a first-rate article that it impairs the quality of literary production, and exercises an influence adverse to the growth of intellectual eminence. Now, what is the remedy? It seems to us to be twofold. First, to direct popular education, not to stuffing the mind with crude aggregations of imperfect knowledge, but rather to the development of its powers of observation, comparison, analysis, and reasoning; to strengthening and instructing its moral sense, and leading it to self-knowledge and consequent modesty. All this, no doubt, is vastly more difficult and far less showy in its results than the present system of competitive cramming, and requires in its teachers a high degree of good sense and sound instruction. The other remedy consists in a powerful re-enforcement of the higher education, and the consequent development of a class of persons, whether rich or poor, so well instructed and so numerous as to hold their ground against charlatanry, and propagate sound and healthy thought through the community. He who gives or bequeathes money to a well-established and wisely-conducted university confers a blessing which radiates through all the ranks of society. He does a service eminently practical, and constitutes himself the patron of the highest and best utilitarianism."

One of the most important influences Parkman had on his times was to stimulate a love of thoroughness in scholarship. This was done through his works, and through his relations with individual men, institutions, and the press. His interest in public libraries needs hardly to be stated. He helped by his membership and counsel a large number of learned societies in the United States, Canada, and Europe. The Archæological Institute of America felt his influence perhaps more than any other society. It was originally projected by scholars of especially classical tastes; but not meeting with sufficient support they soon called on Parkman and others for help. At the organizing meeting the classicists for a time had their own way and imposed European subjects as the aim of the society's labors; but Parkman so ably and vigorously presented the claims of America as to cause the enlargement of those aims to cover a broader field. As long as he served in the executive committee and the council, he remained the champion of American themes. The investigations carried on by Cushing, Bandelier, Captain Bourke, Miss Fletcher, and others, naturally attracted him, and, although he could not read enough to follow their labors closely, he personally aided them in many ways. With no fondness for ancient history and classical subjects, he yet contributed to the fund for establishing the American School of Classical Studies at Athens. All students and societies seeking information found him ever generous with his stores of learning. Some of his hardest efforts, indeed, made at times when labor was most difficult, were put forth to help students of history in collecting or publishing documents, — as in the case of Stevens, Margry, Bannestier, and others.

His interest in our public schools was of the deepest, even as his demands for them were of the highest. He said:

"We are told that, to make a bad voter a good one, we have only to educate him. His defect, however, is not merely intellectual. It consists also in the want of the feeling that his own interests are connected with those of the community, and in the weakness or absence of the sense of moral and political duty. The evil is not to be cured by reading, writing, and arithmetic. The public school may cram his brain with all it is capable of containing, and he will be no whit the better citizen for the process. It might train instead of cramming him, lay the foundation of a sound morality, and teach him something of political and social duty; but such education is more difficult than that now in vogue, and demands more judgment and ability in those who conduct it. To teach the teacher must be the first step; and here, as in everything else connected with public education, we find ourselves moving in a vicious circle. To whom have we entrusted these high and delicate interests? They demand the best intelligence and the best conscience of the community; and yet their control rests, in the last resort, with legislatures and municipal bodies representing in part that very public which needs education the most — wretched, wire-pulling demagogues, ignorant as the constituencies that chose them, reckless of public duty, and without the faintest notion of what true education is. In such education rests the only hope of democracies; but it is vain to look for it unless the wiser half of the public can regain its virtual control."[1]

Parkman's concern for education thus sprang from love of learning and patriotism combined. Speaking of the Catholic attacks on our public schools he said:

"The common school system with its harmonizing and assimilating influences is the life of our institutions; and if New England is not to lose all that is best in her we

[1] *North American Review*, July, 1878, p. 9.

must defend it with a firmness at once temperate and unyielding."

He was, however, opposed to any bigoted anti-Catholic agitation, and believed that "the most effective defence of public schools will be the increase of their teaching efficiency and the maintenance and growth of their superiority over the parochial schools."[1]

But much as he valued popular education, he had little faith in it by itself to safeguard our institutions; insisting that it must be directed by minds of superior culture, and that if common schools are necessary to a democracy, universities of the highest excellence are still more important.

His most important activities as a citizen and a friend of learning were his labors in helping the growth of Harvard College into a university. With his strong sense of civic obligation he maintained that every rich man must give freely, and every educated man must labor earnestly for the welfare of the land that shelters him. The infirmities that imposed so many privations upon his course of life, deprived him of strength for serving in public and exacting positions. Harvard therefore furnished a welcome outlet for his patriotism, and a precious opportunity for discharging a sacred obligation. Nothing outdoes the Board of a great university in the diversity and importance of the questions which come up for discussion; they range over the entire

[1] *Our Common Schools.*

field of civilization, — art, science, religion, industry, war, commerce, politics, — in short, every human interest; and back of all these external achievements lies the heart of the matter: the growth of character. Parkman was especially valuable in this place, and gave himself freely to the duties of his office. As no records exist of his efforts therein, we can only sketch roughly the general lines of his views.

Parkman had strong local attachments, and Harvard College in particular commanded his affection and gratitude. He was indeed closely bound to her, for many of his ancestors were sons of Harvard; his father had been an Overseer and benefactor; he himself had formed there many lasting friendships, and conceived the object of his life-work. "La Salle" was dedicated to the class of 1844, "Montcalm and Wolfe" to Harvard College. His official connection with the college began in 1852, when the Overseers appointed him to a vacancy in the committee for examining in history. By 1868 his fame led the alumni to select him as one of the Overseers for the term of six years; but he was able to serve only half that period. In 1874 he was again elected to the same office by a large majority. In 1875 the most gratifying tribute of all was paid to his worth and eminence — election as a Fellow of the Corporation of Harvard College. In this Board of seven members he served until obliged by infirmities to resign in 1888.

His position on the Board was unique, he being

the first man chosen into the corporation during the present century because of his eminence as a student and author. As thus distinguished from those eminent in the so-called learned professions, he was the last scholar on the Board. His state of health preventing him from attending to practical matters of administration, he was little more than an adviser; but as such distinctly represented the higher scholarly interests. Thus his wisdom had an important influence in the development of the university.

He was always faithful in attendance when his infirmities did not absolutely prevent it. His love of discipline and order showed itself in his punctuality; if ever five minutes late at a meeting, he failed not to apologize; and whenever he met Mr. Eliot, who was ten years his junior, he always addressed him as Mr. President. His attendance at the meetings was often touching, as an evidence of his interest and sense of duty. After sitting perhaps an hour, the knitted brows, the flushed face, and a dazed, oppressed expression showed that his brain could no longer endure the strain of mental application. He would then excuse himself, get up and walk about the room, or go out of doors, returning in a few minutes to his place at the table.

The general lines of Parkman's educational work were apparently irreconcilable with some of his basic traits. Intensely conservative in most things, he represented the liberals in education and the radicals in religion. Out of sympathy as he was with many elements of modern life, he yet labored in unison with President Eliot not merely to expand Harvard College into a university, but to fit it closely to modern needs.

But his deepest concern in culture regarded its influence in the development of character.

> "We of New England," he wrote, "are a bookish people. With us, the idea of education is inseparable from school-houses, schoolmasters, lyceums, public libraries, colleges, and diplomas. Yet these are but secondary agencies — pallid, nerveless, and emasculate, beside those mighty educational powers which spring out of the currents of life itself, the hopes, the fears, the responsibilities, the exigencies, the action or the idleness, the enjoyment or the suffering, the associations, the friendships, enmities, rivalries, and conflicts, which make the sum of each man's vital history." [1]

He thus depended on the cultivation of judgment by close contact with nature and men, quite as much as on the pursuit of technical learning. In his own schooling he had followed this idea and won a rich reward. He hated bookworms and "unproductive digs," fearing the mirage of the study, and continually warning men against "emasculate scholarship." Strangely enough, he cherished great aversion for many elements of the intellectual life, and detested even the words culture and refinement, because of the artificialities connected with them.

Viewing education as the beginning of a growth

[1] A letter to the *Boston Daily Advertiser*, July 17, 1863.

that must continue throughout life, he felt that the student's chief need was manly virtue. His own love of the wilderness clearly reflected itself in his ideals. He demanded that the student should be an improved savage, — virile, natural, full of strength and dexterity, resourceful in emergencies, and intimate with nature; but at the same time governed by delicacy and decorum.

If ever a man believed in the motto, "A healthy mind in a healthy body," that man was Parkman. His contempt was called forth by physical weakness more frequently, I think, than by any other defect of humanity. He would often exclaim, "How I hate 'em," in speaking of weakly or unattractive specimens of the race. The ground on which he built his hopes for America was large families of strong, healthy children. Now and then he uttered strong language against the small families of our Americans; for he saw in the decline of the native Protestant element in our population the gravest dangers to our national institutions.

His admiration for strenuous virility was the chief cause of his amusing aversion for ministers. Despite a long line of clerical ancestors, this feeling sprang up in his boyhood, and under the paternal roof. One day when a pious old lady, who was noted for her admiration of clergymen, called on the Reverend Dr. Parkman, Frank sat down by the window to amuse himself by drawing caricatures. When on rising to depart she went over to see his sketch, she found a picture of three devils carrying off three ministers on pitchforks, gowns and bands fluttering in the air with the speed of their progress. He never lost this dislike of the cloth. In his old age, writing of a boy who had been named after him, he said jocosely: "I hope the youngster will do honor to the name. He should be brought up to some respectable calling and not allowed to become a minister." He had seen in history only too often how prone were theological studies to make men narrow, hypocritical and cruel; and shrank, instinctively, from nearly every element of their training, life, and character, often gratifying his love of humor and of strong language by calling them "vermin." He thought them, as a class, vague, gushing, soft, spoilt by women's attentions, sentimental, unenergetic, and insincere in their professions of faith. It is perhaps needless to add that this instinctive dislike of the profession did not prevent him from counting among his friends several members of it for whom he had the highest regard. Until the Harvard Theological School was made non-sectarian, he could not be induced to take the slightest interest in it, nor did he like any mention of the chair in it that was founded by his father.

The education of woman called forth very few utterances from Parkman; and these were such incidental remarks in the discussion of woman-suffrage that they were hardly heard. While favoring the establishment of Radcliffe College in affiliation with

Harvard, he opposed the granting of diplomas to women, and distrusted the employment of the already fully occupied professors of Harvard as teachers in Radcliffe. Yet his interest in woman's education was sincere and far-sighted. In speaking of maternity he said:

> "It is the root and stem of national existence, while the occupations of men are but the leaves and branches. On women of the intelligent and instructed classes depends the future of the nation. If they are sound in body and mind, impart this soundness to numerous offspring, and rear them to a sense of responsibility and duty, there are no national evils that we cannot overcome. If they fail to do their part, then the masses of the coarse and unintelligent, always of rapid increase, will overwhelm us and our institutions. . . . To give women a thorough and wholesome training both of body and mind; to prepare such of them as have strength and opportunity for various occupations different from what they usually exercise, and above all for the practice of medicine, in which we believe that they may render valuable service; to rear them in more serious views of life and its responsibilities, are all in the way of normal and healthy development. . . . In the full and normal development of womanhood lie the best interests of the world."

Although not sympathizing greatly with the training of woman for any career that takes them away from home, he desired for them breadth of culture in the fundamentals of character.

His term of service in Harvard covered a period of important changes. The adoption of elective courses, the granting of more freedom and self-government to students, the change from the old recitation to the lecture system, the development of all kinds of athletic sports, and the expansion of the curriculum to promote the higher intellectual culture, — these features wrought a complete transformation of college life. And Parkman welcomed them all, for all appealed to manliness and a sense of responsibility. A firm belief in the inductive method led him to a deep interest in the development of scientific lines of education. He took much pleasure in his meetings with Agassiz, Wyman, Gray and other scientists; and showed towards some of this class, whom personally he did not like, a respect and deference not common in his self-reliant mentality. But, although drawn to the scientific, practical, objective side of things, he deprecated any tendency to convert a university into a group of merely technical schools; it should, he thought, remain distinctly the centre of the highest intellectual culture and influence. As to methods of instruction and discipline, he would leave students and professors perfectly free, with the exception of one unfailing demand as to results — thoroughness, without sterilization by too exclusive pursuit of erudition. Perhaps one of his best traits was an utter contempt for superficial education; he had a mission to puncture shams and expose the dangers of pretentious ignorance. It may be noted in passing that his conservative spirit led him always to call the institution by its old name of Harvard College, though it is quite possible this practice was in part due to that high standard of sincerity which would hold back the greater name until the school should really attain its full growth.

In addition to these general interests in the development of Harvard, Parkman held one special aim of prime importance. Having at heart our national welfare, he could never lose sight of the privileges and responsibilities of the university in regard to national growth. He dreaded the levelling-down tendencies of democratic equality. An extract from "The Failure of Universal Suffrage" will show this plainly:

"The slow but ominous transfer of power from superior to inferior types of men, as shown in city councils, legislatures, and Congress, has told with withering effect on the growth of true political ability. Debased as our politics are, they do not invite, and hardly even admit, the higher and stronger faculties to a part in them. Liberal education is robbed of its best continuance and consummation, in so far as it is shut out from that noblest field of human effort, the direction of affairs of state; that career of combined thought and action where all the forces of the mind are called forth, and of which the objects and results are to those of the average American politician what the discoveries and inventions of applied science are to the legerdemain of a street juggler. The professions still remain open, and in these comparatively limited fields the results are good. Literature offers another field; but here the temptation is powerful to write or speak down to the level of that vast average of education which makes the largest returns in profit and celebrity. The best literature we have has followed the natural law and sprung up in two or three places where educated intelligence has reached a point high enough to promise it a favorable hearing. For the rest, our writers address themselves to an audience so much accustomed to light food that they have no stomach for the strong. The public has its effect too on the pulpit. It is pleasanter to tell the hearer what he likes to hear than to tell him what he needs; and the love of popularity is not confined to the laity. From one point of view, the higher education is of no great use among us. It is not necessary to make a millionaire, a party leader, such as our party leaders are, or a popular preacher or writer. So little is it needed for such purposes, that the country is full of so-called 'practical men,' who cry out against it in scorn. Yet, from a true point of view, it is of supreme use and necessity, and a deep responsibility rests on those who direct it. What shall be its aims? Literature, scholarship and physical science, are all of importance, but, considered in themselves, their place is subordinate, for they cannot alone meet the requirements of the times. It has been said that liberal culture tends to separate men from the nation at large, and form them into a class apart; and, without doubt, this is to a certain degree true of the merely æsthetic, literary or scholastic culture. What we most need is a broad and masculine education, bearing on questions of society and government; not repelling from active life, but preparing for it and impelling toward it. The discipline of the university should be a training for the arena."

A man who really believes that the salvation of a democracy depends on its having leaders of worth and culture, will naturally insist on the formation of statesmen. Parkman maintained that orators will always exert great influence over the masses, and not lose their power even with the growth of the press. He therefore proposed and urged the establishment of the course called "English 6," whose object is to develop debaters, and prepare men to discuss questions connected with political science and history.

Parkman's labors in Harvard sprang chiefly from one side of his nature. By inheritance a conservative utilitarian, he became in education a liberal, and almost an idealist. His associates speak of him as distinctly the representative of the higher scholarly interests. From one point of view this is surprising; since he felt little personal interest in philosophical, æsthetic, or spiritual questions. Possibly this estimate sprang from a perception of the purity and energy of his intellectual nature, quite as much as from his particular desires and efforts. He sought especially the welfare of the students in regard to developing manliness, and watched the policy of the university in regard to elevating our national life; he promoted all elements of education that could contribute to these ends, according to the nature of each individual student. He regarded even philosophy, æsthetics, and receptive and sympathetic spirituality not as ends, but as means to the development of character. In short, he would have a society composed of men and women of sound bodies and thorough culture, having intellectual energy and public spirit, and following a high standard of character and manners. He himself was what he once described as a "patron of the highest and best utilitarianism."

The same temperament that fitted him so marvellously for his chosen work placed him in opposition to nearly every characteristic movement of nineteenth century civilization. He was not affected by any one of the great forces, social philanthropy, natural science, or religion. In fact, the various reformatory measures growing out of them were to him irritating topics to be avoided; only now and then would he cast at reforms a bit of his humorous exaggeration or run them through with a thrust of his keen invective.

1. Democratic philanthropies could hardly appeal to such a man as Parkman. A heroic man of martial temper, he was naturally a hero-worshipper; and his enthusiasm for the study of character carried him in the same direction. Yet being more critical than laudatory, more acutely accurate than broadly affectionate, his interest in great men did not include much personal fondness and admiration. They were forces in history rather than objects of partisan devotion.

We are hardly surprised to find in Parkman strong aristocratic tendencies. In this as in many other things his nature was at war with itself. An elevated character will always hate what is vulgar, but, unquestionably, a certain ancestry and environment will predispose a man to esteem birth and social conditions, even in the most highly developed democracy, as very influential powers. Parkman believed in blood. He would continue his confidence in a man of good family even against some serious errors of conduct; and by the same token he seldom hoped much from a man born of a family of inferior quality. It need not be said that he felt no reverence for the arbitrary distinctions of titles; his patent of nobility was personal worth. Thus by temperamental inclination as well as by conviction, he came to regard leaders of worth and capacity as the regenerating powers of civilization.

The limitations of Parkman's sympathy and insight had a decided effect on his political opinions. Instinctively regarding the lower classes from a distance, and practical to the core, he perceived, chiefly, the roughnesses and discords inseparable from the life of average mankind; seldom penetrating to the inner spiritual elements, the fundamental unisons of humanity. He seldom expressed sentiments of pity and tenderness either for himself or for humanity at large. He deplored the modern tendency to discover "objects of sympathy in vagabonds, thieves, and ruffians." Thus, partly from a martial manliness that hated every defect of body and mind, partly from inborn aristocratic tendencies, and partly from an aversion to philanthropic sentimentality, he was temperamentally unsympathetic with the lower ranks of men. On his vacation trip of 1842 about Lake George, he could write in his diary such a passage as this:

"There could be no finer place for gentlemen's seats than this, but now, for the most part, it is occupied by a race of boors about as uncouth, mean, and stupid as the hogs they seem chiefly to delight in."

And even in his full maturity in 1878 he called the working classes "the barbarians of civilization."[1]

Yet a careful view shows these hard utterances to be misleading exaggerations in regard to his faith in humanity taken as a whole. He distrusted the wealthy quite as much as the mired masses. Witness the following:

"Two enemies, unknown before, have risen like spirits of darkness on our social and political horizon — an ignorant proletariat and a half-taught plutocracy. Between lie the classes, happily still numerous and strong, in whom rests our salvation. . . . In the platitudes of democratic society two counter-influences are apparent — the one a curse, and the other a blessing: First those sudden upheavals of accumulated wealth which break with sinister portent that broad distribution of property which once formed our safety; and, secondly, this recent reinforcement of trained intelligence. Each confronts

[1] Article on *Failure of Universal Suffrage*, p. 4.

the other; for culture is no friend of vulgar wealth, and most of the mountains of gold and silver we have lately seen are in the keeping of those who are very ill fitted to turn them to the profit of civilization." [1]

The civil war struck fire from his martial spirit in many ways; and the heroism of the people often won from him expressions of admiration such as this: "Degenerate as our public men may be, the people at large of our time do not lose in comparison with their fathers." [2] He believed in human goodness as the power to work out the regeneration of civilization; and in trusting to this rather than to the remote powers of the Unknown, he only followed his strong common-sense. But, going still farther away from the visionary, he insisted that to be effective human goodness must be embodied in individual leaders of ability and worth. Under such leaders his faith in humanity was unbounded.

It is evident that Parkman must have regarded with profound aversion the so-called democratic principle of equality. He wrote of it:

"Vague and half unconsciously, but every day more and more, the masses hug the flattering illusion that one man is essentially about as good as another. They will not deny that there is great difference in the quality of horses or dogs, but they refuse to see it in their own genus. A jockey may be a democrat in the street, but he is sure to be an aristocrat in the stable. And yet the

[1] *Failure of Universal Suffrage*, pp. 4, 17.
[2] *The Atlantic*, January, 1868, p. 128.

essential difference between man and man is incomparably greater than that between horse and horse, or dog and dog; though, being chiefly below the surface, the general eye can hardly see it. Mountains and molehills, deserts and fertile valleys, and all the universal inequality of Nature, are but types of inequality in men. To level the outward world would turn it into barrenness, and to level human minds to one stature would make them barren as well. The history of the progress of mankind is the history of its leading minds. The masses, left to themselves, are hardly capable of progress, except material progress, and even that imperfectly. Through the long course of history, a few men, to be counted by scores or by tens, have planted in the world the germs of a growth, whose beneficent vitality has extended itself through all succeeding ages; and any one of these men outweighs in value to mankind myriads of nobles, citizens, and peasants, who have fought or toiled in their generation, and then rotted into oblivion."[1] He pictured us as a nation subject to the "tyrant of organized ignorance, led by unscrupulous craft, and marching, amid the applause of fools, under the flag of equal rights."[2]

Such a picture from the pen of an American patriot is startling; but although characteristic of Parkman's independence of mind and vigor of speech, it would not be fair to take it by itself as embodying his political faith. His anti-democratic tendencies were more than matched by an ardent love of freedom and fairness. He strenuously demanded: "A society where liberty is complete, and where all men

[1] *Failure of Universal Suffrage*, p. 5. [2] *Ibid.*, p. 2.

have equal opportunities of development, according to their several qualities."[1] This demand was not incompatible with a distrust of modern democratic methods, and Parkman had his own ideas as to the best means of reaching development and freedom. He said again:

> "Shall we look for an ideal society in that which tends to a barren average and a weary uniformity, treats men like cattle, counts them by the head, and gives them a vote apiece without asking whether or not they have the sense to use it; or in that which recognizes the inherent differences between man and man, and gives the preponderance to power, to character and intelligence, yet removes artificial barriers, keeps circulation free through all its parts, and rewards merit wherever it appears with added influence?"[2]

In all sociological matters he was oddly divided against himself. While his manner was entirely without hauteur, he needed every whit of the common sense, kindliness, and human interest that were his, to restrain a contempt for inferiority of all sorts. He was a "good fellow" with any man of any rank whose character commanded his respect; or even, for the sake of studying life and character, with many whom he did not approve. But, democratic in personal relations, he was an undoubted aristocrat in politics and in his intellectual relations to humanity. He believed in equality of opportunity, but not in equality of power to rule.

[1] *Failure of Universal Suffrage*, p. 2. [2] *Ibid.*, p. 6.

Despite certain idealistic tendencies, he hated abstractions, theories, and sentiments in matters of government. He said: "Iroquois legislation invented nothing; like all sound legislation, it built of materials already prepared."[1] And again:

> "There are no political panaceas, except in the imagination of political quacks. To each degree and each variety of public development there are corresponding institutions best answering to the public needs; and what is meat to one is poison to another. Freedom is for those who are fit for it. The rest will lose it or turn it to corruption."[2]

This passage shows a distrust of all forms of government viewed as essential means to national salvation. A republic was to Parkman not necessarily the summit of political wisdom. But if he distrusted democracy he still more distrusted oligarchy, autocracy, and aristocracy.

His political activities were limited by his disabilities to the writing of a few articles for the press. We find his work more critical than constructive; treating of broad national needs, never concerning itself with party politics. For all this, he was, during the civil war, an ardent Union republican; and, until he became a "mugwump," always voted the republican ticket when able to go to the polls. He was a

[1] *Manners and Customs of Primitive Indian Tribes.* — *North American Review*, July, 1865.

[2] *Old Régime*, p. 446.

regular reader of the New York "Nation," believing its severe criticism of our evils a salutary tonic.

We cannot but look upon this stern, strenuous figure as a prophet calling for political righteousness, and proclaiming the dangers that have grown up under the shelter of our free institutions. He distrusted the very corner-stone of democracy:

"That the ignorant, incompetent and vicious of any color or either sex should vote, I regard as a peril to civilization, and an injury to the entire community, themselves included. Promiscuous suffrage is the deepest source of our present political evils."[1]

He protested against the ballot being "an education in itself, capable of making good citizens out of the poorest material;"[2] and maintained that the unrestricted franchise — a safeguard in the hands of a limited population of patriots such as we had in colonial times — had become a peril in the hands of a mixed population under the domination of demagogues and material interests. He said:

"When a majority of the people become convinced that no aggregate of folly can produce sense, and no aggregate of worthlessness can produce honesty, and when they return to the ancient faith that sense and honesty are essential to good government, then it will become possible — not, perhaps, peaceably to abolish a debased suffrage — but to counteract and so far neutralize it that it may serve as a safety-valve and cease to be a danger."

[1] Letter to Col. T. W. Higginson, June 5, 1876.
[2] *Failure of Universal Suffrage*, p. 9.

His paper on "The Failure of Universal Suffrage" deserves the attention it received both at home and abroad, for its earnest consideration of the gravest topics. Woman-suffrage naturally fell under his disapproval as a part of "promiscuous" suffrage, and for other reasons which we shall consider later.

The lowest deep of Parkman's hatred was reserved for selfish politicians. By as much as he considered statesmanship the highest calling, so did he despise the demagogue as a "political reptile." There was nothing in our national life that he feared to the same degree. Boundless perils were held in store for us by "the machine" and the demagogue's control of an ignorant proletariat. His words on the subject are swords of flame:

"Never, since history recorded the life of nations, was such a people so led, or rather so entangled in such a political mesh-work. We make no allusion to this party or that. Men and parties will change, but the same bad system rules rampant over all. Still the same withering machinery of caucuses and conventions, the same combinations, wheel within wheel, of adroit and selfish managers, the organized scramble of mean men for petty spoils, clogging the avenues and outlets of public opinion, jealously vigilant of the rostrum and the press, and limiting the votes of an acquiescent people to such candidates as may suit, not the national interests, but their own. As freemen and sovereigns we go to the polls and cast our votes, not after our own judgment, but at the dictation of self-constituted knots and combinations of men whom we can neither esteem nor trust. If we did otherwise our vote would be thrown away. A many-headed despotism is exercised in the name of the largest liberty. If to degrade public morals, sink the national reputation, weaken the national counsels, rout out the race of statesmen, and place pliant incompetency in control of our destiny, — if those are the ends of government, then is our political management a masterpiece of human wit." [1]

Parkman's want of confidence in the masses seems to have been aroused by this obedience of theirs to demagogues, more than from any essential lack of respect for humanity. He had full faith in the feeling of the people, though not in their judgment. He wrote thus of them:

"We are told to look at the great popular uprising of the civil war. Here, indeed, democracy revealed itself in its grandest aspect. The degrading elements had not then reached the volume and force that they have reached to-day. There were no doubts and no complications. Victory meant national integrity, and defeat meant national disintegration. Above all, the cause had its visible emblem — the national flag; and thousands and hundreds of thousands of eyes were turned upon it in loving and ardent devotion. We heard a great deal at that time about 'thinking bayonets.' The bayonets did not think, nor did those who carried them. They did what was more to the purpose — they felt. The emergency did not call for thought, but for faith and courage, and both were there in abundance. The political reptiles hid away, or pretended to change their nature, and for a time the malarious air was purged as by a thunder-storm.

[1] Letter to the *Boston Daily Advertiser*, July, 1863.

Peace brought a change. Questions intricate and difficult, demanding brains more than hearts, and discretion more than valor, took the place of the simple alternative, to be or not to be. The lion had had his turn, and now the fox, the jackal, and the wolf, took theirs. Every sly political trickster, whom the storm had awed into obscurity, now found his opportunity. The reptiles crawled out again, multiplied, and infested caucuses, conventions, and Congress. But the people were the saddest spectacles; the same people that had shown itself so heroic in the hour of military trial, were now perplexed, bewildered, tossed between sense and folly, right and wrong, taking advice of mountebanks, and swallowing their filthy nostrums. The head of Demos was as giddy as his heart had been strong." [1]

Parkman felt that the corruption of our political life presented another danger of the greatest magnitude, and that it must be energetically opposed by civil service reform.

"There is no hope," he said, "but in purging and strengthening the republic. The remedy must be slow, not rash and revolutionary. A debased and irresponsible suffrage is at the bottom of the evil, but the state is sick of diseases that do not directly and immediately spring from this source. Something is due to the detestable maxim that to the victor belongs the spoils, and the fatuity that makes office the reward of party service, demands incessant rotation, dismisses the servant of the public as soon as he has learned to serve well, prefers

[1] *Failure of Universal Suffrage,* p. 10.

the interests of a needy politician to the interests of the whole people, sets a premium on trickery and discourages faithful industry. When the scraps and marrow-bones of office are flung down to be scrambled for, the dogs are sure to get the lion's share."[1]

But the immediate evil of vitally injuring the public service is small as compared with the general moral and intellectual ruin it causes. In this regard he was concerned not only for the national conscience and standard of duty, but especially for the higher education and development of character in the cultured class. He said:

"While the faculties that win material success are spurred to the utmost, and urged to their strongest development, those that find their exercise in the higher fields of thought and action are far from being so. For minds that mere wealth and mere notoriety cannot satisfy, the inducements are weak and the difficulties great. The slow but ominous transfer of power from superior to inferior types of men, as shown in city councils, legislatures, and Congress, has told with withering effect on the growth of true political ability. Debased as our politics are, they do not invite, and hardly even admit, the higher and stronger faculties to a part in them. Liberal education is robbed of its best continuance and consummation, and in so far as it is shut out from that noblest field of human effort, the direction of affairs of state."[2]

His deep sense of civic duty made him call on young men of worth and culture to undertake our political regeneration:

[1] *Failure of Universal Suffrage*, p. 12. [2] *Ibid.*, p. 17.

"Here, then, is a career worthy of the best, for none but they can grapple with the complicated mischiefs of our politics. Those gallant youths, and others such as they, who were so ready to lay down life for their country, may here find a strife more difficult and not less honorable. If there is virtue in them for an effort so arduous, then it is folly to despair. If a depraved political system sets them aside in favor of meaner men, and denies them the career to which the best interests of the nation calls them, then let them attack this depraved system, and, in so doing, make a career of their own. The low politician is not a noble foe, but he is strong and dangerous enough to make it manly to fight him ; and the cause of his adversary is the cause of the people, did they but know it ; or at least of that part of the people that is worth the name. No doubt, the strife is strangely unequal ; for on one side are ranged all the forces of self-interest, always present and always active ; and on the other only duty and patriotism. But if the virtue and reason of the nation can be as well organized as its folly and knavery are organized to-day, a new hope will rise upon us, and they who can achieve such a result will not lack their reward." [1]

Patriots, then, were the men for whom Parkman had the greatest admiration, and Washington stood at their head. This grand figure should be the beau-ideal of American youth; and in his estimation one of the worst results of the Rebellion was the relative obscurity into which it had cast Washington by exalting others of less worth. Hamilton came second

[1] *Failure of Universal Suffrage*, p. 19.

only to Washington. Franklin was "a great man," and admirable in many ways, but too thrifty and materialistic. Jefferson he disliked exceedingly for his sentimental following of the French democracy; Jean-Jacques Rousseau was "a depraved and half crazy man of genius." He came at last to admire Lincoln, though thinking him generally over-rated, — a man whose undeniable worth and usefulness were due to circumstances more than to inherent ability. Sumner he considered as not only sentimental, but deficient in courage and manliness: Garrison and Phillips also won little admiration from him.

Parkman's political ambition for the nation embodied his broadest and highest aspirations. As might be expected from his practical and simple way of taking all questions, his creed was short and simple:

"My political faith," he wrote, "lies between two vicious extremes, democracy and absolute authority, each of which I detest the more because it tends to reach into the other. I do not object to a good constitutional monarchy, but prefer a conservative republic, where intelligence and character, and not numbers hold the reins of power." [1]

And again:

"Our safety is in the development and use of the statesmanship latent among us, and long kept latent by the

[1] Letter to Abbé H. R. Casgrain, May 9, 1875.

perverted action of our political machinery. . . . 'Let the best rule' is the maxim of aristocracy; 'let the best serve' is the maxim of the only healthful and permanent democracy. Who are the best? They are gone; their race has died out. Surely as effect follows cause, for a half century they have withered and dwindled away. The race, we mean of legislators and statesmen, minds trained to apply great principles to practice, to grapple with great affairs, to guide the nation with a wise and temperate vigor along the giddy heights of that grand destiny which awaited her, and perhaps awaited her in vain. When will such men return? When a deep and abiding sense of our deep need of them has seized and possessed the national heart, when the fallacies that have deluded us so long shall be thrown from us as debasing and perilous illusions, and the national mind rises to a true conception of republican freedom." [1]

The saviours of civilization were thus to be leaders of ability and worth, men who could direct the masses with wisdom, successfully oppose both selfish demagogues and selfish capitalists, serve the nation as civic officials, warriors, and statesmen, and raise the national ambition above mere material interests. He manifestly sketched his ideal of healthy national growth in thus speaking of England:

"Through centuries of striving she had advanced from stage to stage of progress, deliberate and calm, never breaking with her past, but making each fresh gain the base of a new success, enlarging popular liberties while

[1] Article in *Boston Daily Advertiser*, July, 1863.

bating nothing of that height and force of individual development which is the brain and heart of civilization." [1]

In 1862 he wrote this wise counsel for our own guidance, counsel that recent events and the passage of years only makes more valuable:

> "If the people will learn that no expansion of territory, no accumulation of wealth, no growth of population, can compensate for the decline of individual greatness, if they can learn to recognize the reality of superior minds, and to feel that they have need of them; to feel, too, that in rejecting and ignoring them they prepare the sure though gradual ruin of popular government, — that beneficent lesson would be cheaply bought by years of calamity and war."

Again at the close of his life and labors he sounded the same manly challenge, raised the same standard by which we shall be judged in the procession of races:

> "She [the United States] has tamed the savage continent, peopled the solitude, gathered wealth untold, waxed potent, imposing, redoubtable; and now it remains for her to prove, if she can, that the rule of the masses is consistent with the highest growth of the individual; that democracy can give the world a civilization as mature and pregnant, ideas as energetic and vitalizing, and types of manhood as lofty and strong, as any of the systems which it boasts to supplant." [2]

[1] *The Old Régime*, p. 451.
[2] *Montcalm and Wolfe*, vol. ii. p. 414.

2. Parkman, though much more friendly towards science than towards socialism, was even here not entirely in harmony with his times. We have seen that he favored the fullest development of this side of education, and that he enjoyed an observer's practical knowledge of those sciences which brought him into contact with nature. No doubt he would have gained a broader general knowledge of the subject had his culture not been so restricted by considerations of health. But in truth he cared more for exact knowledge and tangible things than for speculations as to the origin of things. Evolution, and the philosophical investigation that has influenced so profoundly the course of modern life, had but little interest for him. In all phases of citizenship he was still true to his character of historian, and viewed scientific thought as he did other things, as one of the forces affecting civilization. Here came in his idealism, qualifying his admiration of science with disapproval of many of her most notable achievements and most potent influences. He did not look to it alone for the regeneration of mankind.

He regarded the predominance of material interests in our national life as still another danger of great moment. Writing of our condition at the beginning of the Rebellion, he said:

"Luxury and commerce have sometimes emasculated a people naturally warlike. The former has injured us only partially, but the spirit of trade, in the excess of its predominance, has done us a widespread and deadly mischief. The morality of commerce has become confounded with universal morality, and the word 'honor,' to the minds of half of those who use it, means little but commercial honor. The pride of a good bargain has overborne the pride of manhood, and much that is vital to worth and nobleness is treated as illusory. So, from highest to lowest, this influence pervades this vigorous and practical race, courageous, indeed, as all roused and energetic peoples are, but not spurred to acts of courage by the same exacting and unanswerable demands which urge, on the one hand, ruder nations, and on the other, nations of a more balanced and normal civilization."[1]

He saw that "the intellectual growth of the country bears no proportion to its material progress." To give this idea a tangible illustration, we may quote the following passage written in 1875:

"That the present condition and prospects of American literature are not very flattering will hardly be denied. A score or more of years ago there seemed a fair hope that the intellectual development of the country would not be absolutely disproportioned to its material growth; but thus far the hope has not been fulfilled, and, relatively to our vast increase in wealth and population, the value, though not the volume of literary products is less than before. This proceeds, naturally enough, from several causes. The excitement of the war and the inflation of the currency, with the morbid stimulus it applied to trade and industry, were no doubt strong anti-literary influences; but a violent impulse had been given long before to all kinds of material activity by the discovery of

[1] Letter to *Boston Daily Advertiser*, June, 1863.

gold in California. Here, more than anywhere else, began that frenzy of speculation and that race for wealth which have created an atmosphere where the scholar and the thinker find it hard to breathe."[1]

In his diaries we read his regrets that the "Yankee spirit of improvement," in clearing the land of forest, should be "destroying the chief ornament of the country." This feeling led him almost to regret the spread of civilization over the continent, resulting in the extermination of the buffalo, the taming of the Indian, and the building of railroads. This Spartan sufferer had no weakness for luxuries; he liked simple, even primitive modes of life; preferring the saddle or canoe to the stage coach, and the latter to railway or steamboat. For all this, he was actually indifferent rather than antagonistic to modern improvements, accepting them as conveniences, without giving them any thought or admiration.

The material productions of science, however, roused a deeper feeling when viewed in their effects on our national life.

"Nor am I at all enthusiastic for the nineteenth century, many of the tendencies of which I deplore, while admiring much that it has accomplished. It is too democratic and too much given to the pursuit of material interests at the expense of intellectual and moral greatness which I hold to be the true [aim or end] and to which material progress should be but a means."[2] He depre-

[1] Review of Bancroft's *Native Races of the Pacific States,* in *North American Review*, January, 1875, p. 34.

[2] Letter to Abbé H. R. Casgrain, May 9, 1875.

cated our "overstrained and morbid activity, and incessant tension of nerves — the men in the struggles of active life, the women in the ambitions, anxieties, and worries of social existence."

He could not abide the acceptance of material prosperity as proof of our national greatness, and no one irritated him more than the man who regards them as the *summum bonum* of progress. A highly civilized man, he disliked the over-refinements and complexities of civilization. On the other hand, while he loved the wilderness and its adventures, and possessed the hardihood and courage of a Boone, he never would have led the life of an Indian, nor become even a frontiersman. Wealth, especially when concentrated in the hands of men deficient in culture and public spirit, inspired him with a certain suspicion. He condemned our popular admiration for the "self-made man" and the "practical man," had the keenest scent for vulgarity, crudeness, pretentiousness, exaggeration, and spread-eagleism, and the sharpest tongue to denounce them, attributing them to the ignorance and complacency born of undue material prosperity.

3. Of Parkman's religious opinions and feelings, to be dwelt on in a later chapter, it is sufficient to say here that his antagonism to all theological organizations and sectarian aims necessarily limited his influence on the public life of his generation. He had no interest whatever in the religious movements of his time, except a fear of the growing power of the

Roman Catholic Church, and of the proposed "peaceful conquest of New England" by the French Canadians under the leadership of priests.

On other questions of the day, it is interesting to note his clean-cut expressions of independent opinion. The latest extreme form of the so-called temperance movement he condemned as the "corrupting farce of a prohibition which does not prohibit, which in large communities does not prevent or even diminish drunkenness, but which is the fruitful parent of meanness, fraud, lying, and contempt of law."

His love for the wilderness and for certain types of wild men had no force in relation to the Indian question. He never approved of Penn's peace policy.

> "In fact, the benevolent and philanthropic view of the American savage is for those who are beyond his reach. It has never yet been held by any whose wives and children have lived in danger of his scalping-knife."[1]

The effort to educate Indians seemed to him to spoil them as wild men, at the same time failing to civilize them. The following passage is very characteristic of his love of justice and firmness in all the relations of life that were open to his vision:

> "A word touching our recent Indian policy. To suppose that presents, blandishments, kind treatment, even when not counteracted by fraud and lawlessness of white

[1] *Half Century*, vol. i. p. 215.

men, can restrain these banditti [the Apaches, Comanches, and other tribes of Arizona and New Mexico] from molesting travellers and settlers, is a mistake. Robbery and murder have become to them a second nature, and, as just stated, a means of living. The chief enemies of peace in the Indian country are the philanthropist, the politician, and the border-ruffian ; that is to say, the combination of soft words with rascality and violence. An Apache, a Comanche, or an Arapaho neither respects nor comprehends assurances of fraternal love. In most cases he takes them as an evidence of fear. The government whose emissaries caress him and preach to him, whose officials cheat him, and whose subjects murder him, is not likely to soothe him into the ways of peace. The man best fitted to deal with Indians of hostile dispositions is an honest, judicious, and determined soldier. To protect them from ruffians worse than themselves, strictly to observe every engagement, to avoid verbiage and speak on occasion with a decisive clearness absolutely free from sentimentality, to leave no promise and no threat unfulfilled, to visit every breach of peace with a punishment as prompt as circumstances will permit, to dispense with courts and juries, and substitute a summary justice, and to keep speculators and adventurers from abusing them — such means as these on the one hand, or extermination on the other, will alone keep such tribes as the Apaches quiet. They need an officer equally just and vigorous ; and our regular army can furnish such. They need an army more numerous than we have at present; and its business would be to restrain white men no less than Indians. They need in the executive a courage to which democracy and the newspaper sensation-monger are wofully adverse. Firmness, consistency, and justice are indispensable in dealing with dangerous Indians, and so far as we fail to supply them we shall fail of success. Attempts at conciliation will be worse than useless unless there is proof, manifest to their savage understanding, that such attempts do not proceed from weakness or fear."[1]

Feeling, as he did, that universal suffrage was a mistake, especially in a large and mixed population, he took great interest in the restriction of immigration in order to save our institutions from any further strain by a "muddy tide of ignorance rolled in upon us."

The anti-slavery question was by no means a burning one with him, although he recognized "the sound and earnest basis of this agitation." He said further:

"Some half century ago, a few devoted men began what seemed a desperate crusade against a tremendous national evil. American slavery has now passed into history. It died a death of violence, to our shame be it said; for the nation had not virtue, temperance, and wisdom enough, to abolish it peacefully and harmlessly; but it is dead."[2]

The war, however, aroused his utmost sympathy, as shown by the white-heat of his few contributions on the subject to the press. The Union was to be preserved at no matter what personal and national

[1] Review of Bancroft's *Native Races of the Pacific States,* in *North American Review,* January, 1875, p. 43.

[2] *Failure of Universal Suffrage,* p. 19.

cost. Moreover, he regarded martial traits as the most essential and fundamental virtues of a manly personality.

> "Since the world began, no nation has ever risen to a commanding eminence in the arts of peace, which has not at some period of its history, been redoubtable in war. And in every well-balanced development of nations, as of individuals, the warlike instinct and the military point of honor are not repressed and extinguished, but only refined and civilized. It belongs to the pedagogue, not to the philosopher, to declaim against them as relics of barbarism." These instincts, he further insisted, are "always strongest in the strongest and richest nature."[1]

Believing that the progress and stability of civilization depend on force, and despising what he called the "milksop" principle of turning the other cheek also, he was yet the last man to desire an unnecessary or an unjust war.

The woman suffrage movement is the only topic which Parkman treated in a spirit that would seem to require apology or explanation on the part of his biographer. This remark applies chiefly to the pamphlet entitled "Some of the Reasons against Woman Suffrage, printed at the request of an Association of Women." The fuller statement in his article in the "North American Review," October, 1879, is less open to criticism. It is quite unnecessary to our aim of portraiture to discuss his views, but his argument is of interest as a revelation of his mental traits.

[1] Letter to the *Boston Daily Advertiser*, June, 1863.

He thought that by the limitations and inabilities imposed on woman by sex and her maternal duties,

"God and nature had ordained that she shall not be forced to join in the harsh conflicts of the world militant;" that, considering the poor health of American women it is "cruel to add to the excitements which are wasting them other and greater excitements, and to cares too great for their strength other and greater cares. . . . To hold the man responsible and yet deprive him of power is neither just nor rational, for the man is the natural head of the family, he is responsible for its maintenance and order; hence he ought to control the social and business agencies which are essential to the successful discharge of the trust imposed upon him. . . . Woman suffrage must have one of two effects: if, as many of its advocates complain, women are subservient to men, and do nothing but what they desire, then woman suffrage will have no other result but to increase the power of the other sex; if on the other hand women vote as they see fit, without regarding their husbands, then unhappy marriages will be multiplied and divorces redoubled." The danger of "inconsiderate and rash legislation . . . would be increased immeasurably if the most impulsive and excitable half of humanity had an equal voice in the making of laws, and in the administration of them, — abstract right would then be made to prevail after a fashion somewhat startling." The better class of women, instead of controlling others, "will be outvoted in their own kitchens, without reckoning the agglomerations of poverty, ignorance, and vice, that form a startling proportion of our city populations; the female vote would enormously increase the evil, for it is often more numerous, always more impulsive and less subject to reason, and almost devoid of the sense of responsibility. Here the bad politician would find his richest resources. . . . It is not woman's virtues that would be prominent or influential in the political arena; they would shun it by an invincible repulsion; and the opposite qualities would be drawn into it. The Washington lobby has given us some means of judging what we may expect from the woman 'inside politics.' If politics are to be purified by artfulness, effrontery, insensibility, a pushing self-assertion, a glib tongue, then we may look for regeneration; for the typical female politician will be richly endowed with all these gifts, besides the potency of feminine charms aided by feminine wiles. The 'woman inside politics' will not fail to make use of an influence so subtle and strong, and of which the management is peculiarly suited to her talents. If she is not gifted with charms of her own, she will have no difficulty in finding and using others of her sex who are. Delilah has already spread her snares for the congressional Samson. . . . Woman suffragists have done nothing to prove their fitness for a share in government — not having produced a single sound and useful contribution to one side or the other of any question of current politics. . . . As the majority of women are averse to the suffrage" it should not be granted at the request of a minority of agitators. "All usages, laws, and institutions have risen and perished, and risen and perished again. Their history is the history of mutability itself. But from the earliest records of mankind down to this moment, in every race and every form or degree of civilization or barbarism, the relative position of the sexes has been essentially the same, with exceptions so feeble, rare and transient that they only prove the rule. Such permanence in the foundation of society, while all that rests upon it has passed from change to change, is proof in itself that this foundation lies deep in the essential nature of things;" that it is unreasonable to demand woman suffrage as a right. "Government by doctrines of abstract right, of which the French Revolution set the example and bore the fruits, involves enormous danger and injustice. No political right is absolute and of universal application. Each has its conditions, qualifications and limitations. . . . Rights may be real or unreal. Principles may be true or false; but even the best and truest cannot safely be pushed too far, or in the wrong direction. The principle of truth itself may be carried into absurdity. The saying is old that truth should not be spoken at all times; and those whom a sick conscience worries into habitual violation of the maxim are imbeciles and nuisances. . . . The voting of a large non-combatant class is dangerous to civil harmony." The "suffragists' idea of government is not practical, but utterly unpractical, not American but French. It is that government of abstractions and generalities which found its realization in the French Revolution, and its apostle in the depraved and half-crazy man of genius, Jean-Jacques Rousseau. . . . Out of the wholesome fruit of the earth, and the staff of life itself, the perverse chemistry of man distils deleterious vapors which, condensed and bottled, exalt his brain with glorious fantasies, and then leave him in the mud. So it is with the unhappy suffragists. From the sober words of our ancestors they extract the means of mental inebriety. . . . The question is, whether the persistency of a few agitators shall plunge us blindfold into the most reckless of all experiments; whether we shall adopt this supreme device for developing the defects of women, and demolish their real power to build an ugly mockery instead. For the sake of womanhood let us hope not. . . . In the full and normal development of womanhood lie the best interests of the world. Let us labor earnestly for it; and, that we may not labor in vain, let us save women from the barren perturbations of American politics. Let us respect them; and, that we may do so, let us pray for deliverance from female suffrage."

Both advocates and opponents felt that the general tone of this pamphlet did Parkman injustice. It does, indeed, surprise one by the absence of the impartiality and thoroughness of his historical works, by its lack of discrimination as to the different classes of woman suffragists, and by the roughness and discourtesy in some of its remarks on women. But his opinions and feelings as to woman, her development and her rights as a whole, are not to be confounded with his hatred and fear of woman suffrage. In all these matters his views were unconsciously influenced somewhat by his personal tastes; for here, as elsewhere, his preferences were distinct and strong, being quite opposed to the typical "strongminded" and oratorical woman. His social environment and family traditions supported his view of woman's limitations and his antipathy for everything connected with the agitation on her behalf. This pamphlet brought upon him some sharp criticism; but he thus recorded his indifference to such attacks:

"I am occupied as usual with historical matters, varied with other avocations, including (in a literary way) some reviews that have brought as I expected, a beehive about my ears, or rather several beehives, or waspnests, composed of ultramontane catholics, ultra democrats, and woman suffragists. Though their buzzing is great and furious, I do not yet find that they sting."[1]

The other side of his attitude towards woman's functions and rights is plain for those who knew him; but the stranger who should read only this pamphlet might easily be misled as to his total view on this question. The exigencies of an argument which had to be brought into small compass probably constrained him to dwell rather on the incapacities of women than on their abilities and worth. He does express here and there, however, his aims and hopes for women in no uncertain terms; and his demands are both fundamental and far-reaching. Here is his general estimate of their importance in civilization:

"They can, if they will, create and maintain higher standards of thought and purpose, raise the whole tone of national life, and give our civilization the fulness that it lacks; for if they raise themselves they will infallibly raise the men with them."

He believed that the hope of civilization rests upon the most perfect discharge of the maternal functions, that early marriages and large families are most

[1] To B. A. Gould, Feb. 1, 1880.

desirable, and that the home duties of a woman leave little time for any other labors. His friendships with noble women, and their devotion to him, are unquestionable proofs of his chivalric appreciation. What can a man say stronger than this: "Truth itself would seem hardly worth the pursuit if women were not in the world."

In examining Parkman's attitude towards these topics of the times, we have seen something of his intellectual traits; but perhaps we may still pursue this subject for a moment, to get a more intimate glimpse of his general spirit and moral sensibilities. He differed from many writers of his time in having a definite philosophy of civilization. The *laissez-aller* policy was completely foreign to him. His philosophy and hopes of civilization were based on his dominant traits so fully discussed in this book, and his philosophy of life. He took all questions simply and directly, seeking always the practical, positive and exact. He was strongly opposed to many elements of philanthropic reform, and could not accept, either for himself or others, any project that put into the second rank the virtues of independence, industry, and honesty. Indeed he opposed himself so bluntly and broadly to all philanthropic reforms and their advocates as almost to appear indifferent to the welfare of the race. The isolation in which he was compelled to live may have had something to do with this habitual mode of thought; for few men of equal eminence ever had so little personal or intellectual contact with the liberal leaders of their time. As heredity made him stronger in antipathies than in admirations and sympathies, he was necessarily a severe critic of life. His own asperity was hateful to him, but he could not cut loose from that side of his nature. Helped by the warmth of personal contact and friendship, we find him judging men charitably and generously; but in the absence of this humane influence he was neither charitable nor generous. He did not take at their best either causes or champions that he disapproved; on the contrary, his keen eye never failed to find some personal weakness in a reformer, some false assumption or some exaggeration; and he held this up to view with caustic humor. Excepting a vile politician, no one repelled him more than a reformer marked by extreme views and eccentric conduct. Those from whom he differed in questions of life and morals often got themselves characterized as "fools." It seems but just to point out that Parkman's controversial papers offer the only exception to the kindliness and urbanity of his manners. Those of his readers who feel that he was lacking in courtesy and fairness, will understand him better if they remember the continual inward pressure under which he wrote.

A sense of civic duty made him ride hard against idealists and reformers. He considered that transcendentalism was weakening to common-sense and dangerous to practical aims. "The ideal reformer," said he, "is generally a nuisance when he tries to deal with the broad and many-sided questions involved in the government of nations."

But with all his vehemence Parkman made no personal enemies; he was too considerate to talk of people lightly, and he despised gossip; his censure, even the most energetic, was not only free from any mean or personal motives, but made distinctly for the elevation of life and character.

Parkman combined two sharply opposed beings, — a conservative and a liberal. In the firmness of his conservatism he might be likened to a statue; but the marble was aglow with a fiery zeal for growth. In him conservatism was the resistant medium which brought his spirit to expression, defining his aspirations nearly as well as direct statements of liberalism would have done. Environment, moreover, had done little for a not very elastic nature. So he continued to live, with his usual loyalty and persistence, faithful to the traditions of his family and community. His capacity for culture may be thought to have failed in giving him breadth of sympathy in citizenship; nevertheless, it was effective even while not changing the lines of his hopes for humanity. It could have been no common conservatism that mastered a man of such courage and initiative, shown not by ventures but by opposition to ventures. He instinctively regarded changes as evils. And yet, despite the historical cast of his mind, his conservatism was unpoetized by any sentimental regard for tradition; an idea did not attract him because of its antiquity but because of the truth it contained. Though pessimistic he was not a pessimist in the depressing, philosophic sense; his pessimism sprang from doubts not of divine but of democratic wisdom; while especially hating what he stigmatized as "the senseless optimism which leads so many Americans to imagine that all will go well in the end, whatever they may do or fail to do; and that our Ship of State cannot be wrecked, whether the crew do their duty or not,"[1] he recognized that "Faith is indispensable to all achievement; but it must not quarrel with common sense, nor walk with eyes shut." He was a fighting, inspiring pessimist, always ready to lead even a forlorn hope. His essential liberality was no less real because of its confinement to certain lines. While his bugbear was the levelling-down tendencies of modern democratic institutions, his hopes of civilization were unshakable, standing on the worth of the individual citizen. His liberality was intensely earnest in desiring whatever favors the growth of character. With his love of nature — not stopping at the edge of the forest — he wished people to enjoy the utmost freedom for growth, each according to his individual capacities.

Parkman's hopes, then, rested on good birth, the best culture, the subordination of materialism, and the leadership of worthy statesmen. For these things he worked with all the enthusiasm of his nature, along the lines of a conservative and high-minded student of history and of life.

[1] *Our Common Schools*, p. 1.

Part III

SPIRITUAL GROWTH

CHAPTER XII

PARKMAN'S greatest triumph was not the writing of books, but the self-command acquired in remoulding his nature to his conditions. For the peculiar conditions of his nervous system made everything depend upon the issue, — not only the execution of his literary project, but also his physical health, his sanity, life itself. This contest involved all the forces of his being; it showed the most striking traits of his character; it occasioned the most impressive experiences of his career; it moulded his daily life; it modified his spiritual and intellectual growth; and it determined to a certain degree the methods, limits, and qualities of his work. I am therefore reluctantly compelled to ignore his distaste for even the mention of his personal health, and give some space to its consideration.

Self-mastery was doubly necessary, both from the nature of his maladies and from the need of extreme caution in using whatever strength they left him. He literally had to remake himself.

Parkman was a pathetic figure to those who knew his life, though nothing could be farther from his wishes than to appear in any such character. Let us rehearse for a moment the advantages of his career, which made this pathos the more striking. He had a boundless ambition, and his equipment for its fulfilment was all that could be desired. Birth and fortune had united to give him all the advantages derivable from a good social position; he had discovered the bent of his tastes and gifts at a very early age, and followed them closely with zeal and intelligence; he had directed his own education with the utmost economy of forces to secure the special culture needed for his chosen labors; travel had bestowed inestimable opportunities for observing life and character; the stimulus of public appreciation coming early had spurred him on to complete achievement; domestic circumstances enabled him to devote himself wholly to his work; he had the help of a great theme that entirely commanded his sympathies, and focussed all his powers throughout life on a field of definite extent; finally, he possessed in generous measure the moral and intellectual qualities needed for the execution of his task. It would seem that nothing could have been lacking in the happy prospect opened before him.

But almost from the start his progress was made difficult, even dangerous, by shadows about him as strong as the light above. He soon became not only unable to use his eyes with safety, but he was weakened by sufferings that would have paralyzed the powers and courage of most men. "The enemy," like his Iroquois, often held him prisoner, and measured out to him with pitiless atrocity just as much torture as he could endure. Parkman never talked of these trials; he hardly more than hints at them in his autobiographic paper, to which he confided more than he ever said to even his most intimate friends. Our only way of realizing the strain he successfully bore is to note the strength of the faculties opposed by his infirmities. We shall see that nearly every fundamental tendency of his nature was refused its normal action by physical and mental conditions of the most exasperating and discouraging kind. These deep-reaching privations touched the very heart of the vigorous man, the social friend, and the ambitious author. His personal inner life for a long while lacked, to a painful degree, the unity and harmony that marked so strongly his literary career.

Some of Parkman's strongest characteristics were not shown in early youth. His teacher described him as a "quiet, gentle, and docile boy;" this general character, so opposed to his subsequent mercurial activity, may have been due to his lack of abounding health at that time. Patience was not one of his natural traits. Nor was he more truthful and magnanimous than the average boy of his community. We must note another youthful tendency, and one that was not curbed until his moral sense had gained the fullest development: a domineering spirit. This tendency was more an expression of his independence of judgment and force of will, than any mere disposition to tyrannize or command. A masterful spirit at all periods of his life, he never interfered with the freedom of others, or followed petty aims or personal gratifications. Without this quality of strength and mastery he could not have reached his goal; and he seems never to have allowed even its defects to grow beyond the clearest and most imperative needs of his condition and work.

As we often have occasion to say, Parkman's ruling ideal was manliness. It is not easy to give the fullest impression of this quality as expressed in him. It was more of the intellectual and physical or martial type than of the spiritual. Yet fate denied him physical activity and called upon him for the utmost strength of many spiritual qualities. He has told us that his first boyish fancy was "for a life of action and death in battle," and we know that the severest disappointment of his life was his inability to enter the army during our civil war. Rarely in his books does he give any expression to his own feelings and tastes, but he revealed one of the deepest recesses of his nature in speaking, in "The Jesuits," of Maisonneuve, — "The religion which animated him had not destroyed the soldierly pride which takes root so readily and so strongly in a manly nature."

Many of Parkman's traits of mind and character were distinctly those of a soldier. He liked a fight for its own sake, and for the energy, courage, and strength it called forth. Especially did he warm to it if the triumph of justice and freedom were helped thereby. He showed particular pleasure when his little granddaughter beat off two ruffian boys who tried to take a sled from one of her playmates. He never forgave the Quakers for refusing to fight the Indians and defend the country. A newspaper article by him contains the following:

> "In every well-balanced development of nations as of individuals, the warlike instinct and the military point of honor are not repressed and extinguished, but only refined and civilized. It belongs to the pedagogue, not to the philosopher, to declaim against them as relics of barbarism."

He loved the experiences and the objective elements of a military life, — the activity, the adventure, hardship, danger. In a larger view of his mental attitude, his papers on Suffrage show that he counted a great deal on physical force in government; by his temperament and his study of history, he naturally exalted war to a very important rôle in civilization. Moreover, he regarded war as a valuable aid in the development of personal and national character. I do not recall in his writing any recognition of its evil effects on men. Despite all this, however, we cannot find in him any admiration for the bully or the "jingo."

But Parkman's nature had even more of the militant than these feelings and opinions would indicate.

Many of his talents fitted him especially for a martial career. In the first place, he possessed in their greatest force five of the most fundamental requisites of a commander: practical wisdom, energy, courage, prudence, and intellectual power. His love of order and his spirit as shown in self-discipline, promised well for the discipline of an army. Thanks to his exceptional judgment of men, he would have been most capable in selecting subordinates. Although without the overflowing personal magnetism that quickly wins popularity on the largest scale and infuses the masses with enthusiasm, yet he had the dignity, the ability, and the genial sincerity that win friendship and inspire at last the fullest confidence of a people. As for the tenacity and firmness of purpose required to follow a plan to its ultimate issue, no one could give more unquestionable assurance.

When the civil war caused him to look up from his books, Parkman longed for a chance to serve his country and try his hand. Unable to go to the war himself, he gave vent to his feelings by showing a keen interest in young men who could go, and by writing, now and then, for the press a piece that glowed with the fire and elevation of his patriotism. He always remembered with bitterness his inability, and closed his autobiography with an expression of this disappointment, in words that suggest a deeper meaning for himself than a reference to the needs of the hour: "Irksome," he said, as may have been his infirmities, they were "far less oppressive than the necessity they involved of being busied with the past when the present has claims so urgent, and holding the pen with a hand that should have grasped the sword."

His love of action always pulled against his love of study. Such seemingly incompatible passions are rarely seen together in such force. Even in his college days, while still in good health and much interested in physical culture, he was remarked as a man of retirement and industry, a reserved, brooding student, who seldom invited any one to his room, and at the same time an impetuous, social youth. But action was his first instinctive mode of expression, his chief pleasure in life. And it was, moreover, a kind of abnormal, physical necessity, as well as a propensity of his mind. An incident of the Oregon Trail journey shows this trait very plainly. One night when Tête Rouge came to the tent and said that Indians were stealing the horses, Parkman seized his rifle and rushed out, erect as a target, instead of following the more cautious tactics usual with men of the prairies. He did so, not because he was ignorant of the risk, but, having a courage utterly indifferent to danger, he followed his first and strongest impulse. Idleness and confinement were therefore the hardest experience life could impose. Every fibre of the man recoiled from such an existence, and he abominated the spirit of resignation. He tells of the trial in these words to a friend, written in 1849:

"From a complete and ample experience of both, I can bear witness that no amount of physical pain is so intolerable as the position of being stranded, and doomed to lie rotting for year after year. However, I have not yet abandoned any plan which I ever formed, and I have no intention of abandoning any."

The tension of the strain put upon him is well told by Vassall Morton when confined in an Austrian dungeon, p. 208:

"It is but a weak punishment to which Milton dooms his ruined angel. Action, enterprise, achievement, — a hell like that is heaven to the cells of Ehrenberg. He should have chained him to a rock, and left him alone to the torture of his own thoughts; the unutterable agonies of a mind preying on itself for want of other sustenance. Action! mured in this dungeon, the soul gasps for it as the lungs for air. Action, action, action! — all in all! What is life without it? A marsh, a quagmire, a rotten, stagnant pool. It is its own reward. The chase is all; the prize nothing."

And how personal are his reflections on the prospect of no escape from his misfortunes:

"Yet it is something that I can still find heart to face my doom; that there are still moments when I dare to meet this death-in-life, this slow-consuming horror, face to face, and look into all its hideousness without shrinking. To creep on to my end through years of slow decay, mind and soul famishing in solitude, sapped and worn, eaten and fretted away, by the droppings of lonely thought, till I find my rest at last under these cursed stones!"

The passage is only too intimate and painful to any one who knows Parkman's experience and character. Yet there was no melancholy in his temperament, and his consequent cheerfulness sweetened his fortitude.

Parkman's love of study was second only to his love of action. Lowell saw deeply into his nature in speaking of his "aptitude for culture." And Parkman undoubtedly recognized his own gifts and tendencies very clearly; he makes the woman who has the most insight and knowledge of Vassall Morton say to him (p. 372), "You seem to me a person with a singular capacity of growth. You push forth fibres into every soil, and draw nutriment from sources most foreign to you." His weakness of eyes and brain were thus one of the hardest spiritual trials he could meet. And they must have been particularly exasperating in his special pursuit, for historical research is hunting the needle in a haystack.

But strong as was his love of study, the social tendencies, too, had their way. He was never a recluse in spirit, but derived the most beneficial stimulus from society, being specially sensitive to the charms of women. It was no light matter for this virile man, this social being, this hater of asceticism, to be so often restricted to the privations of a monastic rule.

Those of us who knew him only in the latter part

of his life, when he had been reduced to habits of quietude, find it difficult to realize the full force of his ardor. The quiet, reserved manner, the firm stand on common sense, the conservative prudence in all things, the serene self-command in daily life might well deceive even a close observer. His repression of native impetuosity was the more remarkable since this trait was reinforced by great nervous irritability, and this again increased by continued insomnia. After ill health had denied him freedom in exercise, his excess of vital force could find vent only in outbursts of strong language. Mr. Frothingham said of him:

> "Again and again he had to restrain the impulse to say vehement things, or to do violent deeds without the least provocation, but he maintained so absolutely his moral self-control that none but the closest observer would notice any deviation from the most perfect calm and serenity."

Nervousness was never allowed to pass into external agitation, or the irritability seen in so many high-strung and able men. Parkman spared himself and others such waste of vitality and of peace. Fortitude guided by common sense certainly proved his salvation, in enabling him to plan his labors, husband his forces, regulate his habits of living, and make possible the execution of his work. Few men have been so severely tested and have shown these virtues raised to so high a power. His fortitude seems to have been equal to any emergency. Perhaps it received early stimulus from the many examples of endurance he met in the study of his historical personages, — the Indian singing his death-song throughout mortal tortures, the missionary meeting martyrdom with enthusiasm, the endurance of the heroic Jogues, La Salle, and many others.

Parkman's philosophy of life should be included in this account of his basic qualities and their relation to his experience. The average man can live from day to day, blindly obedient to his instincts or ambitions, long before he sees his ideal and grasps it. He is the common sailor, feeling no responsibility beyond the hour of his watch. But a man of Parkman's self-commanding nature must have a port of destination and a compass for directing his course. Referring to his labors as related to his health, he said: "Under the most favorable conditions, it was a slow and doubtful navigation, beset with reefs and breakers, demanding a constant lookout and a constant throwing of the lead." These words are more or less applicable to the dangers he was likely to meet in his mental and moral growth. What could a man do, destined to such a voyage under such clouds and storms, without a beckoning ideal above the mists!

And what was Parkman's philosophy of life? We ask the question with eagerness, but we cannot hope to get complete satisfaction in the matter. His habitual reserve kept him from talking on a subject so intimate; and the only written statement of his philosophy is this passage from his diary of 1846, written at St. Louis, just before starting on the Oregon Trail journey. "The true philosophy of life is to seize with a ready and strong hand all the good in it, and to bear its inevitable evils as calmly and carelessly as may be." This creed, in its general lightness of tone, is not quite in accord with his life and character taken as a whole; but it was probably true to his hopes and aims in the full vigor and freedom of youth. We cannot help observing, however, that it points somewhat away from his self-sacrificing devotion to duty, and sounds a false note in regard to his earnestness. He took life too seriously, albeit calmly, to allow of any carelessness, even at that age. Yet the profession is interesting as furnishing us with his moral starting-point in youth.

The whole aspect of life changed a few years later, when disease had fastened upon him, bringing so much pain and such discouraging obstacles to the attainment of his ambition. But there is no evidence that he added anything to his earliest creed excepting a greater emphasis of endurance. He sat down in his study to his trials and labors with a clenched fist and a set jaw, and took as his motto "Grin and bear it." This motto expressed fully the grimness of his experience and the resistant force of his manhood. Thenceforth it remained his essential philosophy of life, though in later years it was refined by the development of a gentler spirit. The next glimpse we have of his inward feelings was given me by a friend who remembered a conversation with him on shipboard while crossing the Atlantic in 1858. Parkman then expressed a perfect conviction that happiness is not to be expected in this world. Nothing was said of the hereafter. The last evidence of his philosophic standpoint is furnished by a remark made only a year or two before his death. Reading the Thoughts of M. Aurelius Antoninus, he said: "That's about as good a philosophy of life as you can get." This passing remark was taken as an unusual confidence by the daughter to whom he spoke, and from him it indeed meant volumes. Mr. Frothingham said: "The Stoics never had a nobler disciple than Francis Parkman." This is very true in many ways, yet not in all. Parkman must have had little interest in the theories and abstractions on which the Stoics established their physical, theological, and ethical principles, though he found himself at home in the solid elements of their purely practical morality. He was closest to them in his love of their four cardinal virtues, — "wisdom, or the knowledge of good and evil; justice, or the giving to every man his due; fortitude, or the enduring of labor and pain; and temperance, which is moderation in all things." He eagerly accepted their large conception that the end of man is to live in conformity with nature, but was utterly opposed to some of their chief aims. Just because he agreed that we should conform to nature, he probably denied that we should be indifferent to pleasure and pain, and despised any man for being or trying to be devoid of passion. To him feeling was the central force in character. Instead, then, of accepting the passive theory that all things in life are governed by unavoidable necessity, he believed in free will and the power of men to shape events. By all his chiefest virtues he was more Spartan than Stoic.

Parkman apparently derived little or no support from religion in his struggle for self-mastery. None of his writings contain any expression of religious aspirations or reflections; he was a stranger to religious emotion, so far as we can judge; and he never ceased to be more or less in antagonism towards the clergy in general, towards all theological organizations, towards the spiritual elements of life and character, even taken independently of any religious method of culture. Mr. Frothingham says:

"Parkman belonged rather to the ethical than to the spiritual order of men, — those who are so admirably described by Rev. James Martineau in his discourse on the 'Christian Doctrine of Merit.' 'Till somebody has a conscience, nobody can feel a law. Accordingly, we everywhere meet with a higher order of men, who not only comprehend the wishes, but respect the rights of others; who are ruled, not by expectation without, but by the sense of obligation within; who do, not the agreeable, but the just; and even amid the storm of public rage, can stand fast with rooted foot and airy brow, like the granite mountain in the sea. Noble, however, as this foundation of uprightness always is, there may arise from it a self-estimate too proud and firm. If the stern consciousness of personal worth have no kindling of diviner aspiration, it will give the lofty sense of personal merit that makes the stoic and misses the saint. We do nothing well till we know our worth; nothing best till we forget it.'"

Parkman was more a man of action and observation than of worship, — at any shrine whatsoever, whether that of nature, art, humanity, or religion. He would thus naturally remain on the outskirts, mostly a spectator of religious movements. And yet there was a religious side to his nature. It may be said that he moved on with his times in religious opinions. He was one of many distinguished New Englanders, descendants of clergymen, who in their personal development went through the same religious evolution that has been seen in society. Parkman began with the early Unitarian opinions found in Channing; then he embraced the more natural and manly religion of Parker; and he ended in the agnosticism that makes it impossible to subscribe to any definite statement regarding the Unknown. His attitude is shown by this bit of intimate conversation with his sister Eliza. One day when they were rowing on Jamaica Pond she said: "If I should be asked about your religious beliefs, it seems to me I might say that you are a reverent Agnostic." "Yes, that 's about it."

He gave a fuller statement in the following letter,

Francis Parkman.

From a Photograph taken about 1865.

written in September, 1887, on the reception of a book entitled "The Safe Side":

"The opinion that Christ was not a person of superhuman origin has been embraced of late years by many thoughtful men and has been discussed in many places, sometimes by writers with knowledge and reflection, and sometimes by those indifferently provided with either. It seems to me that the world has outgrown the dogmatic part of Christianity which has certainly been the source of misery enough in the past — especially the doctrine of exclusive salvation which is the main source of persecution.

"But when one compares Christianity on its ethical side with all other religious systems, with the partial exception of Buddhism, one cannot but feel that whether we believe in its supernatural origin or not, it is to be accepted with a reverent gratitude as a vast boon to mankind."

It is evident that his interest in religion was limited chiefly to its ethics. He very rarely refers to religion in his books, even in the history of Canada, which turns so largely on this element. We find no more than a bare reference to it now and then, — as "the great principles of Christian truth,"[1] or "that principle of self-abnegation which is the life of true religion, and which is vital, no less, to the highest forms of heroism."[2] Here we catch the personal note, the reflection of his ideal and his experience.

Despite his agnosticism, however, and although

[1] *The Jesuits*, p. 146. [2] *Ibid.*, p. 109.

there is no writing to support the opinion, I think he believed in the government of the universe by a power that directs life continually to better ends. He said in a letter, "My faith, such as it is, is strong and earnest;"[1] and he is reported as believing that the possibilities of a future life were a sufficient motive for striving to develop the best possible character.

It may be interesting now to glance at his philosophy from the opposite standpoint, and see it crystallized in practical virtues. In the following passage, summing up the qualities of his ideal hero, Vassall Morton,[2] he also presents to any one who knew Parkman an autobiographic sketch of the most impressive and touching veracity.

> "Manhood, the proudest of all possessions to a man, is that unflinching quality, which, strong in generous thought and high purpose, bears onward towards its goal, knowing no fear but the fear of God; wise, prudent, calm, yet daring and hoping all things; not dismayed by reverses, nor elated by success, never bending nor receding; wearying out ill fortune by undespairing constancy; unconquered by pain or sorrow, or deferred hope; fiery in attack, steadfast in resistance, unshaken in the front of death; and when courage is vain, and hope seems folly, when crushing calamity presses it to the earth, and the exhausted body will no longer obey the still undaunted mind, then putting forth its hardest, saddest heroism, the unlaurelled heroism of endurance, patiently biding its time."

[1] To Abbé Casgrain, Feb. 13, 1868. [2] P. 362.

To the student of his life the most interesting writing left by the historian is a fragment of an autobiographic letter written in 1868 to his friend the late Dr. George E. Ellis. Parkman was going abroad for medical advice and historical research. His health was such that he feared he might not be spared to complete his series of works. He then wrote this paper, sealed it up, and inscribed it "Not to be used during my life." The following note inclosed with it explains some of the motives from which the paper sprang:

50 Chestnut St., 28 Nov. 1868.

My dear Friend, — Running my eye over this paper, I am more than ever struck with its egoism, which makes it totally unfit for any eye but that of one in close personal relations with me.

It resulted from a desire — natural, perhaps, but which may just as well be suppressed — to make known the extreme difficulties which have reduced to very small proportions what might otherwise have been a good measure of achievement. Having once begun it, I went on with it, though convinced that it was wholly unsuited to see the light.

Physiologically considered, the case is rather curious. My plan of life from the first was such as would have secured great bodily vigor in nineteen cases out of twenty, and was only defeated in its aim by an inborn irritability of constitution which required gentler treatment than I gave it. If I had my life to live over again, I would follow exactly the same course again, only with less vehemence. Very cordially,

F. Parkman.

The autobiographical fragment is considered by some of his friends to be a regrettable production. They think it gives an impression of morbidness quite foreign to the writer's nature and presence; and they regret the publication of such intimate details of his physical and mental condition. The paper reflects the self-consciousness and introspection common to New Englanders. Both Puritan repression and Southern impulse contended for the control of this man's pen. But the morbidness comes from the facts related and the inevitable apprehensions of the hour, rather than from any morbidness of temperament. As for the personal details, they were much better explained by his own hand than by any other; besides, they were quite indispensable to one of his aims in writing the paper, namely, to make known the gravity of the difficulties that had so retarded the progress of his work, and that might prevent its completion. For it may be noted that he had abstained from making any appeal to the sympathy of the public, to its lenience in judging his work, on the score of his infirmities; these are barely hinted at in a preface or two, as an explanation of the delays in publishing the successive volumes of his series. The paper is largely a pathological document that he believed might be of use in the future. We must admit, however, that it seems somewhat out of keeping with his general reserve, and his strong distaste for any approach to the egotistic. And there is to be noted the additional fact that he wrote a second paper in 1886 of the same character; this one he wished to be given, after his death, to the Massachusetts Historical Society. With his remarkable memory it is hardly possible that he could have forgotten the existence of the first one. Perhaps he regarded its preservation in any private hands as less certain than in the archives of this Society. These papers seem to me to have had still another source in a motive very natural to a man of his pride and integrity. He desired, in case of not being spared to finish his task, to make sure of his clearance from the slightest suspicion of having done less than his utmost. At all events, we may be thankful for so full a note of his personality and inner experiences. Still another word may preface it. His most insidious enemy was brain trouble. His physician in Paris, the most noted specialist of his day, had said that he might go insane, and that his cure was extremely doubtful. The wisdom of making known this diagnosis to the patient has been questioned; but it was perhaps the only course, in view of the precautions that had to be an important element of his daily life. In his autobiography he speaks of these medical opinions and his danger in the jocose way frequent with him in mentioning even his worst condition. But the matter inevitably weighed at times upon his mind. He occasionally expressed wonder at not going insane with so much nervous exhaustion from insomnia; and he asked one or two intimate literary friends to watch for signs of mental disorder in his writings. His French physicians were all the more justified in their apprehensions by their ignorance of the New England character. They could not conceive of a man with a will and a power of self-control equal to any trial, however severe or protracted.

Although we have made several extracts from this production, its importance justifies us in presenting it now entire. When the package of posthumous manuscript was opened, it lacked the first seven pages, which for some reason Parkman had decided to reserve. The story begins abruptly thus:

"Allusion was made at the outset to obstacles which have checked the progress of the work, if the name of obstacles can be applied to obstructions at times impassable and of such a nature that even to contend against them would have been little else than an act of self-destruction. The case in question is certainly an exceptional one; but as it has analogies with various other cases, not rare under the stimulus of our social and material influences, a knowledge of it may prove of use. For this as for other reasons, the writer judges it expedient to state it in full, though in doing so much personal detail must needs be involved.

"His childhood was neither healthful nor buoyant. His boyhood though for a time active, was not robust, and at the age of eleven or twelve he conceived a vehement liking for pursuits, a devotion to which at that time of life far oftener indicates a bodily defect than a mental superiority. Chemical experiment was his favorite hobby, and he pursued it with a tenacious eagerness which, well guided, would have led to some acquaintance with the rudiments of the science, but which in fact served little other purpose than injuring him by confinement, poisoning him with noxious gases, and occasionally scorching him with some ill-starred explosion.[1]

"The age of fifteen or sixteen produced a revolution. At that momentous period of life retorts and crucibles were forever discarded, and an activity somewhat excessive took the place of voluntary confinement. A new passion seized him, which, but half gratified, still holds its force. He became enamoured of the woods, — a fancy which soon gained full control over the course of literary pursuits to which he was also addicted. After the usual boyish phases of ambitious self-ignorance, he resolved to confine his homage to the Muse of History, as being less apt than her wayward sisters to requite his devotion with a mortifying rebuff. At the age of eighteen the plan which he is still attempting to execute was, in its most essential features, formed. His idea was clear before him, yet attended with unpleasant doubts as to his ability to realize it to his own satisfaction. To solve

[1] In the second paper he gave some additional facts in regard to his childhood. He there writes: "At eight years I was sent to a farm belonging to my maternal grandfather, on the outskirts of the extensive tract of wild and rough woodland now called Middlesex Fells. I walked twice a day to a school of high but undeserved reputation, about a mile distant, in the town of Medford. Here I learned very little, and spent the intervals of schooling more profitably in collecting eggs, insects, and reptiles, trapping squirrels and woodchucks, and making persistent though rarely fortunate attempts to kill birds with arrows. After four years of this rustication I was brought back to Boston, when I was unhappily seized with a mania for experiments in chemistry, involving a lonely, confined, unwholesome sort of life, baneful to body and mind."

these doubts he entered upon a training tolerably well fitted to serve his purpose, slighted all college studies which could not promote it, and pursued with avidity such as had a bearing upon it, however indirect.[1]

"The task, as he then reckoned, would require about twenty years. The time allowed was ample; but here he fell into a fatal error, entering on this long pilgrimage with all the vehemence of one starting on a mile heat. His reliance, however, was less on books than on such personal experience as should in some sense identify him with his theme. His natural inclinations urged him in the same direction, for his thoughts were always in the forests, whose features, not unmixed with softer images, possessed his waking and sleeping dreams, filling him with vague cravings impossible to satisfy. As fond of hardships as he was vain of enduring them, cherishing a sovereign scorn for every physical weakness or defect, deceived, moreover, by a rapid development of frame and sinews, which flattered him with the belief that discipline sufficiently unsparing would harden him into an athlete, he slighted the precautions of a more reasonable woodcraft, tired old foresters with long marches, stopped neither for heat nor rain, and slept on the earth without

[1] In the second paper he said: "Before the end of the sophomore year my various schemes had crystallized into a plan of writing a story of what was then known as the 'Old French War,' — that is, the war that ended in the conquest of Canada, — for here, as it seemed to me, the forest drama was more stirring and the forest stage more thronged with appropriate actors than in any other passage of our history. It was not till some years later that I enlarged the plan to include the whole course of the American conflict between France and England, or, in other words, the history of the American forest; for this was the light in which I regarded it. My theme fascinated me, and I was haunted with wilderness images day and night."

a blanket.[1] Another cause added not a little to the growing evil. It was impossible that conditions of the nervous system abnormal as his had been from infancy, should be without their effects on the mind, and some of these were of a nature highly to exasperate him. Unconscious of their character and origin, and ignorant that with time and confirmed health they would have disappeared, he had no other thought than that of crushing them by force, and accordingly applied himself to the work. Hence resulted a state of mental tension, habitual for several years, and abundantly mischievous in its effects. With a mind overstrained and a body overtasked, he was burning his candle at both ends.

"But if a systematic and steady course of physical activity can show no better result, have not the advantages of such a course been overrated? In behalf of manhood and common sense, he would protest against such a conclusion; and if any pale student, glued to his desk here, seek an apology for a way of life whose natural fruit is that pallid and emasculate scholarship of which New England has had too many examples, it will be far better that this sketch had not been written. For the student

[1] Referring to this period, he wrote in his second letter to Mr. Brimmer: "I spent all my summer vacation in the woods or in Canada, at the same time reading such books as I thought suited, in a general way, to help me towards my object. I pursued these lucubrations with a pernicious intensity, keeping my plans and purposes to myself while passing among my companions as an outspoken fellow." And of a little later period, when in the Law School, he writes: "Here, while following the prescribed courses at a quiet pace, I entered in earnest on two other courses, one of general history, the other of Indian history and ethnology, and at the same time studied diligently the models of English style, which various pursuits were far from excluding the pleasures of society."

there is, in its season, no better place than the saddle, and no better companion than the rifle or the oar. A highly irritable organism spurred the writer to excess in a course which, with one of different temperament, would have produced a free and hardy development of such faculties and forces as he possessed. Nor, even in the case in question, was the evil unmixed, since from the same source whence it issued came also the habit of mind and muscular vigor which saved him from a ruin absolute and irremediable.

"In his own behalf, he is tempted to add to this digression another. Though the seat of derangement may be the nervous system, it does not of necessity follow that the subject is that which, in the common sense of the word, is called 'nervous.' The writer was now and then felicitated on 'having no nerves' by those who thought themselves maltreated by that mysterious portion of human organism.

"This subterranean character of the mischief, early declaring itself at the surface, doubtless increased its intensity, while it saved it from being a nuisance to those around.

"Of the time when, leaving college, he entered nominally on the study of law, — though in fact with the determination that neither this nor any other pursuit should stand in the path of his projects, — his recollection is of mingled pain and pleasure. His faculties were stimulated to their best efficiency. Never, before or since, has he known so great a facility of acquisition and comprehension. Soon, however, he became conscious that the impelling force was growing beyond his control. Labor became a passion, and rest intolerable, yet with a keen appetite for social enjoyment, in which he found not only a pleasure, but in some sense a repose. The stimulus rapidly increased. Despite of judgment and of will, his mind turned constantly towards remote objects of pursuit, and strained vehemently to attain them. The condition was that of a rider whose horse runs headlong, the bit between his teeth, or of a locomotive, built of indifferent material, under a head of steam too great for its strength, hissing at a score of crevices, yet rushing on with accelerating speed to the inevitable smash.

"A specific sign of the mischief soon appeared in a weakness of sight, increasing with an ominous rapidity. Doubtless to study with the eyes of another is practicable, yet the expedient is not an eligible one, and the writer bethought him of an alternative. It was essential to his plans to give an inside view of Indian life. This then was the time at once to accomplish the object and rest his failing vision. Accordingly he went to the Rocky Mountains, but he had reckoned without his host. A complication of severe disorders here seized him, and at one time narrowly missed bringing both him and his schemes to an abrupt termination, but, yielding to a system of starvation, at length assumed an intermittent and much less threatening form. A concurrence of circumstances left him but one means of accomplishing his purpose. This was to follow a large band of Ogillallah Indians, known to have crossed the Black Hill range a short time before. Reeling in the saddle with weakness and pain, he set forth, attended by a Canadian hunter. With much difficulty the trail was found, the Black Hills crossed, the reluctance of his follower overcome, and the Indians discovered on the fifth day encamped near the Medicine Bow range of the Rocky

Mountains. On a journey of a hundred miles, over a country in parts of the roughest, he had gained rather than lost strength, while his horse was knocked up and his companion disconsolate with a painful cough. Joining the Indians, he followed their wanderings for several weeks. To have worn the airs of an invalid would certainly have been an indiscretion, since in that case a horse, a rifle, a pair of pistols, and a red shirt might have offered temptations too strong for aboriginal virtue. Yet to hunt buffalo on horseback, over a broken country, when, without the tonic of the chase, he could scarcely sit upright in the saddle, was not strictly necessary for maintaining the requisite prestige. The sport, however, was good, and the faith undoubting that, to tame the devil, it is best to take him by the horns.

"As to the advantages of this method of dealing with that subtle personage, some question may have arisen in his mind, when, returning after a few months to the settlements, he found himself in a condition but ill adapted to support his theory. To the maladies of the prairie succeeded a suite of exhausting disorders, so reducing him that circulation at the extremities ceased, the light of the sun became insupportable, and a wild whirl possessed his brain, joined to a universal turmoil of the nervous system which put his philosophy to the sharpest test it had hitherto known. All collapsed, in short, but the tenacious strength of muscles hardened by long activity. This condition was progressive, and did not reach its height — or, to speak more fitly, its depth — until some eighteen months after his return. The prospect before him was by no means attractive, contrasting somewhat pointedly with his boyish fancy of a life of action and a death in battle. Indeed, the change from intense activity to flat stagnation, attended with an utter demolition of air-castles, may claim a place, not of the meanest, in that legion of mental tortures which make the torments of the Inferno seem endurable. The desire was intense to return to the prairie and try a hair of the dog that bit him; but this kill-or-cure expedient was debarred by the certainty that a few days' exposure to the open sunlight would have destroyed his sight.

"In the spring of 1848, the condition indicated being then at its worst, the writer resolved to attempt the composition of the 'History of the Conspiracy of Pontiac,' of which the material had been for some time collected and the ground prepared. The difficulty was so near to the impossible that the line of distinction often disappeared, while medical prescience condemned the plan as a short road to dire calamities. His motive, however, was in part a sanitary one, growing out of a conviction that nothing could be more deadly to his bodily and mental health than the entire absence of a purpose and an object. The difficulties were threefold: an extreme weakness of sight, disabling him even from writing his name except with eyes closed: a condition of the brain prohibiting fixed attention except at occasional and brief intervals; and an exhaustion and total derangement of the nervous system, producing of necessity a mood of mind most unfavorable to effort. To be made with impunity, the attempt must be made with the most watchful caution.

"He caused a wooden frame to be constructed of the size and shape of a sheet of letter paper. Stout wires were fixed horizontally across it, half an inch apart, and a movable back of thick pasteboard fitted behind them. The paper for writing was placed between the pasteboard and the wires, guided by which, and using a black lead crayon, he could write not illegibly with closed eyes. He was at the time absent from home, on Staten Island, where, and in the neighboring city of New York, he had friends who willingly offered their aid. It is needless to say to which half of humanity nearly all these kind assistants belonged. He chose for a beginning that part of the work which offered fewest difficulties and with the subject of which he was most familiar, namely the Siege of Detroit. The books and documents, already partially arranged, were procured from Boston, and read to him at such times as he could listen to them, the length of each reading never, without injury, much exceeding half an hour, and periods of several days frequently occurring during which he could not listen at all. Notes were made by him with closed eyes, and afterwards deciphered and read to him till he had mastered them. For the first half year, the rate of composition averaged about six lines a day. The portion of the book thus composed was afterwards partially rewritten.

"His health improved under the process, and the remainder of the volume — in other words, nearly the whole of it — was composed in Boston, while pacing in the twilight of a large garret, the only exercise which the sensitive condition of his sight permitted him in an unclouded day while the sun was above the horizon. It was afterwards written down from dictation by relatives under the same roof, to whom he was also indebted for the preparatory readings. His progress was much less tedious than at the outset, and the history was complete in about two years and a half.

"He then entered upon the subject of 'France in the New World,'—a work, or series of works, involving minute and extended investigation. The difficulties which met him at the outset were incalculable. Wholly unable to use his eyes, he had before him the task, irksome at best where there is no natural inclination for it, of tracing out, collecting, indexing, arranging, and digesting a great mass of incongruous material scattered on both sides of the Atlantic. Those pursuing historical studies under the disadvantages of impaired sight have not hitherto attempted in person this kind of work during the period of their disability, but have deputed it to skilled and trusty assistants, — a most wise course in cases where it is practicable. The writer, however, partly from the nature of his subject and his plan, though in special instances receiving very valuable aid, was forced in the main to rely on his own research. The language was chiefly French, and the reader was a girl from the public schools, ignorant of any tongue but her own. The effect, though highly amusing to bystanders, was far from being so to the person endeavoring to follow the meaning of this singular jargon. Catalogues, indexes, tables of contents in abundance were, however, read, and correspondence opened with those who could lend aid or information. Good progress had been made in the preliminary surveys, and many books examined and digested on a systematic plan for future reference, when a disaster befell the writer which set his calculations at naught.

"This was an effusion of water on the left knee, in the

autumn of 1851. A partial recovery was followed by a relapse, involving a close confinement of two years and a weakened and sensitive condition of the joint from which it has never recovered. The effects of the confinement were as curious as unenviable. All the irritability of the system centred in the head. The most definite of the effects produced was one closely resembling the tension of an iron band, secured round the head and contracting with an extreme force, with the attempt to concentrate the thoughts, listen to reading, or at times to engage in conversation. This was, however, endurable in comparison with other forms of attack which cannot be intelligibly described from the want of analogous sensations by which to convey the requisite impressions. The brain was stimulated to a restless activity, impelling through it a headlong current of thought which, however, must be arrested and the irritated organ held in quiescence on a penalty to avert which no degree of exertion was too costly. The whirl, the confusion, and strange undefined torture attending this condition are only to be conceived by one who has felt them. Possibly they may have analogies in the savage punishment once in use in some of our prisons, where drops of water were made to fall from a height on the shaved head of the offender, soon producing an effect which brought to reason the most contumacious. Sleep, of course, was banished during the periods of attack, and in its place was demanded, for the exclusion of thought, an effort more severe than the writer has ever put forth in any other cause. In a few hours, however, a condition of exhaustion would ensue; and, both patient and disease being spent, the latter fell into a dull lethargic stage far more supportable. Excitement or alarm would probably have proved wholly ruinous.

"These were the extreme conditions of the disorder which has reached two crises, — one at the end of 1853, the other in 1858. In the latter case it was about four years before the power of mental application was in the smallest degree restored, nor, since the first year of the confinement has there been any waking hour when he has not been in some degree conscious of the presence of the malady. Influences tending to depress the mind have at all times proved far less injurious than those tending to excite, or even pleasurably exhilarate, and a lively conversation has often been a cause of serious mischief. A cautious vigilance has been necessary from the first, and this cerebral devil has perhaps had his uses as a teacher of philosophy.

"Meanwhile the Faculty of Medicine were not idle, displaying that exuberance of resource for which that remarkable profession is justly famed. The wisest, indeed, did nothing, commending his patient to time and faith; but the activity of his brethren made full amends for this masterly inaction. One was for tonics, another for a diet of milk, one counselled galvanism, another hydropathy; one scarred him behind the neck with nitric acid, another drew red-hot irons along his spine with a view of enlivening that organ. Opinion was divergent as practice. One assured him of recovery in six years; another thought that he would never recover. Another, with grave circumlocution, lest the patient should take fright, informed him that he was the victim of an organic disease of the brain, which must needs despatch him to another world within a twelvemonth; and he stood amazed at the smile of an auditor who neither cared for the announcement nor believed it. Another, an eminent physiologist of Paris, after an acquaintance of three months, one day told him that, from the nature of the disorder, he had at first supposed that it must in accordance with precedent be attended with insanity, and had ever since been studying him to discover under what form the supposed aberration declared itself, adding, with a somewhat humorous look, that his researches had not been rewarded with the smallest success.

"In the severer periods of the disorder, books were discarded for horticulture, which benign pursuit has proved most salutary in its influences. One year, four years, and numerous short intervals, lasting from a day to a month, represent these literary interruptions since the work in hand was begun. Under the most favorable conditions, it was a slow and doubtful navigation, beset with reefs and breakers, demanding a constant look-out and a constant throwing of the lead. Of late years, however, the condition of the sight has so far improved as to permit reading, not exceeding, on the average, five minutes at one time. This modicum of power, though apparently trifling, proved of the greatest service, since, by a cautious management, its application may be extended. By reading for one minute, and then resting for an equal time, this alternate process may generally be continued for about half an hour. Then, after a sufficient interval, it may be repeated, often three or four times in the course of the day. By this means nearly the whole of the volume now offered has been composed. When the conditions were such as to render systematic application possible, a reader has been employed, usually a pupil of the public schools. On one occasion, however, the services of a young man, highly intelligent, and an excellent linguist, were obtained for a short time. With such assistance every difficulty vanished, but it could not long be continued.

"At present the work, or rather the series of separate works, stands as follows: Most of the material is collected or within reach. Another volume, on the Jesuits in North America, is one-third written. Another, on the French Explorers of the Great West, is half written; while a third, devoted to the checkered career of Louis de Buade, Comte de Frontenac, is partially arranged for composition. Each work is designed to be a unit in itself, independently of the rest; but the whole, taken as a series, will form a connected history of France in the New World.[1]

"How far, by a process combining the slowness of the tortoise with the uncertainty of the hare, an undertaking of close and extended research can be advanced, is a question to solve which there is no aid from precedent, since it does not appear that an attempt under similar circumstances has hitherto been made. The writer looks, however, for a fair degree of success.[2]

[1] In the second letter he said: "While engaged on these books, I made many journeys in the United States and Canada in search of material, and went four times to Europe with a similar object. The task of exploring archives and collecting documents, to me repulsive at the best, was under the circumstances difficult, and would have been impossible but for the aid of competent assistants working under my direction."

[2] In writing his second letter he said: "Taking the last forty years as a whole, the capacity of literary work, which during that time has fallen to my share has, I am confident, been considerably less than a fourth part of what it would have been under normal conditions."

"Irksome as may be the requirements of conditions so anomalous, they are far less oppressive than the necessity they involve of being busied with the past when the present has claims so urgent, and holding the pen with a hand that should have grasped the sword."

CHAPTER XIII

PARKMAN'S spiritual growth is naturally the most interesting element of his biography, but it is also the most obscure. In attempting to follow it we can see some of his dangers, arising from the defects of his qualities and the demands of his labor and experience; but we cannot so easily follow the aspirations of his reserved nature, or the efforts and influences by which he brought his character to its mellow maturity.

His promontory of a chin and his expression of firmness might well cause some apprehensions as to spiritual qualities. He appears to have recognized a danger in his own strength and firmness, as tending to a certain degree of hardness. It is easy to believe that this masterful spirit in early and middle life was not free from egotism, — a defect which met with little, if any, opposition from the devoted women about him. For his very egotism was always considerate, and, in spite of invalidism, free from the pursuit of personal comforts; singularly enough, it was a means of attaining the aims of the self-sacrificing scholar.

One of the strongest opponents of his growth was an innate conservatism. In many ways, despite his volcanic warmth and energy, he was unchangeable as the hills. Independence and reserve often joined hands in him. He said of Montcalm: "A courage so nobly sustained lifts him above pity;" and he himself asked no pity. His engagement and marriage surprised many of his friends — as an admission of sentiment as a rival to ambition. He never gave himself out, intimately, to any one, though receiving confidences with genuine interest. Thus human sympathy does not seem, at a casual glance, to have been an important source of his spiritual riches. A characteristic incident may be given as an evidence of his extreme reserve in regard to private matters. When he and his devoted sister Eliza discussed the dedication of one of his volumes to her, they both concluded that they did not wish to make such a revelation of their affection to the public. As far as we can judge, his worth and charm attracted more affection than he expressed in return, — so self-sustaining a nature could not feel the dependent kind of affection. He never regarded death or any other event as a dispensation of Providence, or attached to it any degree of mysticism or fatality. When his son died, and some one said: "He was too good to live," Parkman corrected at once any such misinterpretation of life, by saying that such an idea is true of no one; that the world needs the best, and the best can always find a place in it. Again, at the death of his wife when a sympathetic friend assumed that life had no longer any interest for him, he promptly dispelled any such gloomy conception. His patience never included either personal discouragement, fretful rebellion, or passive surrender to the guidance of supernatural powers. He said: "A man must feel that he holds his fate in his own hands." And since we have to take men and things as they are, it would be difficult to find a philosophy better fitted to the man, or a man better fitted to his experience. He often had to face prospects that would have daunted many a man of less firmness and more sentiment. In 1859, for example, he was in one of the "dismallest dens on earth." The previous autumn he had gone to Paris for relief to his spirits after the death of his wife, and for medical help against his maladies, which were then very threatening. He returned in no better health, to what would have been a cheerless hearth but for the devotion of his mother and sisters. The bright visions, the adventures, the sunshine and freedom that had appeared inseparable from the energetic youth, were now replaced by very different elements of life. Shut up in his darkened study, threatened with total blindness, he led at this time a life of monastic solitude; in place of enjoying buoyant activity he sat down to the endurance of pain; his ambition was met either by absolute inability to work, or by exasperating interruptions and petty achievements; worst of all, he was in danger of insanity. The enemy lay ambushed in the darkest possibilities; and how pitilessly must these have pressed upon him in the weakest moments! Yet undoubtedly he stated his own philosophy in giving Vassall Morton's: "Blows are good for most men, and suffering, to the farthest limit of their endurance what they most need."[1] True, there were times when his "faith was wrenched to its uttermost roots. He thought the world was given over to the devil."[2]

All this is too much to contemplate; but it was not too much for Parkman to endure. There is little wonder that he set down his feeling in the following description of the rock off Schooner Head, Mount Desert, when on a visit to his classmate, Mr. George S. Hale, in 1871: "Under a leaden sky the island rocks rest sombre and cold upon the leaden water, as strong men, under the clouds of a dreary destiny, bide their hour in still and stern endurance." The inherent nobility of his nature, however, and his ideals, were too lofty to allow such a spirit permanent control of his life. In "Vassall Morton," he made Edith say of the hero:[3]

> "It was a bitter schooling, a long siege, and a dreary one; but you have triumphed, and you wear its trophy, — the heroic calm, the mind tranquil with consciousness of power. You have wrung a proud tribute out of sorrow; but has it yielded you all its treasure? Could you but have learned that gentler, deeper, higher philosophy which builds for itself a temple out of ruin, and makes weakness invincible with binding its tendrils to the rock."

Yet, with his New England conscience and training, he may have overestimated his defects, and charged a tendency with being an actual condition.

[1] P. 405. [2] P. 414. [3] P. 383.

The details of Parkman's home life were known to me during only his last years, but for the sake of completeness I must give what I can of the preceding epochs in their bearing on his spiritual growth. His married life of eight years, though marked by many severe trials, was happy with mutual affection and devotion. Mrs. Parkman was a woman of excellent understanding, a cheerful disposition, more practical than intellectual, bright in conversation, with a sense of humor to match his own, and a large fund of affection. The twelve years after her death were the most trying period of Parkman's life. It was then that he suffered most from pain and anxiety, from his exaggerated reserve, and from the effects of self-centred efforts to drive on his work. As his need of quiet kept him generally in his study, his isolation was due chiefly to nervous and physical conditions. His domestic relations were never marked by any coldness or constraint; on the contrary, he was always cordial, kindly, and considerate. But some of their friends, who considered the inner life, felt that although he lived happily with his family he was not of them in the most intimate sense; and that for a time he did not appreciate fully and responsively their sympathy and devotion.

His mother died in 1871; Parkman wrote of the event in these terms: "Last week my mother's long and painful illness was calmly and peacefully ended, and a life of rare affection, disinterestedness, and self-devotion came to its close on earth." When on the death of their mother his sister Eliza was able to devote herself thenceforth wholly to him, her intimate friends were concerned for her happiness because of his absorption in his work.

A word may be said here about his relations to his women friends. There are few, if any, literary men who were so dependent on women, or who received so much affectionate service at their hands. Only Wordsworth approached him in this respect. With all his self-sustaining power, Parkman was very sensitive to their influence. It could hardly be otherwise with a man possessing so much imagination, sensibility, and virility. Although he cherished his men friends and talked with them freely on some topics, he never could give himself to any of them so well as he could to a congenial woman. He made Vassall Morton say of himself (p. 358): "Find me a woman of sense, with a brain to discern, a heart to feel, passion to feel vehemently, and principles to feel rightly, and I will show her my mind; or, if not, I will show it to no one."

Besides these qualities he desired a woman to be strong and healthy, bright in conversation, and full of feminine and maternal instincts. He did not care for intellectual tendencies; he even detested the complexities of the "cultured and refined" type. What he desired of women was not inspiration in regard to serious interests, but recreation and amusement. His keenest social pleasures came from his friendships with women; and one of his hardest trials was the limitation of such intercourse by reason of his maladies. He in turn attracted women by many qualities, — his gallant and chivalrous temper, his frankness and love of fun, and his loyalty. As a friend he listened with sympathy and quick perceptions, ever exercising a steadying influence by his wise and practical counsel. One of the marked features of his later life was its richness in the affectionate friendship of fine women. He reaped this reward in some cases even from strangers who knew him only through his histories.

Parkman was remarkably fortunate in the assistance of the women in his own domestic circle. His life was by no means wholly in shadow, for during the fifty years of his work he was never without all the help that affection could give. Some one of the family circle was always at hand to read or write for him, and he was relieved to a remarkable degree from ordinary family cares. Those who thus helped him needed and possessed exceptional tact, intelligence, and devotion to meet the circumstances. For his needs were so imperative and his condition was so fluctuating that only members of his household, close at hand and close at heart, could give him the necessary help. And while he inspired an affection that made such devotion no sacrifice, he was ever generous in acknowledging his indebtedness to them. The helpful friendship that Miss Parkman bestowed on her brother is not often to be matched in literary history; and his success was due in a large measure to her services and sympathy. At the time of their junction in domestic life, her friends felt that she was somewhat alone in her patient devotion. But in spite of some elements of his puritan nature, they were closely united by many traits of character, — by their conservative opinions, common literary interests, and a love of simplicity, decorum, and cheerfulness; as the years passed, Parkman's growth in sympathy brought them nearer to each other; and finally their happiness together was a joint reward for two lives of exceptional experiences.

His brother Eliot, during his infrequent sojourns at home, made the domestic atmosphere sunny with abundant humor and vivacity. In a letter, Jan. 11, 1872, Parkman thus refers to his life and character:

"A telegram from Commodore Stembel, U. S. N., says that my only brother, a lieutenant in the navy, had died suddenly at San Francisco from the effects of a fall. His body arrived last evening. After passing a thousand risks in travel and in war, he died at last by what seemed a trivial accident, but which involved the rupture of an internal artery. He was of a most affectionate and generous nature, and the strongest family attachments."

Parkman was a little above medium height, of an erect, well-built frame, with square shoulders and good muscular development, but spare and sinewy in habit. Only in his last year or two did he allow himself to grow stout, following his physician's recommendation in the hope of thus becoming less nervous and sleepless. On horseback, especially, he was a dashing and martial figure. He had dark hair, and a wholesome color quite foreign to the traditional pallor of the student. His head and features were somewhat angular, with a chin of most exceptional prominence and strength. His gray, penetrating eyes were, in youth, of good size, but in later years they seemed smaller because of chronic inflammation of the lids. He had firm, good-sized hands with square finger-tips. His thin face, always smooth-shaven, generally wore a grave, thoughtful expression, but frank and friendly: strength and alertness combined with kindliness to give it distinction. His mouth, though expressive chiefly of inflexible firmness, was very mobile. His smile was often remarked for its expressiveness; it reminded me always of these traits of Morton: "the heroic calm, the mind tranquil with consciousness of power."[1] Parkman's smile expressed a full consciousness of his strength and victory in life; and it often had a very clear address to you by the penetrating look he sent for a moment into your eyes. Or, at other times, it showed an instant of absence — a turn through far realms of thought; it captured your fancy with a vision of genial companionship on some unknown quest. His laughter was hardly audible, though it was hearty; showing itself chiefly by shaking sides and subdued or repressed sounds. His speaking voice was low and his pronunciation clear.

[1] P. 383.

His appearance was full of distinction; but it shone through a very quiet, unobtrusive manner. There was in him much of the colonial gentleman, but softened and unbent. Eccentricity he hated, and he enjoyed the conventional proprieties of society in his native city. Though not fastidious, he was always neatly dressed, in good London-made clothes, which he wore out thoroughly. In coming to greet you he advanced with an erect bearing and quick, firm step, took your hand firmly and gave it a good but not demonstrative shake; meanwhile looking you in the eye for a moment with a penetrating, frank, and cordial expression. Even when he came on his crutches he brought a manly, cheering presence. There was absolutely nothing of the morbid invalid about him; nor any hint of the assumptions of learning and fame. In full maturity his modesty, simplicity, frankness, gentleness, and patience were given an additional charm by the sympathy with which he met his friends. His modesty was not the modesty of naïveté or humility. On the contrary, he was always, in a quiet way, a masterful rather than a humble spirit. He held his virtues by a firmer grasp than unconscious possession. With an unusual knowledge of himself, he placed the highest value on his qualities as means for achievement and the growth of character.

Parkman's homes were perfectly suited to his tastes and needs. In winter he preferred to live in Boston, with his sister, at 50 Chestnut Street; in spite of his love of nature, he never passed a winter in the country. This street, in the centre of Boston and very near the Common, is yet a quiet, secluded quarter, attractive with trees and old-fashioned houses. The Parkman home is a twilight house of subdued colors, simply furnished with heirlooms, and full of the peace and comfort derived from good housekeeping and a quiet spirit. During the last years of his life, when his lameness was very troublesome, he mounted to his study on the third floor by an elevator which he could operate by the power of his own arms. The room had a subdued light from two windows facing the north. An open stove with a soft-coal fire cast a glow into the shadows; two of the walls were covered with bookshelves, the others with engraved portraits of historic persons. On the mantel stood some of Barye's statuettes of animals, and on the wall were a few Indian relics he had brought from the Oregon Trail. The simplicity of his tastes and the practicality of his mind were shown in this study: it was simply a writer's workshop, without any luxurious or ornamental appointment. He did not approve of large collections of books in private houses, because of the trouble they give, and because such sources of information should be accessible to students, in public libraries. His collection consisted of about twenty-five hundred volumes, which he bequeathed to Harvard College; some of these were inherited from his father. The chief feature of his library was his collection of manuscripts, which far outweighed in value all the other works. Next in importance was a collection of eighty-nine maps, and about fifteen hundred works relating chiefly to his historic labors. All these are now kept together in Harvard College library as the "Parkman Collection." There are almost no notes on the margins; in a very few books he made now and then a mark or sign that was a sufficient aid to his exceptional memory. His contempt for "pallid and emasculate scholarship" is the key to his feeling for books and bookworms. A man of nature and of life rather than a man of books, he had no interest in fine bindings, costly editions, or rare works aside from their contents.

We have seen that during his early and middle life he met his trials with "stern and silent endurance." From the earliest of his married life onward till near the close, the condition of his brain seemed to make it necessary for him to be silent and alone most of the time. But as years rolled on, the improvement in his health, the easier progress of his labor, and the development of his sympathy enabled him at last to meet life with happier moods and habits. Fortunately he was not a man of moods, but one who had in him a wellspring of cheerfulness that rarely ceased to flow. This virtue had exceptional value in his case, because of his inherited affection of the brain; and he was fortunate in early coming to the belief that insanity often begins in moods and mental conditions that at the beginning can be avoided.

Parkman nourished his cheerfulness in the most practical way. His native energy here served him efficiently, aiding him in bringing forward a keen sense of humor which one would hardly expect in looking at his grave, strong face. He and his chief ally, his sister, thus armed themselves with rays of sunshine. The problem they had to meet was to relieve his brain by some lightsome activity, avoiding both serious topics of conversation and gloomy silence. In such efforts he acquired the happy faculty of making much of little things, and casting into the commonplace events and talks of the day a pervading spirit of jocoseness which at last became more or less habitual in the domestic circle. His sense of humor had its freest play in simple, objective, childlike things; it rarely reached the fine point of wit, or entered into the delicate play of psychologic elements. For example, he was presented by one of his granddaughters, on Christmas, with a badge in the form of a cat, cut out of a piece of yellow flannel. For many years when he visited the family he invariably produced this cat with certain miaulings, and stories of her wanderings during the preceding year. He had also, for similar amusement, an Uncle John Frog and a turtle. He liked to hear his brother-in-law, Rev. Dr. Cordner, an Irish gentleman, read Irish ballads; and when his nieces entered the room he often thrummed Rory O'More as a silent greeting and banter.

As still further aid he called into service two faculties that were already highly developed by his literary labors — imagination, and skill in narration. One of the chief elements of his domestic intercourse came to be humorous romancing. At breakfast, after replying briefly to inquiries as to his health, he would begin a tale and carry it on throughout the meal, and even continue it from day to day. He whiled away the time in the same way when driving about the country. The chief characteristic of these stories was a jocose exaggeration. Any subject would serve; now he would reconstruct a character of some novel; or would take a name on a sign as the starting point, and carry the imaginary owner through various experiences more or less impossible. He married off his daughters to persons they detested, and then teased them with making such unwise selections. Frequently he chose subjects more or less theological; he invented a minister in Florida who was so ill supported by his congregation that he had to eat crocodile eggs, which turned him into an amphibious divine; and a Miss Simpkins, who conducted a Sunday School for young demons; as her pupils were rather restless, she passed their tails through holes in the bench, and tied knots underneath. Or he would now and then take up one of the Prophets, and give him a character and history hardly in accord with Biblical traditions. Another string to his bow was humorous verse. During sleepless hours he often composed parodies; one was on the "Psalm of Life" — cats being the heroes. At breakfast he would often make additions to these compositions, and thus enrich and expand a topic to its utmost. Another frequent amusement was the recitation of poetry; he often gave extracts from "Bombastes Furioso" or Byron's "Vision of Judgment." "The Baby's Début," from Horace Smith's "Rejected Addresses," was a favorite with him, because it parodied Wordsworth, whom he disliked as poet and man. His memory was stored with an inexhaustible supply of this whimsical kind of wit; but when insomnia made him too ill for it, he would play with the cat or the children and keep silent. In many instances these diversions were simply a mask for hiding his sufferings.

Naturally he got all that he could from books. Mr. Frothingham gives the following account of his reading:

"In his early life he read a great deal of the best English prose and verse; I recollect years ago, it must have been when he was in college, at his father's house on Bowdoin Square, a question arose in regard to Dr. Johnson, and Francis expressed an idea of the Doctor's character which showed him to be familiar with his writings. This love of the best English literature he kept alive through college and all his life. He had a great enthusiasm as a youth for Milton; Shakespere he always had by him. In mottoes prefixed to his 'Vassall Morton,' I find the names of thirty poets. It would not be safe, of course, to presume that he had read all these, but it is safe to say that Shakespere, Pope, Scott, Byron, the 'Percy Reliques,' Sir David Lindsay, Campbell, Molière, were familiar to him. His taste was for heroic and not for sentimental writing. I should say that he might prefer the book of 'Proverbs' to the book of 'Psalms'; the Gospel of Matthew to the Gospel of John; Scott to Shelley; for he had no relish for metaphysics or abstractions of any kind, scientific or other. His dislike of everything morbid — melancholy, misanthropy, depression — amounted to abhorrence, and if he could not be cheerful he went away if he was able; and if not, he held his tongue or turned to merry thoughts."

This account is true as far as it goes; but it does not go beyond his early manhood. He had taste and capacity for a varied culture within certain lines; but during all the latter half of his life it was necessary for him to avoid serious topics and to seek in reading chiefly amusement. He listened with most pleasure to those works of fiction that are objective in content and treatment, and full of stirring incidents. Jane Austen, Stevenson, Haggard, Dumas, were among his favorites, and he enjoyed every repetition of "Pickwick" as if it had been new to him. The "Nation" was read to him every week, also any article of unusual interest in the periodicals. He would tolerate nothing dreamy, sentimental, untruthful, metaphysical, or philanthropic. He disliked Victor Hugo for exaggeration, as, for example, in making the dwarf on the tower of Notre Dame perform the impossible feat of casting off the ladder after it had been loaded with the assaulting party. He also put Longfellow aside for romancing so much in "Evangeline." And although enjoying Du Maurier's "Peter Ibbetson" up to the mystical part, he refused to hear the rest of the book. Of Lowell he wrote: "I am glad you like 'The Cathedral.' Lowell is equally estimable as a man and as a poet."[1]

His growth was helped again by his labors. He came to see that success could not be won by taking the devil by the horns; that, on the contrary, he must cultivate patience and sweetness as remedies for irritation and nervous excitement. His theme, dealing as it did with character in detail, kept him alive to his own course of development. Ideality was stimulated in him by a disinterested pursuit of scholarship. In following his literary path he was thus led to drop some of his native hindrances, and mount to regions of more light. Again, his life-long study of men and women inevitably brought him more and more in contact with spiritual elements of character and developed his sympathy. An evidence of this was the fact that he expressed in playful ways more affection for his grandchildren than he had shown towards his own children. He was fond of boys; he liked to chaff them for the sake of getting glimpses of their nature. He often saw at a glance the effective forces in a child's personality, and narrated or even imitated its conduct as evidence. His interest in little folks was pleasantly shown at the gathering of his children and grandchildren at Christmas, when he watched from his chair, with lively interest, the changing groups about the tree, and often opened a vein of character by some question or bit of bantering.

[1] To Dr. George Stewart, Feb. 21, 1870.

A more usual and characteristic scene might be enjoyed by any friend who should have called of an evening at the old house in Chestnut Street. The soft colors of the sitting-room were still further subdued by a mild light and a low shade covering the lamp. While the ladies were by the table sewing or reading, Parkman sat at a distance from the light, at the side of the fireplace, in a chair that was erect and firm in form and substance. In the shadows of his corner he was hardly visible. He often rested his elbows on the chair-arms, and meditatively adjusted the finger nails of one hand to those of the other, from time to time separating his hands to see if he could bring them together accurately again with a sharp little blow. Meanwhile the reading or talking of the others went on. He occasionally looked up at a speaker with a direct and decided way to ask a question or pass a remark; but generally he saved his eyes by keeping them lowered on his finger-tips or on the floor. Though he was never a dreamer, absenting himself in mind from his companions, he often passed the evening without joining much in the conversation. At other times he would be full of quiet talk.

His summer home was on the southwestern shore of Jamaica Pond, a small body of water now incorporated in the parks of Boston. The pond is pleasantly surrounded by the groves and grounds of suburban residences. His choice of this location proved to be a very happy one, in giving not only a

*The Landing, Jamaica Pond, and
Mr. Parkman's Boat.*

beautiful site near the city, but especially in affording him facilities for rowing — the only exercise he could take in periods of lameness in the knee. The grounds sloped gently down to the water, and were very inviting with the shade of many fine trees and the productions of his skill in horticulture. The house was an unpretending wooden structure, furnished simply and comfortably, and kept open to the air and sunlight. Social and domestic life in this place was not different from that of the winter home; but Parkman had here one more means of keeping up cheerfulness: the daily row of one hour, which he never omitted or shortened. Such frequent turns on a lake only a quarter of a mile across would have become insufferably tedious without some means of mental entertainment. He therefore enlarged the Pond, by the use of far-off names such as the Cape of Good Hope and Bering's Sea; peopling each region with the lions or the whales appropriate to the surroundings. He kept in its depths a terrible ichthyosaurus and a fearful sea-serpent. To the very cats along the shore — seen or unseen — he gave names, characters, and the most astonishing experiences. The family of muskrats on the bit of an island were visited daily to watch their building and domestic doings. One day he found that a muskrat had brought a leaf of grass and put it on top of a rock sticking above the water, whereupon he named the rock "the shrine." When his sister was with him he would let the boat stop beside it for a minute or two, then ask, with a reverential and serious air, "Are you ready to leave?" and move off in silence.

In these later years he spent a part of each summer with his son-in-law and daughter, Mr. and Mrs. Coolidge, in the Wentworth Mansion, near Portsmouth, New Hampshire. The old farm is approached by a lane winding through pine woods; the stone walls are half hidden by cedars, barberries, and vines; and the outcropping ledges of rock are touched off with juniper and flaming sumac. You come out of the woods at last into a field on the end of a point in the bay, and look off over the channels winding among islands, points, and marshes. On the left in the distance may be seen the spires and masts of Portsmouth, and in front a piece of the ocean with the Isles of Shoals; you hear the surf and the tolling of the bell-buoy on the harbor bar. Passing a few old apple-trees remaining as memorials of old-time cheer, you come face to face with the Mansion. It is a rambling farmhouse of many angles and gables, quaint little rooms, mysterious nooks and queer passages, and one large room where the governor's council used to meet. The unkempt naturalness of the grounds and shore, the colonial plainness of the house within, the spirit of simplicity that pervades it all, and the historic associations, made it a pleasant and appropriate place for Parkman's summer days at the close of his life.[1]

[1] He described the region in chapter xviii. of the second volume of *A Half Century*. Mr. Barrett Wendell also gives an attractive

His strong social instincts were another important help in his growth. It is well to emphasize this side of his character in order to balance the effect of the sterner elements in his personality. He lacked the overflowing geniality and magnetism needed to set the social currents flowing in a large company or club, as well as the special talents required in a successful diner-out. In meeting strangers at a dinner he would at first keep silent, while taking the gauge of those present; and he seldom led in conversation unless drawn out. Notwithstanding this, he was essentially a man of society, liking both the freedom of intimate friendship and the decorum of ceremonious intercourse. Also, having seen much of the world, he was at ease with all sorts of men and in all social doings. People felt him to be a "good fellow." The larger demands made on his social abilities by the presidency of the St. Botolph Club were beneficial to him; in his reserved way he was approachable to everybody. He had an especial fondness for the Saturday Club, where he met a few intimate friends in the freest and most informal intercourse. He was a member also of the Union Club. He often made a painful effort to attend the meetings of these clubs, and sometimes went — when unable to climb the stairs — just to greet his friends in the hall. On his drives about the country he would frequently call

glimpse of Wentworth Mansion and of Mr. Parkman in his paper *Francis Parkman*, in the *Proceedings of the American Academy of Arts and Sciences*, vol. xxix.

on his friends, even if unable to leave his carriage, and enjoy a few minutes of their presence at the door. The range of Parkman's topics of conversation was rather limited, considering his intellectual abilities and his fame. His talk was almost always objective; his greatest pleasure seemed to be the recounting the experiences of his youth. With an excellent memory he recalled these scenes in detail; and often embellished them with imaginary incidents, rehearsing them with all the vividness of recent events. He also talked frequently of nature, telling anecdotes of cats and other animals. More rarely he condemned in his conclusive manner the political and socialistic tendencies of his times, — irritating topics which he generally avoided. Now and then he enjoyed shocking a prig, or taking down the dignity of self-assured superiority. He used to tell of a visit he made to a court-room, where one of his friends sat on the bench, arrayed in his robes and stiffened with official grandeur. Parkman winked at him on entering, and enjoyed immensely the pompous immobility of his old friend in failing to respond. He knew and remembered everything which affected or interested those with whom he was intimate; knew their children and grandchildren by name and by character, and never forgot to inquire after them.

Parkman was more cheerful than humorous, and more humorous than witty. Possessing a quick perception of humor, he was yet not a father of epigrams and witticisms, nor even a stepfather who gathers in the facetious offspring of other minds. He left us no anecdotes; he was not a story-teller. Though often narrating significant incidents that happened to himself or others, he would do this for the sake of some idea brought up by the conversation — never for the sake of causing laughter. Mr. Barrett Wendell gives this truthful impression of his conversation:

"The normal impersonality, the animated objectivity of his talk, the frank, idiomatic raciness of his phrase, the wholesomeness of his nature, made you forget that he had ever written anything. You thought of him, by and by, just as a remarkably friendly human being. You forgot even that he was not exactly of an age with you. Like his own literary style, which kept pace so sensitively with the best literary feeling of his day, the man himself was steadily contemporary."

The spirit and effect of Parkman's conversations were like those of his writings, though more fiery and intense. As he grew older he lost something of his early reserve, and became, at least with intimates, more interesting. In talk he never philosophized, never moralized, never posed as virtuous; all the same, he produced an elevating effect on those who heard him. Professor Fiske says: "What most impressed one in talking with him was the combination of power and alertness with extreme gentleness."[1]

Parkman's friendship brings up the necessity of defining two important terms frequently used in this

[1] *Introductory Essay*, lxxvii.

portrait — spirituality and sympathy. As we have said, he showed little interest in religious, philanthropic, affectional, and æsthetic matters. These limitations marked his lack of spirituality; yet he was free from materialism. In considering his sympathies we must distinguish between Parkman as a citizen and Parkman as a friend. His sympathy had its narrowest range in citizenship, and its greatest force and freedom in friendship. Yet, speaking broadly of his character, he was kind-hearted rather than tender-hearted. The Puritan generally held him in reserve not only as to expression, but also as to feeling in matters relating to the inner life. A few exceptional incidents, however, that involved his deepest affections, revealed a tenderness that struggled almost in vain for expression. Parkman's friendship was most helpful and satisfying. Its distinguishing qualities were persistence and sincerity. Conservatism here served a good purpose, keeping him to the last, in aims, qualities, and opinions, what he was in youth, and thus saving his friendships from variations due to growth on at least one side. He kept all the friends of his youth, and made few intimates outside of this circle.

Sentiment never broke through his reserve, or troubled his wisdom, or cast a doubtful light over his expressions. His quick understanding, sincerity of interest, soundness of judgment, steadfastness, and the winning qualities of his nature — all gave a most assuring sense of value and reliability in his friendship. He was always ready to help a friend to a position, provided the applicant seemed fitted for the post; otherwise, he would not only refuse such aid, but oppose the appointment. Absence never made any break in his feeling; he took up an acquaintance again just where it had been left off. When too ill for social intercourse, the mere silent presence of a friend gave him pleasure. He had a comforting charity for those who were unsuccessful, and for all weaknesses of humanity, outside of unmanliness and meanness. It was not his habit to discuss or criticise his friends, unless their characters were especially under consideration; at such a time he would state frankly his opinions. The needy and suffering, young writers wanting counsel or materials from his ample stores, — all found him patient and generous.

In looking back over his life one is struck with his prodigious strength of character. He was ready to face the universe if nature would play him fair. She had played him foul, yet she could not prevent his victory. In his patient fortitude under suffering, in his persistent industry despite the greatest obstacles, and in his fidelity to his ideals, Parkman was certainly one of the most heroic figures in the history of letters.

APPENDIX A

BIBLIOGRAPHY OF FRANCIS PARKMAN'S WRITINGS

HISTORICAL WORKS

1851. The Conspiracy of Pontiac. 2 vols.

FRANCE AND ENGLAND IN NORTH AMERICA

1865. Part I. The Pioneers of France in the New World. 1 vol.
1867. Part II. The Jesuits in North America. 1 vol.
1869. Part III. La Salle and the Discovery of the Great West. 1 vol.
1874. Part IV. The Old Régime. 1 vol.
1877. Part V. Count Frontenac and New France under Louis XIV. 1 vol.
1884. Part VII. Montcalm and Wolfe. 2 vols.
1892. Part VI. A Half-Century of Conflict. 2 vols.

OTHER BOOKS

1849. The Oregon Trail (first published in the *Knickerbocker Magazine* in 1847). 1 vol.
1856. Vassall Morton, a Novel. 1 vol.
1866. The Book of Roses. 1 vol.

He also wrote the Preface, and a translation of a Sketch of General Bouquet, which were prefixed to the reprint of the "Historical Account of Bouquet's Expedition against the Ohio Indians in 1764," published by Robert Carter, Cincinnati, 1868.

1885. "Historic Handbook of the Northern Tour" — being narratives drawn from "Pontiac," "Pioneers," "Jesuits," "Frontenac," and "Montcalm and Wolfe."

CONTRIBUTIONS TO PERIODICALS

Some of which are advance chapters of the histories.

To the "Knickerbocker Magazine" (not including "The Oregon Trail").

1845, March. "The Ranger's Adventure." By a new Contributor.

1845, April. "The Scalp Hunter."

1845, June. "A Fragment of Family History." By the author of "The Scalp-Hunter."

1845, Aug. "The New Hampshire Ranger." By Jonathan Carver, Jr., a poem.

1845, Dec. "Satan and Dr. Carver." By Captain Jonathan Carver, Jr.

To the "Christian Examiner"

1851, May. "Indian Antiquities in North America" (a review of books by E. G. Squier and Lewis Morgan).

1851, July. "Squier's Serpent Symbol," etc. A short book notice; unsigned.

1853, January. "French's Historical Collections of Louisiana." (A short book notice.)

To the "Atlantic Monthly" [1]

	Vol.	Page	Month	Year
*The Fleur-de-Lis at Port Royal	12	30	July	1863
*The Fleur-de-Lis in Florida	12	225	August	1863
*The Spaniard and the Heretic	12	537	November	1863
*The Vengeance of Dominic de Gourgues	14	530	November	1864
Life and Times of Red Jacket (Stone)	19	383	March	1867
*The Founders of Montreal	19	723	June	1867
Historical Inquiry concerning Henry Hudson (J. M. Read, Jr.)	19	764	June	1867
History of New France (Charlevoix & Shea)	20	125	July	1867
Madame Riedesel's Letters and Journals (Stone)	21	127	January	1868
Charlevoix's History of New France	29	499	April	1872
*Jesuits' Mission of Onondaga in 1654	30	687	December	1872
*Early Canadian Miracles and Martyrs	32	84	July	1873
*A Great Deed of Arms	32	691	December	1873
*Sir William Phips's Attack on Quebec	38	719	December	1876
*Wolfe on the Plains of Abraham	54	339	September	1884
*The Battle of Lake George	54	444	October	1884

[1] The articles marked * were published as advance chapters of his histories.

	Vol.	Page	Month	Year
The Forests and the Census	55	835	June	1885
*The Discovery of the Rocky Mountains	61	783	June	1888
*Capture of Louisburg by the N. E. Militia	67	314	March	1891
	67	514	April	1891
	67	621	May	1891
*Acadia, The Feudal Chiefs of	71	25	January	1893
	71	201	February	1893

To the "North American Review"

Vol.	Page	
74	147	James Fenimore Cooper.
101	28	Manners and Customs of Primitive Indian Tribes.
103	1	Indian Superstitions.
107	370	Morgan's Bibliotheca Canadensis.
*118	225	The Ancien Régime in Canada, 1663–1763.
120	34	The Native Races of the Pacific States.
120	469	Higginson's History of the United States.
*125	427	Cavalier de La Salle.
127	1	The Failure of Universal Suffrage.
129	303	The Woman Question.
130	16	The Woman Question Again.

To "The Critic"

1885, October 31. "Revocation of the Edict of Nantes."

To "Tilton's Journal of Horticulture"

1869 to 1871. Several articles referring to horticulture.

To "The Nation"

No.	
243	The Tale of the "Ripe Scholar."
585	Découvertes et Établissements des Français, etc. (by Pierre Margry).

No.	
618	Montcalm et le Canada Français.
652	Une Colonie féodale en Amérique.
666	Note on Rameau.
680	Note on Rameau (Chronicle of the St Lawrence).
683	Mr. Parkman and his Canadian Critics.
702	Canada under the Administration of Lord Dufferin.
780	Note on Joliet's map.
878	The Rose.
935	A Book about Roses.
1085	A French Memoir of Colonial History.
1143	Note on an Album paléographique.
1189	The Fall of New France.
1193	Note on Indian Sketches.
1237	Une Pélerinage au Pays d'Évangéline.
1347	Appendiculæ Historicæ.
1472	Lake St. Louis.

To the "Boston Daily Advertiser"

(This list is incomplete. His articles were generally signed F. P.)

1861.	Wm. H. Russell and our Duty.
1862, Jan. 8.	Where are our Leaders ?
1862, Oct. 14.	Why our Army is not the Best in the World.
1862, Oct. 17.	Conservatism.
1863, June.	The Weak Side of our Armies.
1863, July.	Aristocrats and Democrats.
1863, July.	Our Best Class and the National Politics. The Nation's Ordeal.
1863, July.	The Chiefs of the Nation.

To "Appleton's Cyclopedia of American Biography"

1866–67. The articles on Frontenac, La Salle, and Montcalm.

To "Harper's Monthly"

1864, November. Exploring the Magalloway.
1890, August. A Convent at Rome.

PAMPHLETS

1887. Some Reasons against Woman Suffrage.
1890. Our Common Schools.

TRANSLATIONS

The "Jesuits" and the "Pioneers" were translated into French and published in 1874 and 1882 by Didier et Cie., Paris. Parkman disapproved of these translations, which were garbled.

Three of his histories were published in German, viz.:

"The Pioneers," Auerbach, Stuttgart, 1875.

"The Old Régime," Auerbach, Stuttgart, 1876.

"The Jesuits," Abenheim, Berlin, 1878.

And "The Failure of Universal Suffrage" was issued by Springer in Berlin, 1879.

APPENDIX B

From "The Knickerbocker," August, 1845

"THE NEW HAMPSHIRE RANGER

"In the Old French War, a body of Rangers were employed on scouting expeditions around Lake George, between the hostile military posts of Ticonderoga and Fort William Henry. Their most celebrated leader, Major Rogers, with a large part of the men, were from New Hampshire. The service they were engaged in was of the most severe and dangerous kind. In parties varying from two or three to a hundred or more, they scoured the woods at all seasons, to seize stragglers, intercept convoys, and encounter the parties of Canadians and Indians that the French were constantly sending out to annoy the English; and whom, unless there was a great disparity of force, the Rangers almost always defeated and beat back to Canada.

"No ordered rank and measured tramp,
  No restless flash of steel;
Nor the long line of dancing plumes,
  And ringing trumpet-peal!
The soldiers of the wilderness,
  A rough and hardy band,
In woodland garb, with woodland arms,
  We guard this forest land.
'T is ours to breathe the battle smoke,
  To range the trackless wood,
To struggle with the howling storm,
  And swim the flashing flood.
Deep in the gloomy forest,
  Unseen by human eye,

We track the foe, we strike the blow,
  And, nameless all, we die.
The scarlet coat, the waving plume —
  Good for the triumph day!
The hunter's frock, the cap of fur —
  Good for the battle fray!
Gay warrior of England,
  Idling the whole day long,
Drink and laugh and gaily dance,
  And shout the camp-fire song.
In William Henry's sheltering walls
  Enjoy thy mirth and cheer,
We guard the dangerous wilderness —
  No danger can come near.
Yet do not deem that I complain;
  Soldier, I would not change,
For thy safe and idle slavery,
  My own free forest range.
I love the savage war-whoop,
  And the whistling of the ball;
The woods, the rocks, the boiling streams,
  I love them, one and all.
And yet their memory is entwined
  With thoughts of sore distress,
Of famine, grief, and danger,
  And bitter weariness.
For the ranger's gun has echoed
  From a thousand pathless mountains;
And the ranger's blood has stained with red
  A thousand limpid fountains.
Some of our band lie wasting
  In the dark noisome dell;
No friendly ear could their death-cries hear,
  None lived their fate to tell.
On stern and wild Agiochook
  The whitening bones are spread;
The fish of crystal Horicon
  Are feeding on our dead.

The ravens of Oswego,
  Slow settling on the plain,
Tear vainly at the sinewy limbs,
  And soar away again.
Some have died by famine,
  Some by the headlong fall,
Some by wave, and some by frost,
  Some by the foeman's ball.
Among these wild green mountains,
  And o'er this gentle flood,
In cold and heat, by day and night,
  Have I in battle stood.
The sultry breath of August,
  December's breezes bleak;
The sleet, the snow, the rushing rain,
  Have beat upon my cheek:
And Nature, I have gazed on thee
  In thy calmest, sweetest hour;
And I have seen thy frowning face
  In all thy wrath and power:
Thy gentle smile, thy whispering voice,
  Have ever a charm for me;
But I love as well thy lowering brow
  Of angry majesty.
I love thee even 'mid winter's cold,
  When trackless lies the snow,
And the boughs of the loaded fir-tree bend
  Into the drifts below:
When in the sharp still evening
  The sky is flushed with red,
And o'er the wide white wilderness
  The crimson glow is shed;
And in the thickest forest
  We heap the snow around,
And spread the boughs of evergreen
  Upon the frozen ground.
And through the long dull night we hear,
  On that cold couch reclined,

The music of the groaning ice,
  The howling of the wind:
While high among the snowy trees
  Swirls up the roaring blaze,
And the bright swarm of dancing sparks
  Far in the darkness plays.
I lie and watch them wandering,
  And gleaming wide and bright,
Like fire-flies by the orchard side,
  On some soft summer night.
But how the blasts sweep moaning
  O'er the solid lake below,
And scatter in the bright moonbeams
  The glistening flakes of snow!
And in the tortured forest
  The pine-trees tough and old
Crack sharply with a sudden sound,
  As if rent with the biting cold.
Woe to the wretch who wanders lost
  In the drear wood to-night!
Like the sculptor's chiselled marble
  He 'll be ere morning light.

But the fierce heats of August,
  The pale sun's noontide blaze,
When each hot mountain slumbers
  Dim in the sultry haze!
No song of bird, no rustling leaf,
  No stirring of the breeze;
Nought but the drowsy hum of gnats,
  Beneath the withering trees!
With the red sun's glare, the breathless air,
  And the faint and pale-blue sky,
With the sleeping flood, and drooping wood,
  The heart sinks languidly.
On yonder rich and verdant shore,
  Where the swelling forests spread,
Glistening beneath the fiery rays
  On the shrinking foliage shed,

I know a cool and limpid spring;
  Its laughing waters gay
Steal rippling through the velvet grass,
  Now murmuring on their way.
I could fling down my weary oar,
  And lay me by its side,
Bathe my hot brow and swelling veins,
  And watch the waters glide;
The cold and gushing waters,
  The pebbles clear and white,
The maples and young linden trees
  That shade them from the light!

Would, by that merry sparkling spring,
  Beneath the fresh cool shade,
I might sit and hear the sweet low voice
  Of Hampshire's blue-eyed maid!
Mark her heart's soft emotions,
  By many a sigh confest,
By the gleaming of her melting eye,
  The swelling of her breast.
Then would I loathe the bugle-note,
  And curse the battle-cry,
And know no other joy on earth
  Than soft tranquillity.
But let the poet muse and moan
  In fancied desperation,
The tame voluptuary melt,
  In selfish lamentation:
Man was made to toil and fight,
  And not to dream and sigh,
And woman fires his failing heart
  To deeds of gallantry.

Best I love the clear cool morn
  Of the bright October day;
When the mountains glow, and the lake below
  Reflects the colors gay.

When the fresh woods are ringing
  With the screaming of the jay;
Where, through the ruddy maple leaves,
  Pours the sun's crimsoned ray:
When the stiffened leaves are rustling,
  And dropping from the trees,
And the dark blue water ripples
  In the light morning breeze:
And far aloft against the sky
  The mountain summits rear
Their black rocks, gay with leafy plumes,
  In the sharp atmosphere.
Then, by the island's grassy bank,
  I fling me on the ground,
And snuff the breeze, like a deer
  That scents the distant hound.
'T is then the fire of health and youth
  Burns high in every breast,
And the wild zeal to dare and do,
  And scorn of slothful rest.
'T is then our thoughts are proudest;
  The dearest joy we know,
Would be to hear the war-whoop ring,
  To grapple with the foe.
The feelings of my earlier youth
  I may recall again,
When I was a lonely wanderer
  In the wild land of Spain.
And up the rough Sierra
  By the faint moon I rode,
And the pale light, so softly bright,
  Rock, gulf, and torrent showed.
I looked on her: it seemed to me
  That I low sounds could hear,
As if the spirits of the rocks
  Were whispering in my ear.
And strange vague thoughts came thronging,
  Thickly and dreamily;

Thoughts of loves and battles
  In ages long gone by.
O'er rock and stone my steed tramped on;
  Wild chafed the haughty beast;
He champed the bit, he shook the rein,
  And tossed his sable crest.
Mine was the youthful recklessness,
  The high presumptuous soul,
Soaring elate, defying fate,
  Disdaining self-control.
Thus up the steep and rocky path,
  Careering carelessly,
Fearing nought and heeding nought,
  Went my brave steed and I.
And then a softening memory
  Rose up within my breast,
Of that, of all things on the earth,
  I 've longest loved and best.
It was of dear New-England,
  Her mountains and her woods,
Her savage rocks, her headlong streams,
  Her pure and gentle floods.
And now, from wandering returned,
  I 've trod thy shore again,
Land barren of the corn and wine,
  Fruitful of fearless men!
Blooming with bright-eyed laughing girls,
  The lovely flowers that spring
Luxuriant from thy rocky soil,
  A matchless offering!
And I have armed me in her cause
  In this her day of woe,
Nor vainly fight to shield her right
  Against her hated foe.
But how in such a scene as this,
  Can thoughts of slaughter rise?
The rich green hill, the waters still,
  The pure and amber skies:

When nature's sweet and powerful voice
  Whispers of peace and rest,
And to a tranquil tenderness
  Would soothe the unquiet breast.
Our toil and woe are well nigh done;
  Strain, comrades, at the oar!
There lie the walls that shelter us,
  On yonder guarded shore.
I see the frowning rampart,
  The rigid palisade,
And slowly rolled in swelling fold,
  Old England's flag displayed.
Hark to the rolling of the drum,
  And the gay trumpet-note,
That, softened on the greedy ear,
  O'er the calm waters float!
And see! and see! on yonder plain,
  The long and glittering line;
The red coats glow in the evening rays,
  The bristling bayonets shine;
How, 'twixt those shadowy western hills,
  Upon the bright array
The sinking sun pours duskily
  His last departing ray!
Where 's the cold eye that would not glow,
  At yonder gallant sight!
Where the tame heart that would not beat
  With a high and wild delight!
I love that broad red banner,
  And the stately soldiery
That bear it on through blood and smoke,
  Always triumphantly.
Brave Briton, I could ever be
  A comrade by thy side
Around the merry camp-fire,
  Or in the battle's tide:
But I cannot brook thy haughty brow,
  Thy bearing proud and high;

Thou 'lt make a cold and disdainful friend,
  But a gallant enemy!
I have dreamed it, and I know it,
  The day is coming yet,
When axe and rifle-butt shall clash
  With British bayonet!
No more through dark and pathless woods
  We 'll hunt the savage foe,
Or track the flying Frenchman,
  By his footprints on the snow;
But hand to hand, and steel to steel,
  On the broad open field,
We 'll try who blenches in the strife,
  Who shall be last to yield!
And I have dreamed it in my sleep,
  How the bullets stormed like hail,
And the red bristling ranks went down
  As wheat bends to the gale!
As I have dreamed it in my sleep,
  That sight mine eyes shall see;
And when that bloody morning comes,
  Right welcome shall it be.

CAPT. JONATHAN CARVER, JR."

"CAMBRIDGE, MASS.,
June 25, 1845.

APPENDIX C

THEODORE PARKER'S CRITICISM OF "PONTIAC"

BOSTON, 22 Dec., 1851.

DEAR SIR, — I have lately read your work on "Pontiac," etc., with much pleasure. I have gained a good deal of information from the book which relates to a period and place where I had not studied the Indians much. On the whole, it seems to me the book is highly creditable to you — to your industry and your good sense. But you will be likely to get mere praise enough, and asked me to speak discriminatingly of the work, so I will write down things which occurred to me in reading the book, and in studying some parts of it. I will speak of the substance, the arrangement and the style; of the *timber*, the *plan*, and the *finish* of it.

I. Of the *substance*, that is the *sentiments* and *ideas*. You evidently have a fondness for the Indian — not a romantic fondness, but one that has been tempered by sight of the fact. Yet I do not think you do the Indian quite justice; you side rather too strongly with the white man and against the red. I think you bring out the vices of the Indian into more prominence than those of the European — which were yet less excusable. The treachery which you censure in the Indian was to him no more a violation of any sentiment or idea that he felt or knew than it was to a Briton to fight with powder and balls. This treachery is not specific of Indians; but generic of all races in a low state of development. It seems to me Pontiac was much more excusable than the Paxton men, the Owens, and the like. It seems to me that the whites are not censured so much as they deserve for their conduct toward the Indians in three particulars:

1. In the matter of *rum*, which the Christian brought to the Savage.

2. In the matter of *women* — whom the Christian took from the Savage as concubines and then deserted when the time came.

3. In the matter of *treachery* and *cruelty* which the whites too often displayed.

I have thought you were a little unjust to the Quakers. But here I have so little direct and positive knowledge that I hesitate in my judgment.

One thing is curious in history: — the Teutonic Race in all its three great divisions, — the Goths, Germans, and Scandinavians — is naturally exclusive, and loves to exterminate the neighboring tribes. On the other side, the Celts and Greco-Italian stock assimilate with other tribes. The history of America shows the same thing in the conduct of the English and the French toward the Indians. It would have enriched your book a little to have called attention to that fact — not generally known. It always enriches a special history to drop into it universal laws or any general rules of conduct which distinguish one nation from another.

The facts of history which you set down seem generally well chosen. The historian cannot tell all. He must choose such as, to him, most clearly set forth the Idea of the nation — or man — he describes. Bancroft chooses one set of facts, Hildreth another, and how different the New England of Bancroft from Hildreth's New England!

So much for the material — which is mainly good *timber*, — now a word of the frame and plan. So

II. Of the distribution of the parts. The title indicates that the conspiracy of Pontiac is the chief theme. But in the book itself it seems to me this is not exactly so, that other things are not quite enough subordinated to the main theme, so as to give unity to the whole book. The *barn* is a little too near the house and the *shed* a little too prominent for the general effect of the house itself. This appears as you look over the table of contents, when Pontiac and his scheme are not the central object about which the rest is grouped. So the book lacks the dramatic unity which is necessary for the artistic treatment of such a subject. Pontiac does not appear so important in the titles of the chapters as the title-page seems to demand. Then the book lacks a sufficient conclusion, and ends abruptly. You do not tell the effect which his death has on Indian affairs. A special history like this requires at the end a general summary with the philosophical reflections which have grown out of the historical treatment of the theme.

It seems to me it would have been better to have divided the matter something after this line:

Introduction. Containing all the general matter relative to the Indians, their origin, geographical distribution, language, arts, agriculture, domestic, political and religious institutions. This is now too much scattered about in the book.

Book I. History of the Indians in the connection with the Europeans up to the time of the general rising.

Book II. History of Pontiac and his efforts to overcome the Europeans.

Book III. Result of the movement on the Indian people, and its effect on their subsequent history. Then it seems to me there should have been more and more obvious unity in the book; now it seems as if the materials have been collected without a definite aim, and that the plan was not quite complete until the book was done. So much of the *plan* and *frame*. Now a word of the *finish*.

III. Of the style of the book. Some passages in it are very well written; in general the style is good, simple, natural, easy. But there is a general lack of severity of style, for which the great Master of Roman history is so remarkable. Some passages remind me of Melville and Headley — whom you would not like to be like. There is a lack of what is characteristic. This appears —

1. In the *description of places*. You do not tell what kind of trees, etc., there were, only trees — leaving us to guess whether they were pines or palms, bushes or tall trees.

2. In the description of persons, the book lacks portraits. Wolfe is well done, so is Montcalm (the account of Braddock is well done). But the picture of Pontiac is not adequate to his important place in the history. It strikes me that Johnson is not very well done. Some passages are left too imperfect. It seems as if you got vexed with the thing and struck out a little recklessly, to hit or miss as it might happen. The style of the book often indicates haste — as do almost all American books — like everything else we do.

There, sir, is not there a list of faults for you? Yes, more than all your critics in the reviews, I suppose, have found with you. But if I did not expect you and think you capable of better things than you have done yet, I should not go to the trouble of pointing out all these faults. You seem to have chosen literature for your profession, and history for your special department thereof, and I do so love to see literary conscientiousness applied to explain the meaning of human history and convey its lesson to mankind, that I have taken the pains to point out particular things in which your book might have been made better. You have already received so much commendation that it is not necessary I should go into the pleasanter business of telling you how many things I like in the book. Believe me,

Truly yours,

THEO. PARKER.

FRANCIS PARKMAN, JR., ESQ.

INDEX

INDEX

ncis
Parkman.

	DATE DUE